AUTONOMOUS **ARCHITECTURE** IN FLANDERS

AUTONOMOUS **ARCHITECTURE** IN FLANDERS

The Early Works of Marie-José Van Hee,
Christian Kieckens, Marc Dubois,
Paul Robbrecht and Hilde Daem

Edited by
Caroline Voet
Katrien Vandermarliere
Sofie De Caigny
Lara Schrijver

LEUVEN UNIVERSITY PRESS

Special thanks to the protagonists of this publication: Hilde Daem, Marc Dubois, Christian Kieckens, Paul Robbrecht, Marie-José Van Hee and their collaborators.

We would like to express our sincere gratitude to the photographers who gave us permission to use their images. This book would not have been possible without the generosity of Stijn Bollaert, Richard Bryant, Els Claessens, Kristien Daem, Marc De Blieck, Mirjam Devriendt and Jean-Pierre Stoop, Christian Galle, David Grandorge, Michiel Hendryckx, Christian Kieckens, Edo Kuipers, Reiner Lautwein, Daniël Libens, Lander Loeckx, Peter Lorré, Jan Mast, Mario Palmieri, Patrick Van Caeckenbergh, Maarten Vanden Abeele, Tania Vandenbussche, Wim Van Nueten, Crispijn van Sas, Frederik Vercruysse, Caroline Voet and Piet Ysabie.

Contents

Prologue

Craftsmanship and Purity
The Architecture of Generation 74 in the Flemish Field

Caroline Voet
Katrien Vandermarliere
Sofie De Caigny
Lara Schrijver

This book is built on the conviction that the work of a group of architects who studied together at Sint-Lucas in Ghent – four of them graduated in 1974 – is more central to Flemish architecture than has heretofore been acknowledged: Marc Dubois, Christian Kieckens Architects, Robbrecht en Daem architecten and Marie-José Van Hee architecten, three architecture firms and one critic, who together have a substantial influence on architecture in Flanders over the past 40 years. They produced a large body of written and built work over their careers. While their work has clearly gained a reputation, and is valued by many critics and architects, their influence might also be seen as more subtle than that of the vocal figures in the architecture debate. Their presence is more implicit than explicit and momentous, their influence is nevertheless extensive. The modesty at first sight is perhaps connected to their restraint in language, and also a resistance to turning to jargon. Furthermore, their engagement and influence in architecture education in Flanders is of prime importance, as well as their providing internships, which may only be truly recognized after many years, in the retrospective gaze and the work of their students and interns.

As such, this book investigates a 'silent school' in Flanders, the result of the generation of 1974 and their quest for an autonomous logic in architecture. Sint-Lucas in Ghent took the initiative as their alma mater, while the Center for Flemish Architectural Archives of the Flanders Architecture Institute and the University of Antwerp helped expand it to the publication as it now stands. The focus is on the early works of Marie-José Van Hee architecten, Christian Kieckens Architects, Robbrecht en Daem architecten and Marc Dubois, in a period (1975-1995) when the autonomy of architecture appeared to be no longer relevant, and attention instead shifted to a semiotic and a social approach. But the protagonists of this publication didn't seem to have much affinity with either postmodernism or a social conscience as guidelines for architectural design. This generation of architects did not follow the doctrine of Rem Koolhaas as did the 'young gods' Xaveer De Geyter or Stéphane Beel, but rather that of his teacher, Oswald Mathias Ungers. Departing from an interest in and awareness of the importance of tradition, they began to investigate the work of Palladio and the Italian Baroque, for example. They developed a research-based design attitude that was rooted in the study of architectural morphology and typologies. Architecture was seen as an autonomous spatial phenomenon, charged with the perspectives of dwelling and experience. Artistry and craftsmanship were seen as central aspects of making architecture.

In this manner they defined an architectural language that grew from spatial analyses, meticulous reflections on art and an intense relationship with craftsmanship. As such, their work focuses more on producing architecture than describing it.

The history of architecture in Flanders is in some ways relatively recent. While there are crucial figures throughout history, such as Victor Horta, Henry van de Velde, Renaat Braem and Léon Stynen, this book addresses the more recent developments. In several articles the publication reflects on the period of the 1970s to the 1990s in order to seek out reference points and events that consolidated architectural culture in Flanders, to which the five in this book contributed greatly. At the same time, as the consciousness of the built environment grew in their wake, the younger Belgian architects often felt (and not wrongly), that architecture as a discipline could count on stronger government support in The Netherlands, thereby also acquiring greater financial support and public visibility. Precisely in the early professional years of the careers of the protagonists of this publication, there was much to be gained in Belgium and Flanders, and many of their peers also worked hard at building up a stronger culture for the architecture profession, built more on quality and competition and less on the basis of intrigue and nepotism.

We are convinced that the work of Marie-José Van Hee architecten, Christian Kieckens Architects, Robbrecht en Daem architecten and Marc Dubois is not only historically relevant for the development of architectural culture in Flanders, but also holds new relevance for contemporary architecture. Supported by the deep appreciation of many of their students and (international) colleagues, we began this project with the sense that their work and influence has not yet been exhaustively studied. This might be due to the unique trajectory of their careers, characterized by a certain obstinacy that perhaps is inevitable for the pioneering role they played. Questions that marked the beginning of this book are: What defines this generation? Why do we have a sense that they share more than a graduation year? What are the foundations of their design practices, and where do they come from? What were they looking for, and what drove them in their early years? This book situates this generation in the Flemish and international developments of the 1980s and 1990s. To what extent did they help develop the contemporary architectural culture in Flanders, and does this type of architecture practice still exist? What is the relation between the growing presence of this group and the nascent architectural culture in Flanders, which might be seen as emancipatory for the discipline? What was the role of an increased willingness to communicate with a broader public? Indeed, manifestations, exhibitions and publications, also in the popular media, started to draw attention to contemporary architecture in the 1980s and 1990s. Especially in the 1990s some of these initiatives became institutionalized, laying the groundwork for the installation of the Flemish Government Architect and the establishment of the Architecture Institute Flanders. This publication addresses the question to what extent the careers of the three architecture firms and Marc Dubois as a critic, and their search for an autonomous language for their architecture, ran parallel with the professionalization of architectural culture in Flanders.

In the trajectory towards this book it not only became clear to us how central their work – from projects, exhibition design and buildings to manifestoes, writings and studio supervision – has been to a quite diverse field, but also how pressing the need is for a publication that offers an overview of the early work and its many networks of influences. At the same time, this marked out the challenge of how to do justice to their contribution to the architectural culture in Flanders. It is in this challenge that we opted for a broad perspective, allowing for a multitude of voices. In the most literal sense, we have incorporated this by allowing for fundamentally distinct contributions, from scholarly essays to brief visual and textual observations.

Attention has been given to not only intellectual evaluations but also to the material projects and the very activity of drawing and designing. In a figural sense, we have incorporated this diversity by ensuring that differing perspectives have been given room to develop along comparable themes.

A number of texts shed new light on the work through an in-depth perspective on single topics. Sven Sterken, for example, shows the importance of the Architecture Museum Foundation (Stichting Architektuurmuseum, S/AM) and its contribution to architecture culture. Fredie Floré departs from furniture design and the interior to offer an understanding of the objects that have not only been influential but also a crucial part of the work. Hera Van Sande and Yves Schoonjans examine the tradition of design thinking at the Sint-Lucas school, which also illuminates the kind of education this generation received as their foundation. Eireen Schreurs and Mechthild Stuhlmacher visited a number of completed projects, and documented their ensuing e-mail conversations in which they exchange their thoughts on notable elements in the design and construction process and how these influence the resulting building. The contribution by Caroline Voet analyses the early work in its most essential features, to show which timeless principles are present throughout the projects.

Other essays offer a spectrum of characterizations. William Mann's essay offers a powerful introduction to the quality of this generation's work, an empathic and pure description of their architecture. Dirk Somers draws attention to similarities with the approach of Venturi, and its influence on the discipline of architecture, while Maarten Delbeke shows how baroque architecture is an important precedent, and which transformations are applied. The relationship between art and architecture, another central element in the work studied here, is the focus of Birgit Cleppe's article.

A number of texts also frame the work in a broader historical and theoretical context. The text by Sofie De Caigny and Katrien Vandermarliere maps out the architecture culture in Flanders between 1974 and 2000, which these five figures have influenced profoundly in different manners. Lara Schrijver's article positions this generation in their time as well as in the broader architecture discourse in Europe and America.

Finally, there are a number of shorter texts by former students, colleagues and *compagnons de route* of this generation. We asked them to explain the impact of this generation through a single critical moment, idea or image. Sometimes an impression or an image can state more than a long discursive description.

Our hope with this book is that it goes beyond the typical tribute, and instead positions these architects within the field of architecture in Flanders – with a critical gaze where necessary. Not as a historically objective condition but rather as a presentation of thematic traits, and their relationship to the context within which these five architects developed their work, and with it, provided a professional, intellectual and educational legacy that still runs under the surface of architecture in Flanders today.

[1] See for example Dirk van den Heuvel, Madeleine Steigenga, and Jaap van Triest, *Lessons: Tupker/Risselada: A double portrait of Dutch architectural education 1953-2003* (Nijmegen: Sun Publishers, 2003).

[2] Geert Bekaert, 'Jonge architecten in Vlaanderen ontmaskeren de architectuur', *Ons Erfdeel. Jaargang 32.* (Stichting Ons Erfdeel, Rekkem/ Raamsdonksveer, 1989).

Lara Schrijver

Breathing Life into Bricks
The Legacy of the 1970s

First, to begin with two snapshots in time.

1974.

In Ghent, a group of graduates from Sint-Lucas Institute of Architecture are determined to leave their mark on the field of architecture in Flanders. A refusal of sleek imagery, the material reality of architecture itself as central. Buildings, ornaments, proportions. These five share a particular view of key issues in architecture, formed by their education, the Flemish context and the time.

Worldwide, it is only a year after the Club of Rome report, and a sense of urgency on environmental issues is increasing. Throughout the western world, the profession of architecture is affected by the economic downturn, and is seeking a new form of legitimacy. In Flanders, the culture of architecture is fragmented and still determinedly non-intellectual.

2014.

In Venice, Dutch architect Rem Koolhaas curates the Architecture Biennale. A turn to the Fundamentals of Architecture, to the elements with which it is constructed. Doors, stairs, roofs, walls. In a retrospective comment, screened on the floor of the Arsenale, he remarks that his first visit to Michelangelo's Laurentian library in Florence showed him that his education was merely the first step in learning to create architecture that had an impact. That even 400 years later, this library touches the visitor, demonstrates the power of architectural space.

Between these two moments, a span of 40 years has passed. Indeed, even the central concerns may appear to be rather distinct at first glance. Yet under the surface lies a similar belief in the value of their profession and in the cultural fortitude of architecture. With some poetic license, we could see the Biennale as the logical result of a soul-searching within the discipline in the latter half of the 20th century. To take these five Sint-Lucas graduates as central figures in this development may extend the license too far, but their particular interests were not as singular a development as a cursory glance at recent histories may suggest. What might be gained from approaching them as a seismographic group – registering and showing, in small amounts, more significant rumblings under the visible foundations of architecture?

The reality of architecture: material, space and light. Marie-José Van Hee, House and practice in Opwijk, 2005-2011. Still from movie, Maarten Vanden Abeele (2015, commissioned by Archipel).

The past 40-some years have been a fascinating period, bringing such developments as postmodernism, deconstruction, and the Congress for New Urbanism, to name but a few offshoots in architectural discourse. Notwithstanding the sombre musings of Hanno Walter Kruft, who suggested in the mid-90s that there has been no significant theory production since World War II, we might instead wonder whether there are things happening that we do not yet have the tools to apprehend and explain.[1] As such, it becomes an embodied knowledge, something residing within the actors in the field, not yet theorized, not yet explicit, but *there*.

Le Thoronet,
Cistercian abbey, France.
Photo Caroline Voet.

TALKING 'BOUT MY GENERATION

What does it mean to be a 'generation' in architecture? Hans van Dijk once suggested that generations last about seven years, based on the coherence of a curriculum.[2] The five architects in this book, Christian Kieckens, Marie-José Van Hee, Marc Dubois, Paul Robbrecht and Hilde Daem, graduated within one year of another. Hilde Daem graduated from the Academy of Fine Arts in Ghent in 1975, and the other four a year earlier from Sint-Lucas in Ghent, in 1974. As such, they fulfil the condition of similar schooling alluded to by Van Dijk. If we take up the history of these Ghent five as bound by more than mere coincidence, as at least determined by their time and their shared experiences, what might this tell us of the developments in architecture, in Flanders and abroad? If we treat these five as not only a biological but also a *sociological* generation, what might this add to their history?[3] While the biological generation, defined by age, implies shared features based on chronological definitions, the social generation is defined by shared events and experiences. May 1968 as such defines a social generation: those who felt part of the student resistance may identify with this generation, whether they were 20-year-old students, 40-year-old sympathizers, or 60-year-old observers. Similarly, the world wars have defined a social generation in confronting all ages with such fundamental life-changing experiences, that they become part of a group, regardless of biological age.

The group presented in this book – once dubbed 'les silencieux' – may seem less clearly defined than the more well-known 'young gods' Stéphane Beel and Xaveer De Geyter.[4] Indeed, within this 'group' they each took on quite different directions. Yet their shared interests are equally striking, and in retrospect, their work is situated in a broader international context of an identity crisis in architecture and the changing conditions under which projects were realized in the 1970s and 1980s. At the time, architecture in Belgium was still seen through the prism of the 'ugliest country', an essay by Renaat Braem on the particular qualities of the modern, semi-urban Belgian environment.[5] Within the national and local context, they were also defined by the focus on the eman- cipatory social role of architecture on the one hand (mostly identified with the legacy of bOb Van Reeth) and the lack of an institutional context and broader debate on the other. As such, we might revisit the work of Dubois as the necessary voice of the group, writing on architecture but also maintaining ties with the few institutions aimed at art and architecture. He played a crucial role in forming more of these institutions as well. The notable feature here is that this little group of silent renegades marked the architecture scene in very distinct ways – from the writings and curatorial strategies of Dubois, to the unassuming craftsmanship of Van Hee, to the clear focus on art and culture by Robbrecht and Kieckens, albeit each in their own fashion.

It is notable that only so recently, in 2014, the most prominent figure in architecture, Rem Koolhaas, the godfather of some of the younger generation in Belgian architecture, evokes a setting in which he was confronted with one of the classical examples of architecture and realized he had much to learn. Koolhaas is, of course, one with dramatic flair for writing and for using retrospective insights based on recollections – perhaps even imagined ones. However, there is an interesting element to his comment – he refers to one of the classic designs of the Renaissance not as an image, but as an entity that goes far beyond the rules of composition. As something that requires a fundamental understanding only acquired through practice, through experience, and through craftsmanship – and then results in a seemingly effortless perfection of space.

It is this positioning that I suggest lies at the heart of the 'generation' presented here. The 'silencieux' sought out qualities that had nothing to do with the media-image of architecture, and everything to do with the classical elements of composition and spatial geometry. This is clear throughout numerous publications and exhibitions.[6] The social function of architecture – at least as approached by the modernists – took a backseat to concerns of space, of material and of design quality. Light, thickness, typology, became more central than the social concerns of their forebears.

In a time when information was rapidly increasing, yet also flattening the experience of architecture, they understood the value of the grand tour, of visiting what they studied. They did these things together, forging the experiential connections that run throughout their work. Above all, they seemed to understand that not all knowledge can be captured in words. This meant that they travelled to projects, they studied drawings, they redrew buildings in order to understand them. They not only formulated their findings in texts, but also in sketches, slides, and drawings. In essence, where possible they circumnavigated words in favour of material, of space, of light.

In this, they were not alone. They shared in some sense a *zeitgeist* that was present in various little pockets of architectural practice in Europe and the United States. Whether it was in response to economic crisis as in the United States or in response to the social unrest in many university cities, or indeed to the emptiness experienced in the culture around them, each sought their answers in the underlying logic of architecture as a craft of composition, within the inner logic of the discipline.

**Diagrammatic facade,
project by Hiromi Fujii,
cover of exhibition catalogue,
drawing and graphic design
Christian Kieckens.**
Hiromi Fujii, Architecture and
Projects in the '70 - '80, *Deetaai* 2
(Brussels: CIAUD-ICASD, 1981).

CONSTRUCTING AUTONOMY

One of the determining features of the 1970s is a general sense that the social ideals of the 1960s had failed. The pressing concern about non-renewable energy, the effects of human intervention on the natural environment, and the destructive aspects of the affluent society, raised a new awareness of the limited resources available. The increased alarm over these issues created a general discourse of limits and restrictions and a renewed concern that was distinct from the 1960s version of social agency.

Steadily, an increase became visible in the questions of what architecture might do. In numerous fields, pressing concerns rose to the surface, which had far-reaching implications for society at large. Questions on the effect of pesticides on flora and fauna raised the dark image of a 'silent spring', and at the same time, the difficulty of allocating and sharing resources illustrated the 'tragedy of the commons'.[7] Modern optimism, driven by the endless promise of technological solutions, began to be toned down by an awareness of problems that are by their very nature unsolvable, so-called 'wicked problems', which require difficult social, political and normative choices to be made.[8]

In the meantime, the professional discourse had become sufficiently embedded in an academic culture, to be raising issues of legitimacy as an academic field. The discussions on the 'minor professions' such as architecture and business management did not go unnoticed. At the same time, this dismissal of the academic value of professional schools was contradicted by the theoretical formulation of the 'sciences of the artificial', which encompassed fields such as engineering, computer science and architecture and planning.[9] Finally, within the architecture debates themselves, the concerns for legitimacy left their own mark. Rather than turn to external conditions driven by industrialization, technologies and modernization, the central concerns of architecture were reflected back onto architectural issues and techniques, such as proportion, composition, and the structure of the urban fabric.[10] In the most diverse guises, these may nevertheless all be seen as driven by a quest for the field's legitimacy if it was not to be found in a directly identifiable and productive social emancipatory agency.

In this context the notion of autonomy is a promising perspective to understand the impact of this generation, as well as the context they operated within. In the 1970s, the role of architecture in relation to the societal questions it faced underwent a fundamental change. On the American side of the Atlantic, one of the most outspoken versions of this attitude is to be found in the work of what was to become known as the 'New York Five': Peter Eisenman, Michael Graves, Charles Gwathmey, John Hejduk and Richard Meier. From quite diverse positions, the work of these five architects was brought together in the 1972 MoMA exhibition 'Five Architects'. Earlier, in the late 1950s, series of visual and formal experiments had already been a substantial part of the curriculum at the University of Texas in Austin.[11] The so-called 'Texas Rangers', which included Colin Rowe and John Hejduk, had helped build an architecture curriculum on the teaching elements of the Bauhaus and supplemented with the visual work of Robert Slutzky. This material shows the early seeds of seeking out the eternal logic of form and composition, which would blossom further into the explicit statements on the logic of the discipline as formulated in the catalogue to the 'Five Architects' exhibition. Of particular importance here are the introductory statements by Arthur Drexler and Colin Rowe, both of whom call attention to the internal and indeed autonomous logic of the discipline. Where the discourse of the 1960s was societally engaged to the extent that architecture was often treated as an extension of social principles, the introduction to the catalogue *Five Architects* marks out the boundaries of this responsibility, and indeed even situates this as a distinction between European architects, and American ones. Claiming that this group of architects exhibit a more humble ambition yet also a more realistic outlook, Arthur Drexler notes: 'their work makes a modest claim: it is only architecture, not the salvation of man and the redemption of the earth. For those who like architecture, that is no mean thing.'[12]

Meanwhile, on the European continent, the social engagement that characterized modernism was still strongly present, albeit transformed by the work of Team 10. Among others, it is this social emphasis that the Ghent group resisted in favour of the material conditions and the logic of architecture. As such, their work shows distinctly more affinity with the New York Five than with their colleagues in Europe, which is also reflected in their choices of reference works – the work of Eisenman shows up in the early pamphlet publications of DEETAAI and Stichting Architektuurmuseum, for example, as well as the work of Hiromi Fujii, and neorationalist European colleagues such as Aldo Rossi and O.M. Ungers.[13]

'Five Architects' shows work that is modest in size and radical in approach. While the diversity of the work is clear – Charles Gwathmey's pragmatic modern residences are difficult to compare with Hejduk's poetic and conceptual proposition for House 10 – one may also in hindsight discern the early hints of what would come to be placed under the category 'autonomous architecture'. Indeed, this marks the first beginnings of a turn inward, to the mechanisms of the discipline, to the logic that underpins design. Coming particularly from an English school, these concerns and questions return in various guises throughout this time, with Denise Scott Brown offering a brief history and analysis of the gap between architectural design and urban planning.[14] Her article suggests that the social concerns of architecture are indeed also misunderstood.

As such, a broadly shared question on the role and effects of architecture becomes apparent in many areas of architecture discourse. There are the outspoken statements against the social interpretation of architecture such as those of Oswald Mathias Ungers, who states that the many external conditions of architecture do not offer sufficient principles for architectural design: 'it is useless continuing to discuss architectural problems if it is only a question of satisfying the existing requirements in the most rational way... The work's destination does not contain in itself elements of formal choice.'[15] There are also those who turn ever more to the social discourse in order to legitimate the use of extensive symbolism in postmodernism, where the emancipatory ideals of modernism are transformed in the right to expressive building.

This context also shapes the environment of Kieckens, Robbrecht en Daem, Van Hee and Dubois, who found the social focus of their mentors overbearing, and questioned

Spatial archetypes.
Louis Kahn,
**The Dominican Convent.
First Floor Plan, Media,
Pennsylvania, 1965-1968.**
Michael Merrill, Louis Kahn
Drawing to Find Out:
The Dominican Motherhouse
and the Patient Search for
Architecture (Zurich: Lars Müller
Publishers, 2010).

Architectural logic.
Peter Eisenman,
**House II (1969-70),
diagrams.**
Peter Eisenman, Inside Out:
Selected Writings, 1963-1988
(New Haven:
Yale University Press, 2004).

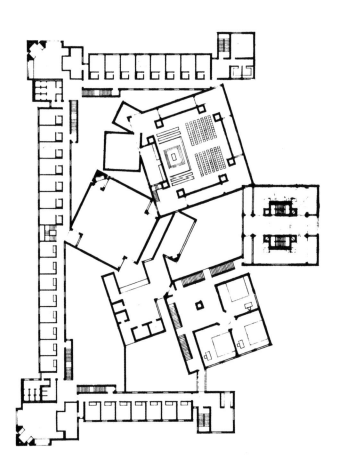

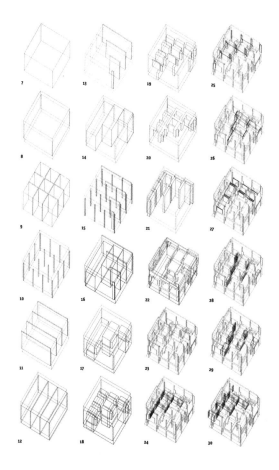

whether design attitudes did not offer more room for human comfort.[16] In this sense, they perhaps share certain premises with architects like John Hejduk, who seeks the poetry in life, and with Oswald Mathias Ungers, who seeks a sensible and autonomous disciplinary logic to form the basis for a design. The interest in art and its impact on architecture and everyday life, is one of the elements that speaks to the necessity of cultural production as more than mere functionalism or economic necessity. As a number of the articles in this publication also show, they often sought out similar international projects, as they found in them a resonance with their own intuitions on architecture's essential qualities.

Within the discourse of autonomy, the overall social impact of architecture and its mechanisms shifts to a more individualized cultural appreciation. Earlier positions were often founded on the modernist principles of emancipation and the conviction that architecture and urban design would have a fundamental impact on the behaviour of users. Moreover, a transformative capacity was often attributed to the fields of design. While much of this was rhetoric that perhaps spoke more to hope and opti-mism than to an actual conviction that architecture was transformative, it nevertheless marked the time. In contrast, those working in the aftermath of this period turned to a more humble interpretation of both their responsibilities and their impact. Still, the convictions remained a fundamental element in the profession. In 1977, sociologist Robert Gutman published an analysis of the heated discussions within the architecture discipline, and concluded that architects needed to rethink their claims to legitimacy.[17] He suggested that they should take a more entrepreneurial approach to their profes-sion, founded less on the notion of cultural necessity, and more on communicating the added value of architectural services. Nevertheless, the intrinsic convictions of architects have remained throughout the 1970s and 1980s. Indeed, while the effects of these convictions were expressed in fundamentally different forms – from the social and political engagement of the 1960s to the faith in autonomy and disciplinary concerns in the 1970s, to the poetic and deconstructive gestures of the 1980s – the undertones of a deeply felt fervour remained present.

RESPECTING CULTURAL CONTINUITY

As the 1970s melted into the 1980s, the presence of history became more important throughout the architecture debates, as a way of addressing the vast number of problems confronting the discipline: it had worked for so many generations before, and the significance of historical examples was not to be denied. As such, the turn to history is neither momentary nor local. The first architecture Biennale in Venice in 1980 is titled 'The Presence of the Past' to remind us of the long duration of architecture.[18] An outright statement against the *tabula rasa* of the modernists and also the progres-sivism of the 1960s, this Biennale is a plea for awareness of the existing urban fabric, of building conventions and of the presence of history throughout the discipline. In this sense, it is not a surprise that around the same time, Alan Colquhoun writes the essay 'Form and Figure', in which he argues that it is not just the Platonic form of the Modernists that we should take into account, but a broader understanding of form as guided convention and symbolism.[19] As such, he appeals to the notion of 'figure' in rhetoric, where it is the understanding of convention that also 'fills in' the diagrammatic statements that formal gestures inevitably are.

In this manner, it becomes clear that much of the ado is related to the legitimacy of a profession that is not immediately and critically necessary. In fact, as Robert Gutman points out, while architects often like to compare themselves to lawyers and doctors, the services of the architect are significantly less crucial than legal and medical services.[20] Gutman suggests that the architect needs to become more entrepreneurial, to create the desire for his services. It is perhaps ironic that this message seems to have been strongly incorporated in the culture of the 1990s onwards – certainly the very notion of 'city branding' and the 'creative class' are clear expressions of an entrepreneurial spirit – of situating architecture at the heart of economic activity. This is what many young architects did – they created a desire for new, radical architecture.

Through the discourse of autonomy, the legitimacy of architecture is shifted to a domain internal to the field. In stark contrast to the preceding generation, which found its legitimacy in the social impact and concerns of architecture, the architecture of the 1970s and 1980s finds a stronger argument in the particularities of a discipline, in its own logic and structure. Yet in later years, as the economic viability of architecture was increasingly emphasized, it was its role as economic motor that took centre stage. As such, the most mediagenic or sharply provocative statements (material or textual) began to take precedence over works less immediately mediagenic.

In essence, this 'generation 74' built a foundation for a return to the cultural weight of architecture, and the craftsmanship that it requires. As such, we might indeed argue that this group forms not only a biological generation, responding to its 'fathers' – but also a cultural generation, marked by a time of economic downturn, of disillusionment in 1960s ideals, of a return to poetic license, of a return to foundations of discipline. The lack of an architecture culture in Flanders made this a difficult conversation to have at the time, but the work of these five was central to building up a culture of exhibitions and debate.[21] Where New York's MoMA – by accident of social network perhaps – at least offered a platform for the New York Five to propose a renewed sense of the discipline, the culture in Flanders was still highly informal in the late 1970s. This required a slow and steady building up of cultural institutions and fabric that was not previously available, in the broadest sense. In this, the group of architects presented here are formative, and their deeply developed knowledge of historical precedents, from medieval architecture to Renaissance geometries and baroque compositions aided not only in their own designs but also in determining themes for architectural and cultural debate.

CULTURAL TURNS AND NEW GENERATIONS: MATERIAL PRESENCE

Culture is something that is not only consciously disseminated, but also formed, recreated and solidified in everyday habits. As such, cultural transformations are best seen in hindsight, unhindered by the obviousness of habit. The late 20th century has been decisively shaped by numerous ruptures, yet the underlying continuity in cultures also remains visible. In Flanders, the influence of the five architects in this book is both visible and culturally embedded. This presence is perhaps most visibly notable in their buildings. The historical continuity upon which their work is based, has offered a reference point for many young architects currently practicing in Flanders. Culturally their contribution can be traced in the founding of architecture platforms for debate such as the publications of *Deetaai* and the Bulletin of the Stichting Architektuurmuseum (S/AM), thus contributing fundamentally to an awareness of architecture, urban planning and design in Flanders.[22] Yet for the immediate future, one might surmise that their most fundamental influence will be on the next generation. For one, they have been an important part of the educational curriculum, both as teachers and as examples. But more importantly, they have provided timeless experiments in the material realizations of architecture, which still stand to be examined, discussed and above all experienced. Instead of turning to more words about buildings, they built. And some of them, such as Marie-José Van Hee, were particularly silent, leaving their buildings to speak for themselves.

Fragment from: Pierre de Crescens, Rustican ou Livre des profits champêtres, Jardin en ville – enluminé par le Maître de Marguerite d'York, 1480, Flanders.
Marie-José Van Hee, 'Beschouwingen omtrent tuinen in de middeleeuwen tot in de tijd van Lodewijk XIX' (Thesis, Hoger Instituut Sint-Lucas Ghent, 1973-1974): 24.

Cultural production is increasingly dependent on scientific methods for its legitimacy. Yet scientific research is also increasingly attuned to visual, material and spatial concerns. In this, the work of these five architects holds special resonance, in showing what cannot be told. As early as the mid-19th century, Viollet-le-Duc voiced a concern from the perspective of an educator that may still resonate today: what indeed should we teach our students if so much information is already at their fingertips, in the form of books, or photographs, or travel descriptions? If indeed they can also visit the projects described in mere days or weeks, rather than the months it would have once cost?[23] His conclusion was that judgment was the key skill to train: a manner of sifting through the vast amounts of information and seeking out what was best, or most appropriate. One in fact may argue that these architects did precisely that: they travelled to projects together, they discussed them, and in so doing they formed a sense of what architecture meant, what cultural continuity could be, and how they positioned themselves within this greater cultural narrative.

The work of these architects, from their writing to their building, shows a precise architectural, aesthetic and spatial judgment. Their sheer focus on architectural logic, composition and the discipline in general, laid a foundation for the next generation to avail themselves of architectural techniques, historical precedent and an embedded sense of cultural responsibility. And the sense of judgment that runs throughout their work stands testimony to the endless series of decisions involved in producing an oeuvre.

Hadrian's Villa, Tivoli (begun 117 A.D.). S/AM, Monography 1: Architecture Museums (Ghent, 1984), back inside cover. Scan APA.

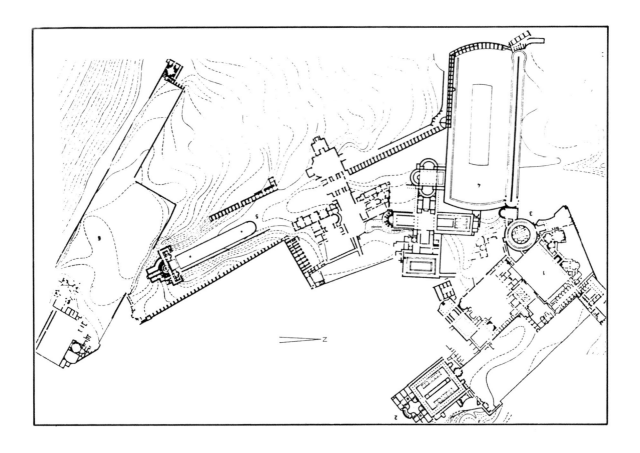

1   Hanno Walter Kruft, *A History of Architectural Theory from Vitruvius to the Present*. (New York: Princeton Architectural Press, 1994), 434-446.

2   Hans van Dijk, *Bouwmeesters. Portret van een generatie* (Rotterdam: 010 Publishers, 2009).

3   Karl Mannheim, 'The Problem of Generations', in: Paul Kecsemeti, ed. *Essays on the Sociology of Knowledge* (London: Routledge, 1952) 276-322. Originally published in 1928.

4   See for the 'silencieux' for example William Mann, André Loeckx, *Marie-José Van Hee, architect*. Gent: Ludion, 2002. The 'young gods' were seen as a breath of fresh air and received due publication, having worked for the Office of Metropolitan Architecture in Rotterdam.

5   Renaat Braem, Het lelijkste land ter wereld. Brussels: ASP and CVAa, 2010 [orig. Leuven: Davidsfonds, 1968].

6   See the articles of Sven Sterken, Sofie De Caigny and Katrien Vandermarliere, Hera Van Sande and Yves Schoonjans, in this publication.

7   Rachel Carson, *Silent Spring* (1962), Garrett Hardin, 'Tragedy of the Commons', Science, v.168, n.3859, 1243-1248 (1968).

8   Horst Rittel and Melvin Webber, 'Dilemmas in a general theory of planning', *Policy Sciences* 4, 1973, 153-169.

9   Nathan Glazer, 'The Schools of the Minor Professions', *Minerva*, v.12 n.3, 1974, 346-364. Herbert Simon, *The Sciences of the Artificial*, Cambridge: MIT Press, 1969.

10 Colin Rowe, The Mathematics of the Ideal Villa, *Architectural Review*, 1947; Robert Venturi, *Complexity and Contradiction in Architecture*, 1966.

11 Alexander Caragonne, *The Texas Rangers: Notes from an architectural underground* (Cambridge, MA: MIT Press, 1995).

12 Arthur Drexler, 'Preface'. In: *Five Architects* (New York: Oxford University Press, 1972).

13 See DEETAAI Study Group (Jos Vanderperren, Christian Kieckens), *CRESCENDO 1. architectuur 1980* (Wezenbeek-Oppem: DEETAAI, 1980); Kieckens, Christian (ed.), *Architectuurmusea* (Gent: Stichting Architektuurmuseum, 1985). See also the article of Caroline Voet in this publication.

14 Denise Scott Brown, 'On Architectural Formalism and Social Concern', *Oppositions*, 1975.

15 Oswald Mathias Ungers: 'Architecture's Right to an Autonomous Language', in: *The Presence of the Past*. First International Exhibition of Architecture, La Biennale di Venezia, 1980, Exhibition Catalogue, Venezia: Edizione La Biennale di Venezia, 1980, 319-324.

16 See the articles by Sven Sterken and Hera Van Sande and Yves Schoonjans in this publication.

17 Gutman, 'The Entrepreneurial Profession', *Progressive Architecture* 5 (1977): 55-58.

18 Paolo Portoghesi, ed., *The Presence of the Past*. First International Exhibition of Architecture, La Biennale di Venezia 1980, Exhibition Catalogue (Venezia: Edizione La Biennale di Venezia, 1980). The work of Portoghesi is also a common reference point for the architects discussed in this publication, see also the articles by Sven Sterken and Caroline Voet.

19 Alan Colquhoun, 'Form and Figure', *Oppositions* 12, Spring 1978, 28-37.

20 Gutman, 'The Entrepreneurial Profession', 55-56.

21 See in particular Sofie De Caigny and Katrien Vandermarliere, 'More than punctual interventions' elsewhere in this publication.

22 See also Sven Sterken, '*Ghostwriters* of the Young Flemish Architecture' elsewhere in this publication.

23 Viollet-le-Duc, *Discourses on Architecture* book V. transl., Henry Van Brunt. Boston: James R. Osgood and Co., 1875. [orig. Entretiens sur l'Architecture 1863].

A Constellation of Scattered Points
Crisis in Design Mentality at the Sint-Lucas Institute (1969-1974)

Hera Van Sande
Yves Schoonjans

In September 1987 the subject of recent architecture in Belgium was covered in a special issue of the Dutch magazine *Archis, Maandblad voor Architectuur, Stedebouw en Beeldende Kunst.*[1] To outline this complex problem the magazine opened up the floor to three prominent critics of Belgian architecture: Geert Bekaert, Francis Strauven and Marc Dubois. Though each had a different take, all three mentioned a void, an absence of any distinct architectural culture. Bekaert felt that Flanders' present context made it difficult, if not impossible for its architects to create anything beyond the commonplace. The prevailing mood, among the population and government alike, was one of historical and social indifference to good architecture. The pressing drive for liberalisation brought with it a full reinforcement of individualism.[2] That this had affected spatial structure, collective space and architecture goes without saying. Marc Dubois likened the new architectural production of the day to an archipelago, islands of individuality between which every effort to achieve quality drowned in a sea of indifference.[3]

It was in the midst of this indifference that a group of young architects including Paul Robbrecht, Hilde Daem, Eugeen Liebaut, William Lievens, Christian Kieckens, Marie-José Van Hee, Stéphane Beel, among others, sought to determine their own position in this discourse during the second half of the 1980s. Theirs was the architecture shown in this and the subsequent special edition on Belgian architecture in 1989. Though Francis Strauven would later describe a group of them as the Flemish Minimalists, the authors of these special editions had great difficulty identifying the new generation of architects with any single group or school. This 'atomisation' was fomented by the very structure of the architectural firms (they worked individually, upon a plethora of small commissions), by the scope of their design idioms, their frames of reference and the highly individualist dispositions of the architects. Nonetheless, for very young architects such as ourselves, recent graduates and undergraduates, something very special was about to come.[4]

In 1987-1989 the architectural duo Paul Robbrecht and Hilde Daem saw their plans for the BAC bank building in Kerksken realised. This was the first actualisation to confront us. Even just the image of the building in the street had a tremendous impact. The street was so recognisable, yet so hard to place. It could have been any street in the Flemish countryside. It was exactly this generic recognisability that we found so intriguing in 1989.

'Architecture or Picking Strawberries', Student exhibition at the Sint-Lucas Institute, Photos Christian Kieckens.

The *Archis* magazine described the environment as a chaotic, urban situation that yielded no real frame of reference for the design, 'It makes no sense to ask how anything could be integrated in this'.[5] And yet the design was clearly entangled with this Flemish townscape. Various essays and articles described how the freestanding colonnade engages in dialogue with the context. They pointed out that the street's contours and rhythm had become part of a new field of tension; that the free space between the dual shell of the colonnade and the volume it encapsulated served as a collective hiding or mooring; that shell and solid volume created an interplay of colour, light and shade. The project illustrated that when it came to taking an intelligent position, Flemish architecture had no need of a separate plot. In other words, that both poetic dialogue and broader architectural discourse was actually achievable within the banality of commonplace Flemish street buildings; a rationale that would later be expanded upon by architectural firms such as B-Architecten, architecten de vylder vinck taillieu, Barak, noAarchitecten, and others.

But the design's entanglement with the townscape was more than just local. Both its clarity and its complexity seemed to bind it firmly to the then topical international architectural discourse on typology and autonomy. Unlike many architectural projects of the 1970s and 1980s it did not use effusive design idioms to make a direct emotional appeal to the public in the hope of reintroducing the idea of identity. However, in no way did it lack ambition. The project attempted to redefine the actual role of architecture and to test its capacity as an autonomous discipline. Architecture was forced to reassess its responsibilities. These responsibilities underpinned the discipline of architecture and urban development that Robbrecht en Daem had in mind. To be worthy of this right the architect would need to show commitment to the community as well as the profession. They saw architectural autonomy not as an escape from social responsibility but as the forging of a stronger link between use and experience of the building and the town itself. Though the architect's role was not confined to architecture, responsibility lay in the quest to discover the discipline's core and boundaries. It was the duty of every architect, claimed Robbrecht, to recover the laws and principles of architecture. This was perceived as gaining a sense of a community's historical continuity. From this perspective the design of the BAC bank in Kerksken connects with the design strategies of Álvaro Siza, Luigi Snozzi and Aldo Rossi, who set up a strong poetic dialogue not only with the local context, but with the theoretical rationale behind the discipline of architecture. One important aspect in this is 'design mentality', a sort of *analogon* of architecture, in which drawing and design not only feed the theoretical discourse, but become an essential part of it.

We might wonder whether the seed of design mentality had already been sown at the Sint-Lucas Higher Institute in Ghent in the late 1960s and early 1970s, when Marc Dubois, Christian Kieckens, Marie-José Van Hee, Paul Robbrecht and Hilde Daem pursued their studies there. In various interviews they all describe this period as dark, disillusioning and almost pointless. At first sight, nothing to them seemed to have contributed to the development of their architectural path. It was as if their particular practice of design had been fuelled by elements before, outside and after their studies.

In the period shortly after May 1968 the Higher Institute, which still had one foot firmly rooted in the past, wasn't entirely sure how to cope with the accelerating pace of society's transformation. Though brother Urbain, the principal at the time, would have had a clearly defined curriculum in mind and made every effort to implement it, reality, as is always the case, was not necessarily compliant.[6] In actual fact, the course was composed of separate events and activities, as if modelling a constellation of scattered points for transient moments in time. For more than a hundred years Sint-Lucas had remained faithful to tradition, an approach that had adapted slowly (and with some delay) to the present day. A certain distrust of all things modern, of all things fashionable, still prevailed. The past couldn't simply be uprooted. Its merits could never be outweighed by an all-too-rapid acceptance of contemporary trends, although they seldom could be entirely avoided. However, the courage to do so was not always present. New trends would be criticised, but no inspirational alternatives were suggested in their place. Long held ideas were discussed laboriously and indecisively, one after the other. This led to a sort of fragmented ideology. It was this very reluctance to adopt a compelling new position, something, which had been key to the school's foundation in the 19th century that now brought it under heavy fire.[7] The early 1970s were no exception to this. The senior lecturers tended to hold key positions over last year students, upon whom they would push their own practice forward as sole reference point. At the same time, the institute had recruited young architects like Herman De Witte to run the design studios for the junior years. The young guard of dynamic new lecturers in the junior years left their students with high expectations, none of which were satisfied during their final studies. Seldom was there room for architectural debate. This deficiency was only partially remedied by exceptional teachers, the odd interesting assignment or trip, the students' influence on each other and the general artistic milieu.[8] The curriculum led to disillusionment, rebellion, dissatisfaction and mental conflict with the teaching staff.[9] In 1974, his graduation year, Paul Robbrecht was asked to organise an architectural exhibition in the Institute's White Room gallery. With the title 'Architecture or Picking Strawberries?' twenty or so students, including Paul Robbrecht, Hilde Daem, Marie-José Van Hee and Christian Kieckens, rebelled against the indolence of the lecturers in the design studio. When senior lecturers like Paul Van Maele and Rutger Langaskens refused to take the initiative seriously, the students hung their derisive slogans on the wall in huge gothic letters. 'Architecture? Child's play', 'Basic architecture is shit architecture', 'Architecture and the pill, license to do as you please'. The exhibition was a revolt for a new architectural discourse. Echoing pop art and the new international cultural scene, the exhibition consisted of a series of readymade and everyday objects. Lego farmhouses, flashing statuettes of the Virgin Mary and Jesus, knitted sweaters by Myriam Callebaut with the letters NY, etc., were displayed. Three toilet bowls were set up in the display cabinet at the entrance. Through this the students made a statement about the mental state of their school, responding less to its sterility, and more to the absence of debate. At the same time the desire for a substantive discourse was reinforced.

No matter how dark the education may have appeared to their generation then, and today, one can still identify several elements that may have shaped and driven their design mentality. In the article *Zie Tekening: Uitdaging voor een Tekenpedagogie [See Drawing: the Challenges facing the Pedagogy of Drawing]* Robin Schaverbeke describes the evolution of the drawing and redrawing of architectural details in the course (only Gothic and neo-Gothic elements until the First World War). In the 1970s sketching was, by way of tradition, still high on the curriculum. Erik Boone, an artist of impressive architectural and drawing fluency, taught observational sketching in the first year, followed by live model drawing with sculptor Maurits Witdouck in the second year. The architect Pierre Pauwels taught the subject of complex stone cutting, which was designed to give the students spatial awareness. The students' eyes were opened by the complex analyses they encountered in the subject of geometry, taught by brother Urbain. Every week they spent two hours sketching at the institute and one hour sketching in town. They would complete three sketches over the weekend. These sketches were kept and filed to monitor the students' progress. Brother Alfred's conviction that the art of sketching could only be learned by training and exercise was clearly still alive.[10] This is why sketching continued through the final year of the course and why students received mandatory sketching exercises as homework. The discipline of constant exercise led to manual technical proficiency, for which drawing was clearly the most appropriate tool.

However, the drawing method involved more than rational and technical elements, and went beyond a recording skill. The ability to see -'L'érudition des yeux" - was the precondition for artistic creation; drawing was the means to that end.[11] In observational drawing and live sketching the students drew subjects from real life to learn to interpret and capture their expressive, spatial and constructive characteristics. Brother Alfred identified three elements in sketching: *la lecture (voir)* learning to observe an object mindfully, *l'analyse (comprendre)* using reason to analyse the form in order to better understand its structure, *la réproduction (écrire)* putting to paper what the eye has seen and the mind has understood. Since its foundation the Sint-Lucas school had employed the 'descriptive' design methodology.[12] Sketching the architectural fragments in the school's sculpture garden was less about understanding the concepts of proportion and perfection, and more about developing an alphabet and rich vocabulary.[13] The power of the Sint-Lucas tradition lay in the combined study of Neo-Gothic and Gothic historical models, whose descriptive character made room for contemporary interpretation. In a self-evident manner, old and new blend together. A comprehension of the existing models (provided by the school up to 1970 and not left in the hands of the students) would lead to a moral, emotional and aesthetic juncture centred on architectural creation.[14] It was the ground for the design of a new architecture, albeit within the established framework. Drawing was an autonomous art form that helped refine observation, analysis and synthesis. It was in this sense that for decades the technical skill of drawing was the basic tool employed to develop design mentality at Sint-Lucas. It was a foundation from which the student could set about creating new architecture.

L. Van Mechelen, Het Gulden Getal: Dekmantel voor de proporties in de Kunst. Course syllabus on the Golden Section and the Plastic number, Sint-Lucas, 1980.
Cover of course syllabus, personal archive Christian Kieckens.

Drawing was not just the sole instrument by which to arrive at an architectural design, or even communicate it. It was also a medium between seeing and creating. The architect was seen as the craftsman/craftswoman, who in creating must never lose touch with the material. This attitude permeates the architecture of Marie-José Van Hee. Her student drawings were legendary - everything was determined, delineated and calculated minutely, to the millimetre. She aspired to create good architecture in every sense of the word. Drawing was the basis for design mentality, and the significance of the margin between drawing, design and execution was sought out as an essential factor in this. Individual details played a fundamental role. The 'thinking hand' was the point of departure in the quest for architecture itself. The drawing, the hand, the craftsman/craftswoman takes centre stage. 'The Craftsman', says Peter O'Neill in *Crafting a Better Life*, 'revolves around the idea that craftsmanship - the sustained act of making physical things - often shapes our identity and cultivates a communal sensibility. In terms of quality of life, craftsmanship enriches one's being: more specifically, using one's hands leads to self-awareness and vocational identity'.[15] The result of this work, in this case architecture, is embedded in society and is what allows us to make it our own. And, of course, this 'thinking producing culture' was a familiar concept at the Sint-Lucas school. It was an *Arts & Crafts* institute and, as such, its art and architecture departments had always been closely related, even if only by their physical proximity in the 1970s. In the final debate of the 'Point Zero' event Paul Robbrecht made explicit reference to the benefit of studying at an art school, of being confronted with other arts on an almost daily basis and of sensing, observing and absorbing the creation of paintings, sculptures and glass art at close quarters.[16]

Nonetheless, there are many layers to craftsmanship and it chafes against architecture's own discipline and autonomy in many ways. The drawings produced by Van Hee, Kieckens, Robbrecht en Daem are not merely images and writings, but a medium

'The sculpture garden of Sint-Lucas Zwartezusterstraat with gothic elements made by students of the academy, shown here as background to the exhibition Lapides ad Initium. 'The works of art included in the Lapides-project (...) were added to the historical collection of stones. Works of art that make us think about material and its reworking by human hands, the relation between nature and culture, the principle of stacking and tension, the column as primal element of architecture, the relation between text and material.' Dubois, Marc, Lapides ad Initium, exhibition initiative Yves De Smet. With work by among others Paul Gees, Jean-Marc Navez and Jean-Georges Massart, 1986.
CAO Tijdingen, volume 3 no 1, October 1986.
Photos Piet Ysabie.

through which both can be meaningfully interpreted. It is an investigative gesture, to be interpreted in a movement of two parts. Architecture's main justification lies in the value of its appearance and how it is experienced, in its content and consequently its own *being*. Architecture is a discipline with its own laws and rules, which each and every architect must discover. The form and spatiality, which he or she achieves, should be seen as the end product of a substantive process. On the other hand, any resumption of this relative autonomy implies a resumption of the architect's responsibility. The search for architectural autonomy is connected to the discovery of the history of architecture, of craftsmanship and of the architect's social responsibility. It is for this reason that we recognise in Van Hee, Kieckens, Robbrecht en Daem the desire and the will to redefine the architectural taxonomy by combining it with an in-depth study of historical typologies and architectures. Bringing autonomy to architecture did not imply the wholesale adoption of a set of universal laws. On the contrary, a building's design had to fit uniquely within its own, obvious context. In which case the architect was less responsible for the social aspect than for the building that housed and facilitated that same social dimension. In this way architecture did not determine the social aspect, but prevented it from being determined. And knowledge of the past played a major role in this.

The reapplication of ideas required to draw lessons from the past, was present in several of the courses and in several forms. Paul Kongs taught the class in architectural history in a way that was not purely historiographic, but presented the knowledge as themes, which allowed its implications for the present to be conveyed. For the subject of topical art and architecture Gilbert De Roeck took the students on a memorable trip to the Netherlands to visit Henry van de Velde's Kröller-Müller Museum, Herman Hertzberger's Montessori school in Delft, and the Frank Van Klingeren project in Dronten. As a young lecturer Jacques De Visscher taught philosophy in a profound and captivating manner, drawing connections with contemporary art and film. We can assume that this representation of knowledge was most explicitly conveyed in the lessons on architectural theory. Brother Urbain asked his colleague, brother Alfons Hoppenbrouwers, lecturer and director of the Sint-Lucas archives in Brussels, to teach this subject between 1972 and 1974.[17] The course was a ray of hope in the curriculum, opening the way to a new architectural thinking. Past and present were set in direct opposition. As in the Sint-Lucas tradition, knowledge of one's own past was never cast in doubt. But the aim of this course differed. Hoppenbrouwers defined building as explicit, architectural theory, through a series of historical texts and books, from the futurist manifesto to *Architectural Principles in the Age of Humanism* by Rudolf Wittkower. Interesting examples of this cast iron theory include the interpretations of baroque by Christian Kieckens, the impact of Adolf Loos on Van Hee, and of Louis Sullivan on the building of the BAC bank in Kerksken, to name but a few.[18]

On its own, of course, craftsmanship (aesthetics, sketching techniques, building techniques, history of architecture, composition, etc.) is no guarantee of the ability to create interesting and meaningful work. Often, the determining factors will also

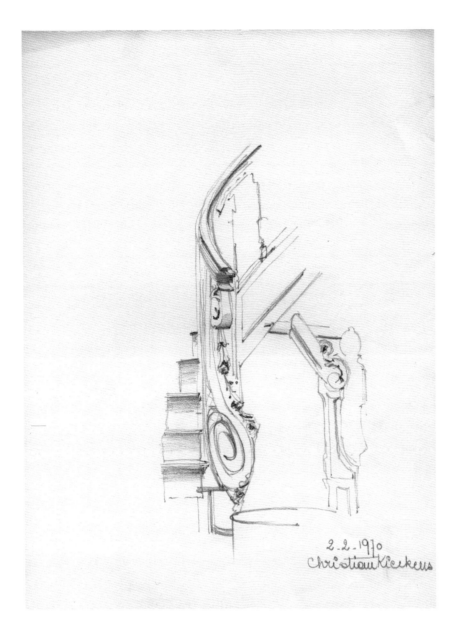

Christian Kieckens,
sketch for course in perception
drawing, Architecture studies
first year, Sint-Lucas, 1970.
Personal archive
Christian Kieckens.

lie in the peculiarities of the designer's line of reasoning and his or her interaction with others.[19] Philosopher and architect Irina Solovyova tells us that design thinking exists in relation to emotional significance derived from autobiographical experiences.[20] Significant emotional events are embedded in the memory and affect the way we picture architectural concepts. The mind registers significant experiences and captures them in its memory. It is an ensemble of scattered elements and influences, which the architect brings together in the design process to form a meaningful constellation. Architects draw on the past: they use the power of their imagination to abstract and combine it to create future design solutions. The latent, subconscious knowledge of the designer is unlocked and often serves as an indispensable stimulus for new insights. It is not so much storage, but a representation of knowledge in their own discipline, of the building itself.

Design thinking at the Sint-Lucas institute is not based on a pre-determined architectural style, nor is it theoretical or practical. The curriculum in general has always been open to all kinds of styles and influences. Sint-Lucas may have taught skills and doctrines, but it did not impose a doctrine of art. Architecture is an ongoing search, in which drawing and the creation of meaning have formed a crucial pairing. To put it in the words of bOb Van Reeth, who taught briefly at Sint-Lucas while the generation of 1974 were there, analogous with brother Urbain:

> 'For me architecture is: the search for architecture. I don't actually know what architecture is. For me, design means carrying out research: I'm not someone who knows, but someone who searches. That's the only way to discover things.' [21]

Herein lies the seed of the quest for an autonomous logic in architecture. What can a school do other than provide a scatter of interesting points, which a motivated student might then transform into meaningful constellations?

**Christian Kieckens,
sketch for course in life
drawing, Architecture studies
fifth year, Sint-Lucas, 1974.**
Personal archive
Christian Kieckens.

Marc Dubois,
sketch for course
in life drawing,
Architecture studies first
year, Sint-Lucas, 1970.
Personal archive Marc Dubois.
(top)

Jury for the international
competion 'Kuip van Gent',
1987. 125 years Sint-Lucas
Gent. Initiative and
coordination: Marc Dubois.
From left to right: Jo Coenen
(NL), Evert Lagrou, Marc
Dubois, BrunoVayssière (F),
Fabian Van Sande, Charles
Vandenhove, Jean Barthélémy.
Photo Christian Galle.
(below)

1 Special issue 'Recente Architectuur in België', *Archis* 9 (1987).

2 Francis Strauven, 'De Negatie van de Eigen Bouwcultuur', *Archis* 9 (1987): 12-17.

3 Marc Dubois, 'Jonge Architecten in België', *Archis* 4 (1989): 14.

4 Yves Schoonjans had graduated just a few years earlier, and Hera Van Sande was midway through her studies.

5 Marc Dubois, 'Jonge architecten in België', *Archis* 4 (1989): 14-25.

6 Dirk Van de Perre, *Op de grens van twee werelden. Beeld van het architectuuronderwijs aan het Sint-Lucasinstituut te Gent in de periode 1919-1965/1974.* (Ghent: Provincial Government of East Flanders, 2003): 44.

7 Christophe Van Gerrewey, 'Saintluquismen - 150 jaar Kritiek op Sint-Lucas', in *Tekenen & Betekenen: Opstellen over het architectuurinstituut Sint-Lucas 1862-2012*, eds. Rajesh Heynickx, Yvs Schoonjans, Sven Sterken (Leuven: Leuven University Press, 2012): 94.

8 Geertrui Vandist, 'Christian Kieckens en de Barok', Interview 2008, University of Gent. Available online in *TXT_INT_CK* [http://www.christiankieckens.be/downloads/pdf/236.pdf, last consulted on 8 September 2015]. 'Each of us had investigated a particular architect or area, Paul Robbrecht studied Louis Kahn for example, and we 'taught' each other. We also went off in Paul's little Citroën 2CV to look at houses by Juliaan Lampens, Paul Felix, etc. I personally subscribed to *Domus* and *L'Architecture d'Aujourd'hui*, so I had a good idea of what was going on in the international world of architecture.'

9 Vandist, 'Christian Kieckens en de Barok'. So rife was the dissatisfaction that when he received the Godecharle prize in 1979, Paul Robbrecht reported Alfons Hoppenbrouwers and Paul Kongs as his studio lecturers instead of the official ones, Rutger Langaskens and Paul Van Maele.

10 Van de Perre, Op de grens van twee werelden, 66.

11 Van de Perre, *Op de grens van twee werelden*, 44.

12 Karel Wuytack, 'De beeldentuin - Een plek van educatie, reflectie en contestatie', in *Tekenen & Betekenen: Opstellen over het architectuurinstituut Sint-Lucas 1862-2012*, eds. Rajesh Heynickx, Yves Schoonjans, Sven Sterken (Leuven: Leuven University Press, 2012).

13 Van de Perre, *Op de grens van twee werelden*, 44.

14 Robin Schaeverbeke, 'Zie tekening - Uitdagingen voor de Tekenpedagogie op Sint-Lucas', in *Tekenen & Betekenen: Opstellen over het architectuurinstituut Sint-Lucas 1862-2012*, eds. Rajesh Heynickx, Yves Schoonjans, Sven Sterken (Leuven: Leuven University Press, 2012): 36.

15 Peter O'Neill, 'Crafting a Better Life', in *Applied Research in Quality of Life 4 (2009)*: 312.

16 *mOments lecture series: The generation of 1974 revisits the moments that have been characteristic of their vision*, Closing debate of 4 June 2015, Faculty of Architecture KU Leuven, Sint-Lucas Ghent campus.

17 W. Goossens, 'De AH-Erlebnis - Dagboekaantekeningen over een geïntegreerd architectuurdenken', in *Tekenen & Betekenen: Opstellen over het architectuurinstituut Sint-Lucas 1862-2012*, eds. Rajesh Heynickx, Yves Schoonjans, Sven Sterken (Leuven: Leuven University Press, 2012): 29.

18 Whereas the prevailing mood during these studies was one of boundless faith in the future, the cultural crisis of 1968 was followed by economic crisis in the mid 1970s. Construction work declined, and there was no work for the new graduates. A long period of independent study began for Van Hee, Robbrecht, Daem and Kieckens. Each of them gradually became 'immersed' in the history of architecture. Robbrecht en Daem had a huge interest in the development of visual art and the effect it might have on architecture. They took their inspiration not just from contemporary art but from the classical tradition of architecture. After winning the Rome Prize (1979) and the Godecharle Prize (1979) Robbrecht went on an educational trip through Italy, where he immersed himself in the Renaissance and became a member of the Centro Palladio.

19 Harold Rugg, *Imagination* (New York: Harper and Row Publishers, 1963): 192.

20 Irina Solovyova, 'The role of the autobiographical experiences with emotional significance of an architect in design conjecturing', (PhD diss., Texas A&M University, 2008): 1.

21 bOb Van Reeth, interview in *B-nieuws*, no.16 (2003).

Concentration consummates a certain line of technical development in the hand. The hands have had before to experiment through touch, but according to an objective standard; they have learned to coordinate inequality; they have learned the application of minimum force and release. The hands thus establish a repertoire of learned gestures. The gestures can be further refined or revised within the rhythmic process that occurs in, and sustains, practicing.

Richard Sennett, *The Craftsman* (New Haven: Yale University Press, 2008): 178.

The Thinking Hand

Tracing the Design Process of
Marie-José Van Hee, Paul Robbrecht
and Christian Kieckens

The following series are stills from interviews.
The interviews took place as part of the mOmenten series organised by Fragile,
Faculty of Architecture, KU Leuven, Campus Sint-Lucas, 2014-2015.

Tutors:	Carl Bourgeois and Caroline Voet
Student team Marie-José Van Hee:	Ghan Oudhuis, Willem Devos, Karel Sucaet and Fran Pieters
Student team Paul Robbrecht:	Matthias Decleer, Pieter Dossche and Matteo Lampaert
Student team Christian Kieckens:	Reintje Jacobs, Hannelore Pauwels and Kelly Coomans

Marie-José Van Hee elaborates on her design for the house in Opwijk

Stills taken from the interview with Marie-José Van Hee
at her house in Varkensstraat in Ghent, 26 November 2014.

'I will tell you how I designed the house in Opwijk. The previous house was positioned orthogonally on the terrain...

...and the adjacent building followed this direction cutting off the oblique pathway so everybody had to walk around it. We proposed a withdrawn facade, so the town received a triangular piece here...

...while we filled this triangle in the corner. In such a manner as to allow such the pavement to continue nicely, and the corner disappears.'

'...still it was the goal to tilt the bedrooms over the practice in the front building block.'

'So actually the stair here bends to arrive at the facade line.'

'Then you get the further organisation such as the double carport, serving as a parking space for the patients with their children.'

'...because behind it you have the garage. I wanted to take some distance from that.'

'It becomes a kind of strong buffer against the garage boxes at the back.'

'In this strip you have a shower and toilet, and storage space...

'So the pool story became almost political, a totally different history altogether...

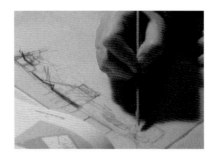

...and then here we have a shed for the chickens.'

'In the back we planted a couple of trees to mask the back facades of the other houses deeper in the plot...'

'So this was one of the starting points.'

'Then we had the idea to bring in light here, so we brought in the rotation at the back.'

'The living space found its place around the rotated strip and then an intermediate space was made in order to separate the practice from the private part...'

'Then you get a passage through everything, outside...

...and then the passage inside, first hallway, second hallway, and so on.'

'Actually this entire wall, the wall that you have there, is a cabinet wall that unfolds into a storage room to then become a cabinet again along this whole passage ...

...meant for the swimming pond that we will make here.'

'So here there is a planted piece, a water piece, brick and here we position a small sauna.'

'The neighbor objected to this pool, while he filled his lot with garage boxes with plastic roofing!'

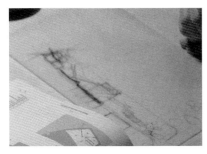

'...and also because as such we continue the line of trees already situated within the inner area of the wider building block.'

'That is grosso modo the design. It grows from an initial starting point, through an idea!'

'The initial design is nothing more than a series of conditions that are present, that need to be witnessed and taken as starting points.'

Paul Robbrecht explains his design for a pavilion with a stage for the Horst Arts & Music Festival 2015, in collaboration with Guy Mouton

Stills taken from the interview with Paul Robbrecht
in his office in Ghent, 19 November 2014.

'In one way or another, whatever we design is connected to this place, where we live, reside and work. Each time it holds a kind of reference to this situation,...

...that we actually use to embark upon other projects, in particular this project that I want to talk about. Horst.'

'More specifically, we are designing a stage for a dj-festival there and this departs from the space of our office residence: to create an arch around a space, as a basic condition of making architecture.'

'... from rain and wind.'

'The most special feature is the direct confrontation of the place with the beautiful water castle of Horst, only a bit more than a hundred meters away but very present.'

'During the festival, several art projects will reside around the castle lake.'

'We hope for and count on the light, also daylight. The sunset takes place in this direction from the river.'

'Because of the clear plastic it will create a kind of luminosity, a halo.'

'I almost don't dare say it, but in the past Speer also designed such a light dome for the large assemblies of the Nazi's in Neurenberg.'

'For this project we are collaborating with Guy Mouton. We never worked together before, but we taught together. This time we felt like doing something...

...and Guy is working on it intensely, because it is not a straightforward project. There are no laboratory tests for what those plastic boards can and can not handle.'

'For the fence we need to provide for a series of poles, partially drilled in the ground. We saw it as a kind of demarcation, literally, of a place.'

'We will do this as a kind of demarcation of that place. We will place a series of four woven spans and wooden planks.'

'And this is like our own hall here that serves as a kind of inspiration. A kind of structure, that will carry the roof in transparent wavy plastic.'

'It is a kind of envelope and of course protection for the techniques that will be placed underneath...'

'So we thought about a vault but also a kind of enclosure and housing of that place. We want to expose it a little...

...but also hide it a little. You don't need to see everything when you arrive. It becomes a very readable enclosure of the landscape...

... amidst those strong elements there, that castle, that great pond. To isolate something and offer a place for 1500 people, young people I think, that will experience the festival.'

'Don't suspect me of being inspired by that, but he made light beams to flow over the masses.'

'So on the one hand there is the sun that sends a kind of changing light over the scaled walls of the enclosure, and on the other hand of course artificial light; simple TL-lights with bright white light.'

'Still we think a kind of chromaticism, a kind of color will be created. Continuously changing colors that with the production of sound will create a kind of momentum.'

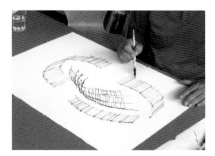

'Then we are not far from the manner in which the Roman solders built their camps. By knocking one pole besides the other. So we named the project Castra...

... that is the name of that place. Sounded nice, too. The only thing I need to add is the small stage, that stands as a kind of almond shape under the dome.'

'Let's see how we will succeed, it will be a miracle. But there is a lot of energy at that place, I met the people, young people, fantastic! They want to completely go for it, and I like to take part in that.'

Christian Kieckens, geometric scheme of the San Carlo alle Quattro Fontane by Francesco Borromini in Rome

Stills taken from the interview with Christian Kieckens
in his office in Brussels, 19 December 2014.

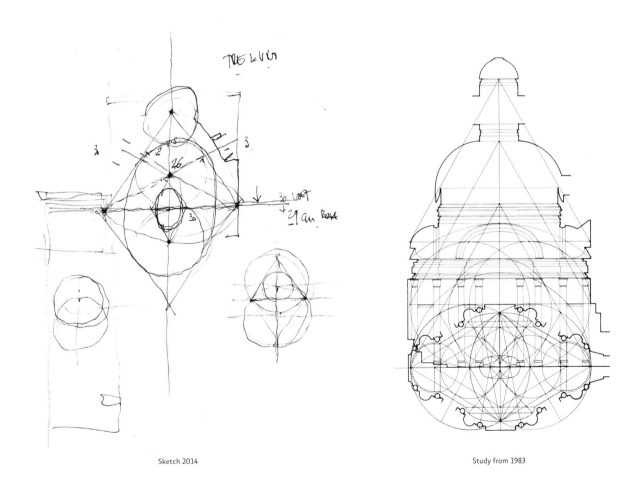

Sketch 2014

Study from 1983

'To explain the proportion 26:30, and to show the proportion of the Borromini church...

...starts with the drawing of a crucifix horizontal and vertical plane...

in one direction divided in 30 feet, one feet being 29 cm as determined by the Romans.'

'Then this gives something else: when you draw the perpendicular from the triangle, the intersection divides the height of the triangle into a 2 : 1 proportion.'

'From that point you can inscribe a circle.'

'You can do this twice, the construction of the anchor points important for the triangles and the inscribed circles.'

'... if we then rotate it, and add this element here... Scarpa!'

'There are uniform systems in this Scarpa design, uniformity between man and female in relation to the two circles...

...and that resemblance, we see it at a moment that we come together in the 1970s and 80s.'

'...and as such, you can trace the complete geometric pattern of the church.'

'Furthermore, you can draw the section with the drawing of the plan and so on. But this I don't remember completely by heart.'

'To define this... it means ' tre et uno assieme', three and one together.'

'The system is based on the drawing of a quarter circle in that direction, and in the other...'

'...forming a square.'

'The proportion 26:30 is formed at the intersection of the two axes.'

'This means that we have this story, of two overlapping circles.'

'So these circles serve to define the inscribed geometry, the whole Borrominian systematic.'

'This can also be seen, I redraw the two points here, then the two circles...'

'I take this anecdote to explain that these things don't stand on their own, you see it in all kind of elements.'

'Now, if you continue in the Borromini church, you see that passages are situated in the extension of the perpendicular, here to the atrium and here to the crypt.'

'You can then draw another circle at the top of the triangle...'

'Then you see here the dome, and here a smaller interstitial space, here the lantern.'

'You have the plan, you have the dome, you have the lantern and the light. The light that falls down in this direction. That is the complete Borrominian scheme.'

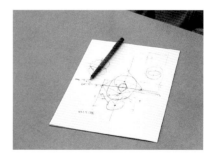

'Beautiful, no? We architects do not work like that anymore now, but I think it is beautiful.'

More than Punctual Interventions
Cultural Events, Competitions and Public Debate as Impetus for Architectural Culture in Flanders, 1974-2000

Sofie De Caigny
Katrien Vandermarliere

1974. Belgium was in the midst of an architectural crisis. Between 1965 and 1975, according to Geert Bekaert, architecture was slowly going under.[1] Due to the economic malaise the building industry went into serious decline after 1973, and in particular young architects found it difficult to find work. Francis Strauven diagnosed the situation in 1980: 'Once Belgian architecture had, and not without difficulty, assimilated functionalism or some derivative of it, and learned to concentrate on the production of 'functionally' expressive objects, it lost all sense of urban character and contextuality, and now finds it extremely difficult to recapture those qualities'.[2] The malaise was caused by a mix of an ineffective or non-existent architectural policy, a politicised process of commissioning, inadequate conservation of historic buildings (with only few protected monuments) and architectural education that generally was not very inspiring and that gave short shrift to the discipline's social responsibilities. Moreover, architects could not rely on a vivid architectural culture in Belgium.[3] There were no exhibition spaces in which architecture could be shown, nor places where it could be discussed from a cultural perspective. Brussels has two architectural archival institutes since 1968 (Sint-Lukas Archives and Archives d'Architecture Moderne), but they were more concerned with the loss of Brussels' valuable heritage of art nouveau and art deco than with contemporary architecture. There were no competitions, the workings of the Association of Architects was heavily criticized and there was no critical magazine for architecture, despite the foundation of A+ in 1973. The lack of a forum for critique and the deteriorating Belgian construction climate was made painfully evident in a polemic by Geert Bekaert which, though refused by A+, was published in a special edition on Belgium in the Dutch magazine Wonen TA/BK in 1983.[4] One of the consequences was that there was no such thing as Belgian architecture abroad. Another was that a group of orphaned young architects without commissions were forced to make their way in a professional environment that was anything but challenging. Such was the climate in which the protagonists of this book found themselves.

2015. Architects of the 1974 generation, as well as younger (particularly Flemish) Belgian architects, are winning competitions abroad. They are invited to teach at highly qualified international architectural schools, to exhibit their work, to curate exhibitions and to give lectures. Foreign architectural magazines publish on architecture in

Charles Vandenhove Architecture, fragment façade Design Museum Gent, for exhibition Chambres d'Amis, Ghent, 1986.
Charles Vandenhove, Art and Architecture (Doornik, 1998): 259.

Flanders.[5] What has happened in the last four decades? How could an architectural culture develop in Flanders that is influential abroad? What characterises this culture and who has played a leading role?[6]

A BURGEONING ARCHITECTURAL CULTURE

In hindsight it seems that two moments in 1983 proved important to recent architecture in Belgium. At that time the Carrefour de l'Europe was the subject of the Bonduelle competition, according to Geert Bekaert this was the first time the new generation could brandish their talents in a public architecture commission. In addition to the acclaimed Georges Baines, the architects Jo Crepain, Georges Volcrick and the Hoogpoort team (Stéphane Beel, Xaveer De Geyter, Arjan Karssenberg and Willem Jan Neutelings) submitted entries. The competition did not pass without discussion, because the results demonstrated the potential that existed to turn this blot on the Brussels North-South Connection into a lively, urban setting. Despite the dynamic unleashed by the competition, the Carrefour de l'Europe ended up being privatised and cheapened by pastiche hotel architecture that stemmed from a tangle of political interference and lobbying by promoters. This was tremendously disappointing.

In 1983 too, Marc Dubois and Christian Kieckens set up the Architecture Museum Foundation (S/AM), which had a far-reaching effect on the development of an architectural culture. S/AM functioned as a platform for discussion about architecture. Its exhibitions and publications provided a stage for young architects whose relatively small commissions from 'enlightened' clients enabled them to experiment and almost soundlessly they changed the course of architecture in Flanders. Additionally, S/AM organised foreign trips to inspiring examples of architecture. The foundation's magazine evolved from a fairly amateurish rag to a respectable series of architectural monographs. Along with an international programme of lectures these publications satisfied the architects' demands for foreign and historical references and for criticism, information and reflection on architecture.[7]

S/AM was not the first of Dubois and Kieckens' initiatives. In 1977, at the age of 27, Dubois became one of the youngest members ever of the Royal Commission for Monuments and Landscapes.[8] He was also involved in founding the architectural association Archipel in 1979, and Interbellum in 1980, another non-profit organisation dedicated to the study and conservation of valuable patrimonial heritage from the 1920s and 1930s. In 1980 Dubois began to publish articles in Wonen TA/BK, where he frequently expressed his interest in contemporary architecture, architectural history and the preservation of historic buildings. He wrote about the legacy of modernism in Belgium, studying figures such as Gaston Eysselinck (1907-1953), and about contemporary architecture and (the lack of) government policy in this area. More than ten years later, when publishing the first Flanders Architectural Yearbook in 1994, he noted that in his eyes architectural culture meant 'the creation of conditions to enable the development of an architectural culture, a culture cultivated on historical reflection and topical critique'.[9] From the very beginning this layering of ideas was present in his efforts to nurture an architectural culture and help generate awareness for the built environment. Before the foundation of S/AM, Christian Kieckens had also proven to be an architect who not only looked to the present and the future, but used valuable elements from the past, when honouring his intellectual patron Pieter De Bruyne (1931-1987) in 1981. The two founders of S/AM had never intended to gloss the past with nostalgia, but to study it in order to translate its qualities to the present. How they might lend shape to this in a contemporary way was the challenge that Kieckens and Dubois took on. In addition, Kieckens sought to discover the boundaries of architecture as a discipline, by, *inter alia*, incorporating visual art and design. He was more inclined than was Dubois to bring his interest in art to bear on his architectural research. These two lines, i.e. historical reflection and dialogue with the visual arts, were extended by two initiatives in Ghent in the second half of the 1980s.

In 1986 the arts events Initiatief 86 and Chambres d'Amis took place in Ghent. For the Chambres d'Amis, artists created works of art in private homes that often intentionally reflected on the surrounding architecture where the piece of art was created. Luc Deleu's art installation of two power pylons on St. Peter's Square, Paul Robbrecht en Hilde Daem's scenography for a section of the Initiatief 86 group exhibition and Charles Vandenhove's intervention on the 16th-century façade of the Museum of Decorative Art made it quite clear that architects could play a challenging role in the world of art.[10]

Robbrecht en Daem, Scenography, Initiatief 86, Sint-Pietersabdij, Ghent: works by René Heyvaert, 1986.
Photo Piet Ysabie.

Two years later a new event in Ghent placed architecture itself centre stage. Architectuur als Buur (Architecture as Neighbour) was an architectural festival organised by Architectuurpromotie, a non profit organisation of several public and private organisations, such as the Union of Architects, the Historic Buildings and City Archaeology Department of the City of Ghent, the S/AM, the Royal Association of Master Builders of East-Flanders and the National Association of Architects. The highlights of the event were an exhibition, visits to interesting buildings, a debate, a publication and an architecture guide, all of which had clear educational objectives. The architectural festival sought to be a 'call to create a positive architectural climate, in which a collective sense of responsibility would lead to a high quality urban development and architectural modernisation process'. It used the 'strategy of creating a broad public platform to discuss contemporary architecture.'[11] Notably, the administration of the city was aware of the city's responsibility concerning contemporary architecture, given its role as both commissioner, and as the administration for approval (or rejection) of building permissions. From an administrative viewpoint it took quite some time before an official response came to the underlying demands of Architectuur als Buur, through the foundation of the unit of architecture at the Historic Buildings Department, a relatively independent urban development service and the Chamber of Quality. What did come fairly quickly was a tax on abandonment. The main effect of Architectuur als Buur in the short term was that public awareness for contemporary architecture grew, and that architecture was taken seriously as a cultural discipline. Young architects were given interesting private commissions, partly because of the attention the event received in popular media. In hindsight Architectuur als Buur functioned as a catalyst for the many town festivals and architectural events that became popular in Flanders in the 1990s and through which urban (re)discoveries and city development became linked to tourism and the promotion of the city.

In the meantime, in the mid 1980s, an initiative originated in Antwerp that would make an enduring contribution to the burgeoning architectural culture. Under the directorship of Frie Leysen, the international arts centre deSingel launched a series of architectural exhibitions in 1985. Architectural programmer Carolina De Backer worked in close collaboration with Geert Bekaert and Mil de Kooning. The deSingel exhibition programme featured Belgian architects such as Charles Vandenhove (1986), AWG (1987), Luc Deleu (1987), Marc Dessauvage (1987), Paul Robbrecht and Hilde Daem (1989) alongside international designers such as OMA in 1985, Aldo Rossi in 1986 and Luigi Snozzi in 1989. In addition, themed exhibitions focused on topical subjects through reflection on the past, such as 'Adolf Loos - Le Corbusier. Raumplan versus plan libre' in 1987-88. This gave architecture a place in the arts scene and the arts centre devoted resources to professional architectural activities, something which remained quite unique for many years. Soon a synergetic relationship grew between the S/AM and deSingel, and in the spring of 1988 the exhibition entitled 'Young Architects in Belgium' presented the S/AM's selections from 1985 to 1987. At the opening of this exhibition Jo Crepain read a letter to four ministers out loud, in which he pleaded on behalf of '28 angry young men' for good clientship and for a system of public competitions in which quality (and not political relations) were the most important criteria.[12] The action of this group of young architects, who had nothing to lose, showed how critical questions and demands could be expressed to policymakers from the refuge of a cultural niche.

Architectuur als Buur.
Panorama view of Ghent and surroundings
(Turnhout: Brepols, 1988).

AWG Architecten,
Floating theater De Ark,
Antwerp, 1993.
Archive AWG Architecten.
Photo Wim Van Nueten.

GATHERING MOMENTUM

A year after Crepain's statement at deSingel there was hope of an about-face. In 1989, nine renowned architects from Belgium and abroad were invited to take part in a restricted competition for the construction of a new Sea Terminal in Zeebrugge. Projects were submitted by Rem Koolhaas, Charles Vandenhove, Fumihiko Maki, Aldo Rossi in association with Claude Zuber, and bOb Van Reeth. Although Geert Bekaert described the competition as an 'innovation' and a 'point at which the Zeebrugge policy gave rise to a hope that architecture would be taken seriously in Belgium', the project wasn't realised.[13] But things seemed to be gaining momentum and initiatives followed in ever quicker succession, including architectural competitions and shows on architecture from Flanders, both at international and local platforms. It seemed that change might actually be possible. Following the letter of the '28 angry young men' in deSingel, the S/AM managed to sweep from the table a clichéd design for the Belgian pavilion at the World Exhibition in Seville, and the contract was won on the back of a public competition (1991) by the young firm of Giedo Driesen, Jan Meersman and Jan Thomaes.

The dynamic caught on in smaller Flemish towns and cities. Local architectural associations such as Architectuurwijzer (1991) and Stad en Architectuur (1997) were formed and city councils set up competitions. In 1990, for example, Kortrijk and the intermunicipal organization Leiedal invited tenders for the development of Hoog-Kortrijk, a contract which was won by Bernardo Secchi. With its Domus Flandria project the Flemish government hoped in 1990 to catch up on its social housing stock, and sought to employ good architecture in the process. In Ghent, for example, a project for 129 social housing units on the Hollainkazerne site was awarded to Willem Jan Neutelings following a competition in 1993. Competitions for Wonen in Gent (WIG) and the WISH competitions organised by the Minister for Housing, Mr Buchmann, originally sparked hope of better architecture through a public procedure, although the results turned out to be a disappointment when local networking swayed the decision-making process.[14]

Of a different magnitude and with a greater impact on later developments was Stad aan de Stroom in Antwerp. This study group, which was made up of architects, civil engineers and representatives of civil society, sought to generate ideas through an international architectural competition for the districts Het Eilandje, Zuid and the Scheldekaaien, three former port areas that were in decline following the loss of harbour activities nearby the city centre in the 20th century. The competitions were a success: invited international designers submitted proposals for the three former harbour districts. The competition also boosted the local architectural dynamic since more than 100 young Belgian architects submitted proposals. There was a public debate on the feasibility and desirability of the projects, and in 1992 two detailed proposals (from Toyo Ito for Zuid and from Manuel de Solà-Morales for Het Eilandje) were approved in principle by the city council and presented to the public.

One of the effects was that architecture was given a central position in the Antwerp Cultural Capital of Europe '93 program, under the program Studio Open Stad which was curated by Pieter Uyttenhove. The focus lay on urban culture, through which the city's past, its image and representation, and research by design were connected to each other. The 19th-century city belt became the working space in which these three pillars were developed. Antwerp '93 and Stad aan de Stroom were extremely important to the architectural climate in Flanders. Neither of the two events led to specific architectural or urban projects in the short term (only general disappointment in the decisiveness of politics where Stad aan de Stroom was concerned), with the exception of a few significant restorations (such as the Bourla Schouwburg) or one-off projects in the city, such as the Ark, a 77-metre floating theatre/café designed by AWG for Antwerp '93. But they both lent a powerful impetus to the rediscovery of the city as a place of economic and cultural activity and creativity, to public awareness, to a vision for urban development and the role that architecture can play in this. In addition, Studio Open Stad served as a catalyst for getting the various Belgian architectural schools to rethink urban problems, by bringing together research by design, historical reflection and the theoretical basics of architecture and urban development.[15] Studio Open Stad remained operational for ten years after Antwerp '93 and turned its attention to Brussels, where the arts centre Beursschouwburg played a prominent role as its host.

While it became increasingly obvious that foreign architects should be asked to develop plans and conduct discussions in Flanders in the early 1990s, architecture from Flanders was also able to hold its own in an international context. Meanwhile the discourse on contemporary architecture took a noticeable swing from 'Belgium' to 'Flanders'. Whereas the term 'Belgian' architecture had been used until the late 1980s, and the exhibitions organised by S/AM were entitled 'Young architects from Belgium', the focus quietly shifted towards architecture from Flanders. This shift was linked with the Belgian State's federalisation into Communities and Regions, which was first felt in the domains of education and culture. Given the fact that the young architectural culture in Flanders was able to unfurl in the wake of a dynamic set up by cultural players, for example through its embedding in deSingel and its association with urban culture festivals, architects looked primarily to new possibilities that the emancipatory Flemish cultural policy created. With Flanders' newfound independence and the installation of its own government ministers,

Poster invitations deSingel: Van Hee, Robbrecht en Daem, Kieckens, and Herzog De Meuron. Archive deSingel.

including a minister for Culture, it made more sense for architecture to profile itself as 'Flemish' rather than 'Belgian'. Indeed, it may have had more to do with opportunities and finding resources for (international) presentations, and with the possibility of winning contracts, than with a strong political ideology. Moreover, the growing interest in urban culture in Flanders, through events like Chambres d'Amis, Architectuur als Buur or Antwerp '93, was more than a decade ahead of French-speaking Belgium. On the other hand, the continuity of historical architectural culture was much greater in French-speaking Belgium, due to for example the emancipatory role of the La Cambre school of architecture, which was a reflection of Bauhaus' avant-garde education.[16]

The fact that education was no longer organised by the Belgian government under the state reform of 1988-89, but shifted to the Flemish and French-speaking Communities, helped remove even more of the formal ties between Dutch-speaking and French-speaking architects. This does not mean that architectural developments across the language border were ignored: figures such as Charles Vandenhove and Bruno Albert were still important in Flanders. A big difference between developments in Flanders and French-speaking Belgium was that the evolution in the south of the country was associated with works and figures who were much less concerned with the culture around architecture than was the case in Flanders, despite the fact that on the initiative of architect Philippe Rotthier the Fondation pour l'Architecture was set up in Brussels in 1986 to disseminate an architectural culture through exhibitions and publications.[17] In this dual speed landscape of federalisation, the Belgian magazine *A+*, which issued parallel editions in French and Dutch, played a connecting role as an island between the two cultural communities.

The state reforms implied that there were two speeds and strategies in support of an architectural culture, one on each side of the language border. The succession of state reforms and the emancipation of Flanders made it worthwhile for Flemish policymakers to employ a cultural policy that placed Flanders on the international map. In 1990 the Flemish Community invested for the first time in presenting Flemish architects at an international forum in Berlin and Moscow, using retakes of deSingel exhibitions by

Christian Kieckens,
installation 'Table-landscape',
deSingel, Antwerp, 1997.
Photo Reiner Lautwein.

Luc Deleu (T.O.P Office), bOb Van Reeth (AWG) and Stéphane Beel. However, more significant was Flanders' first participation in the Venice Architecture Biennale in 1991. Marc Dubois had persuaded the minister of Culture, Patrick Dewael, of the importance of the presence of the Flemish Community at this international architectural event, and was appointed as curator. Christian Kieckens' sober and subservient scenography was used to display works by Paul Robbrecht en Hilde Daem, Marie-José Van Hee and other architects of their generation. Artist Johan Van Geluwe brought the surrealist Belgian undertone to light for an international audience, to evoke the context in which architects worked in Flanders. The exhibition did not go unnoticed. Two years later Italian publisher Electa produced an overview of architecture in Belgium since 1970, and in 1994 the French journal *Architecture d'Aujourd'hui* dedicated a special issue to architectural developments in Flanders.

Flemish designers seemed able to enter the international architectural scene with a new flair and self-confidence. Cultural projects were a major instigator. From 1990 onwards, the exhibition policy at deSingel, curated by Katrien Vandermarliere, rested on several cornerstones: monographic exhibitions of work by the young generation of Flemish architects and quirky post-war modernists, high-profile international designers and related disciplines that broadened the perspective of architecture, such as landscape, art and photography. The exhibition space in the Léon Stynen building - 80-metre long and 6-metre wide corridor - invited the architects to address the scenography as an architectural intervention. Along with this exhibition programme deSingel steadily built up a series of architectural publications which were later taken up by publishers Ludion and Lannoo. With exhibitions such as 'Mein erstes Haus' (Amsterdam 1994), 'Nouvelle architecture en Flandre' (Arc-en-Rêve, Bordeaux 1997) and 'Homeward' (which took place in six European cities and the Venice Biennale 1999-2000), deSingel picked up where S/AM had left off after its dissolution in 1993, as regards the international presentation of Flemish architecture.[18] With the professional organization of an international arts centre behind it, Flemish architecture had the capacity to be contrasted, discussed and even held up as an example at international forums. In addition, deSingel offered the space and freedom to help shape the burgeoning architectural policy from a critical perspective. In the mean-time, Dubois continued his work as a critic and curator and kept on making efforts to win international recognition for Flemish architects. For example in 1997, he curated the exhibition Arquitectura de Flandres in the Col.legi de Arquitectes de Catalunya in Barcelona.

ARCHITECTURAL CULTURE AS THE CATALYST FOR POLICY

While architects, lecturers, critics and cultural professionals were building an architectural culture from the ground up, they continued to press for structural government support for quality in architecture. The international exchange helped get things going on a structural level. Architecture may have withstood comparison to neighbouring countries to some degree, at the same time the official architectural policy faltered on crucial aspects, such as the procedures for awarding projects, the quality of public contracts, an appropriate urban development framework, the opportunity to carry out innovative research and the lack of possibilities to publish on architecture. However, the political emancipation of Flanders offered real potential in those areas. In 1992 the Flemish coalition agreement stated for the first time that 'architecture and design must be given a place in culture policy'.[19] The fact that in all that time the most spectacular steps in the development of an architectural culture had taken place in arts centres and at events, now received permanent recognition and possibilities were created for the story to further unfold. An Architecture Study Group started to operate from the Visual Arts and Museums depart-ment of the ministry of the Flemish Community and worked on developing an architec-tural policy.[20] In addition, resources were earmarked for cultural projects on architecture and for (international) grants, and a newly formed Architecture and Design Commission assessed the quality of the applications.

Also in 1992, Stéphane Beel became the first architect to win a Flemish Community culture prize. Since architecture did not have a 'prize of its own', Beel received the prize for visual arts. This recognition of the cultural importance of architecture became permanent when the Flemish Community biennial cultural prize for architecture was introduced in 1995.[21] Also the publication of the first Flanders Architectural Yearbook in 1994 was a breakthrough: from then on there was a permanent tool to hand to analyse the better projects, to start a dialogue on the subject of architecture with policymakers and the general public, and to broadcast recent developments in Flanders abroad. Over the same period Johan Sauwens, minister for Monuments and Sites, made up ground in the area of historical buildings preservation by protecting a large number of monuments, and in 1993 awarding the first Flemish Community monument prize. Historical building

**Marie-José Van Hee,
Installation in Bordeaux, 1996.**
Archive Marie-José Van Hee
architecten.

**Bernardo Secchi & Paola Vigano,
Spoor Noord, Antwerp.**
Photo Stijn Bollaert for Flanders
Architectural Yearbook 2008-2009
edition 2010: 106-117.

preservation and qualitative contemporary architecture were firm allies in the fight for a better architectural climate. This was evidenced once again at a workshop on 'Public buildings and space: a cultural challenge' in Antwerp in 1995, an organisation set up by the Open Monument Day Coordinating Committee, the Flemish Community's Art adminis-tration and deSingel.[22] It was articulated that contemporary architecture and historical building preservation were strongly linked as a fecund medium for a lively architectural culture and as the basis for an integral vision on the quality of the built environment. It was quite clear that environmental planning had a role to play here too. With the approval of the Ruimtelijk Structuurplan for Flanders in 1997, a general spatial zoning plan for the entire region of Flanders, hope grew of bringing into practice an alternative for urban sprawl, the spread of business parks, roads and allotments, which had led to the degeneration of the landscape in Flanders.

In the years before, architects had stressed the necessity to award contracts on the basis of public competitions. The international architecture competition for the renovation of the Beursschouwburg in Brussels in 1997, won by B-Architecten, was a turning point in this. The theatre, with the Flemish Community behind it, revealed itself as an exemplary commissioner and gave hope of a fundamental turnaround.[23] This came one year later when the minister for Finance, Budget and Health, Wivina Demeester, established the Flemish Government Architect (Vlaams Bouwmeester). In the early years, the Flemish Government Architect set up procedures to stimulate the quality of public architecture. This generated a snowball effect of interesting projects and building sites through which the young guard and established archi-tectural firms were given opportunities to create public buildings. These opportunities grew again after 2002 with the installation of Stedenbeleid, an integral urban policy through which strategic urban renewal projects could effectively be realised in 13 Flemish cities.[24]

In the meantime the minister of Culture, Luc Martens, had completed his preparations for the foundation of the Flanders Architecture Institute (VAi). His successor Bert Anciaux inaugurated the VAi in 2001. The VAi was given the tasks of handling the biennial

publication of the Flanders Architectural Yearbook and organising Architecture Day. The idea was established that the quality of the built environment rests not only on the level of the contemporary architecture but also on knowledge and respect for the past, and in 2003 the Centre for Flemish Architectural Archives (CVAa) was incorporated within the VAi. The VAi and CVAa were housed in deSingel and so their incorporation in the arts centre continued.

AN (INTERIM) BALANCE

This article discusses how, as the result of cultural projects and events on architecture, and following the public commotion in relation to certain commissions and competitions, a process of emancipation took place in which Flemish architectural culture reached adulthood. Of course, this focus on the genesis of the contemporary architectural culture through a cultural programme of exhibitions, journeys and events cannot be viewed separately from other developments which also contributed to the current dynamic of the architectural culture. For example, architectural education evolved in the same period, through, *inter alia*, the development of research by design and the installation of chairs of architectural theory, and there were important initiatives such as the *Vlees & Beton* publication series. The history of the present architectural culture is also closely connected to the way in which architecture was discussed in newspapers and other popular media by critics like Geert Bekaert, Mil De Kooning, Marc Dubois, Hilde Heynen, Francis Strauven, Paul Vermeulen and Koen Van Synghel. The sector of art and design also led to intellectual exchange and to opportunities to critically assess architecture, including the efforts of the Interior Foundation in Kortrijk, with its design competitions, guest curators and commissions for scenography, and with the foundation of the Centre for Architecture and Design in 1996, in which Marc Dubois was involved.[25] All these initiatives contributed to public debate and awareness of the added social value of qualitative architecture.

What makes the evolution fascinating from the perspective of a cultural policy on architecture, is that the architects involved were always expected to engage in a process of intellectual input and of exchange with contemporary artists. This created a tension between the actual building process on the one hand, and the development of a more theoretical discourse on the other. The incorporation of programming architecture in cultural institutions was important for this, and possibly a determining factor, in continuing to enrich the architectural scene. It created the possibility of permanently challenging experiments, multilingualism, peculiarity and criticism. The freedom to programme architecture in a cultural institute did not imply practical or political restrictions in setting ambitions, however unachievable they might have seemed at the time. Exotic countries and neighbouring countries could offer inspiration or could be held up as a conceptual standard, without having to wonder if this was realistic. It seemed that the cultural framework was a playground or laboratory in which foreign standards could be measured against the Flemish context, in order to develop a proper idiom. All levels of scale in design could be treated in the same way: from furniture and scenography to architecture, infrastructure, urban development and landscape, and even related arts like photography and film. But there was a clear agenda behind the cultural architectural programming, which sought to have an impact on the building process itself. Not only did it bring a broad audience, including future clients and policy makers, into contact with architects through exhibitions and lectures. Often the same architects were invited to advise the government on developing an appropriate architectural policy.

This model was strongly entwined with the dynamic in visual arts, theatre and fashion in Flanders, and differed greatly from the developments that were taking place in other countries. Architectural policy in France supported 'Grands Projets' for Paris and the major cities, which then built cultural infrastructure through large international competitions, such as the FRACs. In time this top-down approach led to what is probably the biggest architecture institute in the world, the Cité de l'architecture et du patrimoine, in Paris. As opposed to Flanders, the connections with contemporary architectural education and art, and a critical disposition were not as high on the agenda. The Netherlands also had a blossoming architectural policy in that period and garnered international attention for years through the image it cleverly created around the architecture of several larger firms that completely dominated the architectural debate. Under the 'Superdutch' denominator the Netherlands focused almost exclusively on object-related architecture with a pronounced contemporary idiom.[26] At the same time an accommodating grant system supported a large section of the architectural corps, which produced research studies and publications. The Dutch Architecture Institute (NAi) was the elder, much bigger and stronger brother of the VAi, which helped promote Dutch architecture internationally.

Against these top-down models of the neighbouring countries, stood the Flemish architectural scene, being smaller and the result of a series of bottom-up initiatives, but nonetheless ensuring that the discourse on architecture was always lively, alert and international, feeding itself with historical reflection, a strong relationship with architectural education, mutual influences with other arts and critical debate. Herein lies the legacy of the S/AM. From the very outset the S/AM strove for international exchange, originally due to the lack of interesting developments in Flanders/Belgium. Foreign architecture and architectural policy were initially admired with envy, later to be critically analysed. It gradually became apparent that the Flemish architectural scene could actually withstand international comparison. Self-confidence grew, and was used to convince policy makers. Also in this, the S/AM went ahead. From the 1980s on, it had always tried to be closely connected to policy preparations. In open debate and behind the scenes it helped think of ways in which architectural policy might be shaped, and about the appropriate values and instruments for this. Finally, the permanent concern for new generations of architects is a third aspect of architectural culture in Flanders that was initiated by S/AM, and was later continued by deSingel and VAi amongst others. In the cultural realm of exhibitions and series of lectures, young designers are always given opportunities. Taking the lead in this with its much talked about series of 'Young Architects' exhibitions, the S/AM is without doubt the fountainhead of Flanders' present architectural culture.

1   Geert Bekaert, *Hedendaagse architectuur in België* (Tielt: Lannoo, 1995): 169.

2   Francis Strauven, '150 jaar architectuur en stedenbouw in België. Hoe België zijn huidige aanblik kreeg,' *Wonen TA/BK 12* (1980): 20. In his reference work *Moderne Bouwkunst in België*, Pierre Puttemans also reported the 'intense disorder' that reigned in Belgian architecture around 1968: the student revolts in La Cambre and the support these actions received from respectable professional associations were in sharp contrast with 'the sombre hush' that returned after 1968. Pierre Puttemans, *Moderne Bouwkunst in België* (1975): 243-244.

3   Geert Bekaert, 'Belgische architectuur als gemeenplaats. De af-wezigheid van een architectonische cultuur als uitdaging,' *Archis 9*, September, (1987): 10-11.

4   Geert Bekaert, 'Wie over architectuur wil spreken, sta op en zwijg,' *Wonen TA/BK 11* (1983), 10-11.

5   Christoph Grafe et al., Normcore. Die Radikalität des Normalen in Flandern. *Arch+ Zeitschrift fûr Architektur und Städtebau* 220 (2015).

6   In preparing this article Katrien Vandermarliere interviewed Pieter Uyttenhove, Paul Vermeulen and Hilde Heynen. The authors would like to thank these respondents.

7   For more information on the Architecture Museum Foundation see Sven Sterken's contribution in this book.

8   Between 1977 and 1985 he was member of the Royal Commission for Monuments and Landscapes of the province of West-Flanders, and from 1985 to 1995 of the Commission for East-Flanders.

9   Marc Dubois, 'Algemeen opzet van het jaarboek,' *Jaarboek Architectuur Vlaanderen 1990-1993* (Brugge: Ministry of the Flemish Community, 1994), 12.

10 *Luc Deleu. Postfuturisme?* Antwerp: deSingel. (1 January – 1 March 1987) catalogue (Antwerp: deSingel, 1987); Geert Van Doorne and Jo Lefebure, eds., 'Naar een architectuur-beleid voor Gent?', *Architectuur als Buur*. (Turnhout: Brepols, 1988), 10; Bart Cassiman, Paul Robbrecht and Hilde Daem, eds., *De architectuur en het beeld*. Antwerp: deSingel, 2-28 May 1989), catalogue (Antwerp: deSingel, 1989). The relationship of Paul Robbrecht and Hilde Daem to visual art is further covered in the contribution by Birgit Cleppe in this book.

11 Van Doorne and Lefebure, 'Naar een architectuurbeleid voor Gent?', 10.

12 'Open letter to ministers De Wael, D'Hondt, Geens, Olivier, and anyone else who becomes involved in building and renovation at one point or another', archive S/AM, APA. The letter was signed by Bernard Baines, Peter Cornelis, Willem De Beus, Henk De Smet, Klaas Goris, Jean-Michel Huyghe, Georges-Eric Lantair, Eugeen Liebaut, Kris Mys, Mauro Poponcini, Stephane Beel, Jo Crepain, Philips Deceuninck, Giedo Driesen, Pierre Hebbelinck, Luc de Maesschalk, Patrick Lefebure, Guy Mertens, Willem Jan Neutelings, Frank Stals, Paul Wintermans, Jan Bruggemans, Marc Dubois, Christian Kieckens, Paul Bellemans.

13 Geert Bekaert, *Sea Trade Center Zeebrugge* (Antwerpen: De Standaard Uitgeverij, 1990): 196.

14 Marc Dubois, 'Prijsvraag WISH'84: een nieuwe impuls voor Vlaanderen', *Wonen TA/BK* 4 (1984), 7.

15 Pieter Uyttenhove, *Tussen kant en wal. De 19de-eeuwse gordel van Antwerpen. elementen voor een cultuur van de stad* (Turnhout: Brepols and Studio Open Stad, 1993).

16 Christoph Grafe, 'Die Erfindung einer Architekturkultur. Bemerkungen zu den Wurzeln der Architektur und ihrer Lehre in Flandern', Normcore. Die Radikalität des Normalen in Flandern. *Arch+. Zeitschrift fûr Architektur und Städtebau* 220 (2015), 7.

17 In 2000 the Foundation integrated the International Centre for Town, Architecture and Landscape (CIVA).

18 Katrien Vandermarliere, 'Het experiment is een constante geworden', *A+ nr 253* (2015), 36-40.

19 Marc Dubois, 'Subsidies architectuur 1996 en 1997', *Jaarboek Architectuur Vlaanderen 1996-97* (Ministry of the Flemish Community, 1998), 220.

20 The members included: Jan Verlinden (chairman), Mil De Kooning, Marc Dubois, Hilde Heynen, Francis Strauven, Herman Stynen, Jan Thomaes, Pieter Uyttenhove, Katrien Vandermarliere, Jan Vermassen and Luc Verpoest (Subsidies architectuur 1998, 220).

21 The Architecture Prize has been awarded to the following people: Luc Deleu (1995), Paul Robbrecht, Hilde Daem and Marie-José Van Hee (1997), Christian Kieckens (1999), Eric Antonis (2001), Filip De Pau (2003), Wim Cuyvers (2005), Ralf Coussée en Klaas Goris (2007), bOb Van Reeth (2009), Paul Vermeulen (2011) and Kristiaan Borret (2013).

22 Hilde Heynen, 'Ter inleiding. De plaats van architectuur in Vlaanderen', *Jaarboek Architectuur Vlaanderen 1994-95* (Brussels Ministry of the Flemish Community, 1996), 17.

23 Koen Van Synghel, 'Schouwburg tussen grunge en gadgets', *De Standaard*, 7 February, 2004.

24 André Loeckx, *Stadsvernieuwingsprojecten in Vlaanderen. Ontwerpend onderzoek en capacitybuilding* (Amsterdam: SUN Publishers, 2009): 10-16.

25 For the interaction with interior, see the article by Fredie Floré in this book.

26 Bart Lootsma, *Superdutch* (Rotterdam: NAi Publishers, 2000).

'Torn between Two Loves'
Tentative Encounters between Art and Architecture by Christian Kieckens, Robbrecht en Daem architecten and Marie-José Van Hee

Birgit Cleppe

'Our work is characterised by a great belief in architecture as a form of expression, the architectural form of expression, which possesses a high degree of autonomy. It is a form of expression that refers to itself.'[1]

The trepidation with which Christian Kieckens, Robbrecht en Daem architecten and Marie-José Van Hee relate visual art to their architectural practices may come as a surprise. They appear, each in their own way, to want to emphasise architecture's autonomy with regard to art, not from any lack of affinity, or to reject or outshine art, but rather to allow both disciplines to preserve their value and to coalesce while retaining their own individuality. Christian Kieckens talks of being 'torn between two loves' where 'the two disciplines flirt with each other, but where it is patently obvious that they stand side by side. They use each other.'[2] Undoubtedly this self-awareness, the yearning to see architecture affirmed as an independent discipline, is rooted in the miserliness with which architecture was already treated when they completed their studies in their home country.[3] However, it is not an absolute autonomy. Architecture is also a form of art, is part of 'the arts', and is linked to values inherent to modern art: experiment, originality, renewal, authenticity and complexity, etc. At the same time their architecture is never arrogant or vain, and Kieckens, Robbrecht en Daem architecten and Van Hee distance themselves so explicitly from international trends in museum architecture, which have emerged since their graduation.

In 1977, the Centre Pompidou opened its doors in Paris. The apparition of the glass museum temple was to provide an accessible and spectacular encounter between contemporary art, contemporary architecture and the general public. With their design Renzo Piano and Richard Rogers didn't just herald the beginning of a boom in museum construction in the last decades of the 20th century. The architecture also expresses the far-reaching institutional and societal transformations of the museum as an institution.[4] Hereby the traditional museum programme is transformed into 'a grand cultural emporium in which the museum itself is reduced to one of the departments.'[5]

Marie-José Van Hee,
House and practice
in Opwijk, 2005-2011.
Photo Lander Loeckx.

Museum buildings are mushrooming all over Europe, the United States and Japan, where the architecture's spectacle value overwhelms the artworks on display.

The three largest museum institutions for modern and contemporary art in Flanders also saw the light of day during this period. In Ghent the City Museum for Contemporary Art (*Vereniging voor het Museum van Hedendaagse Kunst*, or MuHKA) had already been founded in 1957, under the impetus of Karel Geirlandt. Its great ambition was to create an autonomous museum. Yet the Ghent City Museum of Contemporary Art only came to existence in 1975. The basis of the MuHKA collection in Antwerp was established in 1977, when Gordon Matta-Clark created his work Office Baroque in an empty office block on the Scheldekaaien, at the invitation of Flor Bex from the ICC. A number of art lovers worked hard to ensure the property's continued existence and integration in a new museum of contemporary art. Artists from all over the world donated work to support this project and although the property was eventually demolished and the plans were stored, this art collection was later used as an argument in favour of launching MuHKA.[6] Since 1957, West Flanders continued to build its collection of modern art, which only acquired a definitive location with the foundation for the Provincial Museum of Modern Art (Provinciaal Museum voor Moderne Kunst) in Ostend in 1986.

A sound architectural framework that can house the collections and exhibitions did not appear to be a priority. In 1975, the City Museum of Contemporary Art in Ghent was allocated a small wing at the back of the Museum of Fine Arts (Museum voor Schone Kunsten). It was only in 1999 that S.M.A.K. moved into its own building. In 1964, the West Flanders collection of modern art was afforded temporary shelter in the Groeninge Museum in Bruges, in the Lakenhalle in Ypres in 1972, and in the conversion of a former warehouse in Ostend in 1986, by Gaston Eysselinck. After a rather sketchy award of the architectural assignment, the MuHKA was housed in an unfortunate conversion of a former grain silo on the muted Zuiderdokken in Antwerp. In 1985, the Dutch trade publication Wonen/TABK published an opinion article by Marc Dubois lamenting the fragmented museum policy and the overhasty construction plans for the MuHKA by former Minister of Culture, Karel Poma:

> This purchase, as well as the appointment of the Antwerp architect Michel Grandsard, who was commissioned to convert the building, took place under suspicious veil of secrecy... With regard to the museum one could ask why more talented Antwerp architects such as bOb Van Reeth, Georges Baines or Jo Crepain were not taken into consideration... With this in mind one could ask whether the policy can, or indeed has the ambition to establish the right priorities. In Ghent the curator Jan Hoet has been looking for a new location for his internationally acclaimed collection of contemporary art for years.[7]

It was only in 1996, with the subsidy for Stéphane Beels' design for the Roger Raveel Museum (Raveelmuseum) in Machelen-aan-de-Leie, that the authorities would, for the first time, invest in qualitative museum architecture for contemporary art. As Steven Jacobs points out in De Witte Raaf, the question is also whether such a monographic project is a priority while the operations of the 'ordinary' museums, which are occupied with collecting, storing and exhibiting modern art, which in part is due to the scant financial intervention from (central) government can be said to be problematic at the very least.[8]

In his opinion article Dubois advocates for targeted and adequate investments in museum infrastructure as well as for qualitative architecture in the same breath. The government's dysfunctional museum and architectural policy is forcing both the art and architectural sectors into fewer institutionalised straitjackets. If more established names such as Georges Baines and bOb Van Reeth are not able to rake in any large projects, it is no wonder that Christian Kieckens, Robbrecht en Daem architecten and Marie-José Van Hee predominantly express their affinity with art in smaller, often temporary design projects. This affinity stands out first and foremost in the work of Paul Robbrecht and his partner Hilde Daem, and has already been discussed at length in multiple publications.[9] They maintained close contact with artists such as Jan Vercruysse, Philip Van Isacker, Gerhard Richter, Raoul De Keyser, Isa Genzken, Juan Muñoz and Cristina Iglesias. In their first assignments, the City Museum of Contemporary Art in Ghent played a crucial role since its programme devoted attention to museum and exhibition architecture. In 1983, it dedicated an exhibition to the issues related to constructing an autonomous museum of contemporary art in the 'Museum zoekt Museum (Museum seeks Museum)' project.[10] In 1986, the director Jan Hoet agreed to the request submitted by the S/AM '(Stichting Architektuurmuseum or Architecture Museum Foundation)' founded by Christian Kieckens and Marc Dubois, to exhibit the designs for their 'Architectuur voor een Zee-land (Architecture for Zeeland)' project at the MVHK. Models including those by Luc Deleu, Christian Kieckens, Paul Robbrecht en Daem architecten, John Körmeling, Benthem Crouwel, Frank and Paul Wintermans and Wim Cuyvers were on display for a month in the Hemicycle of the Museum of Fine Arts.[11] However, it is with the scenographies for the MVHK exhibitions outside the museum walls 'Kunstzicht (Art view)' in a student restaurant at Ghent University and especially Initiatief 86 (Initiative 86) in St. Peter's Abbey - that Robbrecht en Daem architecten are able to develop their own distinctive model for their exhibition designs. In addition, as Steven Jacobs pointed out, the exhibition space was domesticated:

> In this respect Robbrecht en Daem will always view their task as an attempt to harmonise the existing architectural context with the artworks. The existing architecture is recognised as a fait accompli and afforded added value with the help of minimal forms, without detracting attention from the works of art. The ensemble is frequently characterised by a pre-museum, homely intimacy, which is mainly achieved through a sensitivity for diverse materials.[12]

Initiatief 86 was organised in the slipstream of the art project Chambres d'Amis. Artists invited by the MVHK create work for specific locations, predominantly private residences in Ghent. It is one of the first art events in Belgium that explicitly explores the boundaries between contemporary art and architecture. The fact that the project enjoys major international acclaim also reflects on Robbrecht en Daem. After Initiatief 86 they received several commissions abroad. They design, for example, the scenography for 'Floor for a Sculpture – Wall for a Painting' (1987) in de Appel Arts Centre in Amsterdam and for 'Theatergarden Bestiarium' (1989), an exhibition by Chris Dercon in The Institute for Contemporary Art in New York.

Also Christian Kieckens and Marie-José Van Hee developed their work addressing different disciplines. Kieckens' activities encompass other applied arts such as graphic design and furniture design in addition to architecture. He gives lectures (often related to his teacher Pieter de Bruyne), compiles exhibitions and catalogues (often for the Architecture Museum Foundation) and publishes texts for diverse publications such as Archis and Openbaar Kunstbezit in Vlaanderen as well as Winkler Prins. In 1983, he collaborated on the initial phase of the renovation of the Mys House with Paul Robbrecht and Hilde Daem. The house, which was only completed in 1993 pursuant to several phases of renovation, is one of their first completed projects in which artists' interventions deliberately engage in dialogue with the architecture. 'Artworks, ranging from the impressive scale of a Lili Dujourie in the entrance hall, to the barely perceptible accent of a Jan Vercruysse on the kitchen window, are supported by architectural interventions that now constitute Robbrecht en Daem's standard idiom.'[13]

In the first years of her practice, Marie-José Van Hee stood out with a series of housing projects that testify to a marked consistency. Her work was included in publications and exhibitions by the Architecture Museum Foundation in 1986. In 1991, she was part of the selection for 'Architetti [della Fiandra] / Architects [from Flanders]' at the Venice Architecture Biennale and in 1993, she was the subject of a monographic exhibition including catalogue in deSingel in Antwerp. Robbrecht en Daem and Kieckens follow a similar course. However, besides their architectural projects they also published texts during this period, about their own work and that of others, and also about artists. Van Hee does not. Her silence is consistent with the radical modesty that typifies her work. Nonetheless, she engages in a broad network of personal contacts with architects and artists. She maintains a close friendship with Hilde Peleman, who founds the first art and architecture bookshop in Ghent, Copyright, in 1983. In 1988, Peleman even organises the 'Architettura è donna' exhibition about three female architects: Marie-José Van Hee, Monique Stoop and An Wirtz. Peleman is also in touch with Christian Kieckens and between 1989 and 1992, allocates him several design projects for the furniture and refitting of the shop in Jacobijnenstraat.

Originally Copyright occupied the same building as and its operations were closely associated with, Het Gewad, a centre for contemporary art. It had been founded a few years earlier by Jan Debbaut (then curator of the Van Abbemuseum in Eindhoven), collector Anton Herbert and gallerist Joost De Clercq. In addition to organising exhibitions, Het Gewad - given a second lease of life between 1986 and 1992 as 'Galerie Joost De Clercq' - published a magazine every two months, which included articles by, for example, Paul Robbrecht.[14] Years later, Joost De Clercq would act as the adviser for art acquisitions by the town of Knokke-Heist, otherwise playing a role in the art integration of the statues by Franz West on the Rubensplein designed by Robbrecht en Daem in 2003. The group of artists that exhibited work there between 1979 and 1992 is impressive: Joseph Kosuth, Laurence Weiner, Dan Graham, Daniel Buren, Sol LeWitt, Marthe Wéry, Guissepe Penone, Gilbert & George, Rebecca Horn, Jan Vercruysse, Thomas Schütte, Jef Geys, René Daniëls, Cindy Sherman, Jean-Marc Bustamante, Gerhard Merz, Lili Dujourie, Juan Munoz, Cristina Eglesias, Ettore Spalletti, François Hers, Niek Kemps, Tony Cragg, Jan Van Oost, Koen Theys, Berlinde De Bruyckere and Sophie Ristelhuber, etc. In the 1980s, Het Gewad may have made a similar contribution to the dynamic that ruled in the field of visual art in Ghent as the MVHK. Moreover the gallery must have played a key role in the affinity and relationships that Kieckens, Van Hee and Robbrecht developed with visual artists at the beginning of their careers. In any case, it is a fact that a large number of the artists with whom Robbrecht en Daem collaborated, previously exhibited at Het Gewad or in the Galerie Joost De Clercq.

In the glow of the 1986 Chambres d'Amis art event's success, the initiative for an international prize for architecture was launched for the MVHK, coordinated by Professor Charles Vermeersch and with for example Geert Bekaert as member of the jury. The tug of war between Hoet, Bekaert, Ghent's city council and the Order of Architects about which architects should be allowed to enter the competition, resulted in its eventual cancellation. Besides advocating for Frank O. Gehry, Hoet apparently supported

Marie-José Van Hee, Modenatie, Antwerp. Interior view and plan, 1999-2002.
Photo Mario Palmieri.

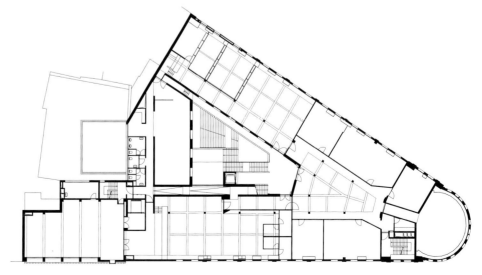

the participation of Rem Koolhaas, Aldo Rossi and bOb Van Reeth, who had already confirmed their participation, as well as Fumihiko Maki and Paul Robbrecht: a request that the competition organisation did not grant.[15]

The work of Robbrecht en Daem architecten did not go unnoticed by a number of enlightened private individuals and gallerists either. They were assigned design projects for the residence and Galerie Greta Meert (1991), a penthouse in the existing Art Nouveau building in Brussels, with the integration of the Camera piece by Isa Genzken. Along with Marie-José Van Hee they built a residence and gallery for the art dealer Xavier Hufkens in Ixelles (1992). The middle-class residence was radically transformed with a shaft that brings overhead light far into the house and a new layout in which the library on the first floor acts as the fulcrum between the public exhibition rooms downstairs and the private residence upstairs. The project is reminiscent of the 'domestic' framework for art that was already visible in Initiatief 86 by Robbrecht en Daem.[16] The complex circulatory structure with double and concealed staircases, which we also find in earlier house designs by Van Hee and that was later elaborated in her design for the ModeNatie, generate paths that intimately position the visitor in relation to the art and lead them ever deeper into the house's private atmosphere.

The route, the promenade, also formed the backbone of the exhibition concept for the Aue Pavilions at Documenta IX in Kassel. In 1992, the administrator Jan Hoet commissioned Robbrecht en Daem architecten for the project's design. It signifies the first major, albeit initially temporary, museum project for Robbrecht en Daem architecten. The five slender, train-shaped pavilions almost, but not quite touch each other, just like carriages in a shunting yard. They are still connected by transverse crossings, creating a linear exhibition route. Thanks to their location on the edge, parallel to the dominant lines of sight in the park, and their light, elegant legged forms, the unusual structures still exude serenity. Inside they offer space for the work of around thirty artists, such as Isa Genzken, Gerhard Richter, Raoul De Keyser, Thomas Struth and Dan Graham. 'Architecture and art engaged in real

Robbrecht en Daem with Marie-José Van Hee, Galerie Greta Meert, Brussels, 1981-1991.
Photo Kristien Daem.

Robbrecht en Daem, Leopold De Waelplaats, Antwerp, 1997-1999.
Photo Kristien Daem.

interaction there ... We wanted ... works by Dan Graham with his glass pavilions and their play on reflections. He was enthusiastic from the outset; it was ... two years before the opening. At the time Graham was not part of the selection, but he was invited at our suggestion.'[17]

Collaborations also represent an important constant in the practices of Marie-José Van Hee and Christian Kieckens. For Van Hee, the encounter, the dialogue, does not play so much on the dividing line of two disciplines, but centres on the core of her own professional field, to the extent that she based her practice at the same location as that of Robbrecht en Daem. In their collaborations, the Galerie Hufkens (1992) for example, her signature is unmistakably present, without having to permeate each square centimetre of the design. The house is separated from the city with a similar vigilance, and harbours a complexity that we also find in her other houses, through, for example, double staircases and diagonal perspectives. For the renovation of the Leopold De Waelplaats for the Royal Museum of Fine Arts in Antwerp (1999), Van Hee, Robbrecht en Daem joined forces with Cristina Iglesias and Ann Demeulemeester, who respectively designed a fountain sculpture and seating.

At Robbrecht en Daem architecten, artists are actively involved in the design process, such as in the case of Iglesias who designed the skylights for Katoen Natie (1997). However, by no means does this result in the work and the architecture blending into each other as if they are one and indivisible. As Steven Jacobs points out, 'In this project the exceptionally fragile light sculptures by Cristina Iglesias are in stark contrast to the rudimental nature of the building. The artworks form a critical presence in comparison to the ... harshness of the architectural interventions.'[18] Christian Kieckens' work is characterised by what he refers to as a 'constantly changing hierarchy. Either my role disappears - and I act as a kind of foundation for the artist - or the work of the artist.'[19] In David Claerbout's intervention in de XPO Halls in Kortrijk (1999) the artwork is, for example, absent in visual terms. Claerbout inserts sound installations in the columns, and thus does not intervene in the architecture's spatial articulation. In the double

Robbrecht en Daem with Marie-José Van Hee, Hufkens gallery: section with lightwell, Ixelle, 1992.
Photo Kristien Daem.

Robbrecht en Daem with Marie-José Van Hee, Hufkens gallery: double stairs, Ixelle, 1992.
Photo Kristien Daem.

Robbrecht en Daem, Rubensplein Knokke, with sculptures by Franz West, 1999-2003.
Photo Kristien Daem.

exhibition with Marthe Wéry in the Synagogue de Delme (1995) the opposite occurs. Kieckens is present during the work process and produces an analysis of the exhibition space. Only his analysis drawing is exhibited. Marc Dubois writes: 'With his clarification of the compelling architectural subject, he undoubtedly supported Wéry's idea of developing her painting as a structure - four units and six panels - squeezed into the space with her power and aura. It was a refreshing dialogue, where painting gave voice to the silence of the architect's drawing.'[20]

Vice versa the painting by Niele Toroni, who was a guest at Robbrecht en Daem on the occasion of Chambres d'Amis, caused Paul Robbrecht to formulate reflections on architecture.

> The work demonstrates that painting, when compared to other visual artistic disciplines, such as sculpture, is an astonishing activity that defies the obvious. Creating an image on a flat surface by applying colour is irrefutably no mean feat. Painting is far from sculpture's direct Darstellung (depiction)... This is precisely why there is solidarity (created) between the art of painting and the architectural profession.[21]

As Maarten Delbeke pointed out, pictorial influences in several works by Robbrecht en Daem are also fundamental, such as the colour palette of the stones on the Rubensplein (2004). 'It is, after all, a square, and the treatment of its surface demonstrates that Robbrecht en Daem do not see the application of refined materials as a way of conquering the third dimension, but of complicating the surface.'[22] A palette of colour combinations was also sought for the interior of the Concert Hall (2002) and the Boston in Lincolnshire (2007). The pictorial aspect, the colour, also plays a decisive role in the work of Marie-José Van Hee. The façades of her buildings are often monotone - Kristiaan Borret refers to 'a whitewash' - in soft shades of grey. The focus is on the large volumes and resulting building compositions as a whole, which con-

Marie-José Van Hee architecten with Robbrecht en Daem architecten, central square with colour planes by Benoit van Innis, Deinze, 2009-2012.
Photo Frederik Vercruysse.

Robbrecht en Daem, Whitechapel Gallery, London, 2003-2009.
Photo Richard Bryant.

Robbrecht en Daem, The house where it always rains, Barcelona, 1992.
Photo Kristien Daem.

jure up images of Morandi's still lifes.[23] The Van Aelten Oosterlinck home and practice project (2005) in Opwijk is typical. The red shades of the brick are broken up by the thick, pale cement pointing. It creates a pointillist effect with red-coloured notes. Van Hee herself refers to Sigurd Lewerentz's mantle pointing, but as Anna Luisa Schubert remarks in Arch+, the façade feels almost like textile.[24] Creating a pictorial skin, with an honest play on materials, is also emphatically present in the mosaic parquet in the forum of the ModeNatie building. The diagonal construction of dark and light-stained strips prevents a seam from forming between the floor pattern of the V-shaped room. Together they create a canvas that teemingly colours and connects the different rooms - whose walls, columns and ceilings are smooth and white. The fact that her collaborations with artists are often interventions on the surface of the design is also noteworthy. For the public tender related to Zoersel town hall (2003), Van Hee collaborated with her former student Kris Martin. Martin created a sculpture of 'snails crossing over' the surface of the footbridge, and in this way brought the life of the surrounding forest to the building. The redevelopment of the banks of the Leie and Deinze central square (2012) involved another collaboration between Van Hee and Robbrecht en Daem in which Benoît Van Innis was invited to participate. His interventions - coloured tiled surfaces on the square and on the underside of the canopy - refer to the seasons and the colouring of the Latem School.

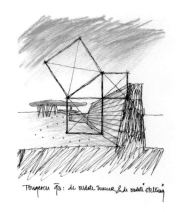

Tongeren 93: de oudste muur & de oudste stelling

Of the three, Christian Kieckens is without a doubt the one who has experimented most with the boundary between architecture and visual art. In the context of the 'Archi-Archè-Toon-stellingen' project in Tongeren in 1993, he exhibited an installation of metal scaffolding pipes as graphic depiction of the Pythagorean theorem: three squares that form a right-angled triangle where they meet. The installation reads like a sculpture rather than an architectural project. Its aim is not to design the space, frame views or orient bodies, much less is its existence based on a functional necessity. It is, just like a sculpture, carefully positioned in the space, present and bearer of the questions and references that the creator, as well as the spectator project upon it. Similar objections could be raised with regard to Brique de verts, a glass brick-form object. In 1995, Kieckens had four examples made for the occasion of the Designers WeekEnd in Brussels. The most famous is his Tafel-Landschap (Table Landscape) installation that he built in deSingel in 1997. For the inclined plane in the foyer next to the Red Hall, Kieckens designed a horizontal platform on legs that is high enough to walk underneath at the bottom of the incline, and is as high as a table at the top. The 'furniture piece', which is intended as an empirical introduction to his retrospective 'De Plaats en het gebouw (The place and the building)' in the corridor around the corner, combines his beloved themes, such as intervals, labyrinth, construction, scale and perspective in a single representation.[25] The exhibition concludes with an installation by the artist Peter Downsbrough, with whom Kieckens organised the 'Densities (downtown Aalst)' exhibition in 1996 in Galerie S65 in Aalst. In 1998, he exhibited a series of photos of baroque domes 'Lichtbeelden Lantern Views', also in Galerie S65. The pictures date back to 1981, the year that Kieckens was awarded a travel scholarship as the Godecharle prize laureate, with which he studied baroque churches in Bavaria, Bohemia, Moravia and later Rome.

In spite of Paul Robbrecht's lyric articulations - and by extension, those of the broader architectural community - about the success of the relationship between art and architecture in the Aue Pavilions, Jan Hoet disappointed with the architecture of his own museum, the SMAK, whose doors opened in 1999. In his text 'Als de dood voor de Architectuur (Like the death of Architecture)', Geert Bekaert complained about the 'Cinderella-like role' that museum director Jan Hoet bestowed on architecture in the project. This was a somewhat perplexing statement given Bekaert's earlier claim that Hoet had already demonstrated 'how unique the dialogue between art and architecture could be.'[26] However, in this case, according to Bekaert, Hoet had chosen an architect in the spirit of the predominant political culture.

> With an obedient architect-cum civil servant, he thus built his museum himself, and accomplished his dream of a subservient architecture, an architect for art. ... The building's personality is just as indispensable as the curator's personality in affording art place. Architecture cannot adapt to the art, because in doing so it makes itself and the art impossible. Architecture is the place where art is granted its freedom.[27]

Perhaps it was the temporary nature of the art pavilion, or the clarity of its programme that afforded the architecture of Robbrecht en Daem its freedom in Kassel - however sober and obeisant - to allow it to be wholeheartedly true to itself. In any case, we find an identical self-awareness in other art pavilions they have designed such as 'The House

Christian Kieckens, Archi-Archè sculpture, 1993. De oudste muur en de oudste stelling / The oldest wall and the oldest teorema.
Archive Christian Kieckens. Scan APA.

Christian Kieckens, Brique de verts (Green glass brick), 1995.
Personal archive Christian Kieckens.

Christian Kieckens, exhibition design 'De Plaats en het Gebouw / The place and the building' and installation 'Table landscape', deSingel, Antwerp, 1997.
Photo Reiner Lautwein.

Where It Always Rains' (1992) in Barcelona for Juan Munoz, and *Het Huis* (2012) in Middelheim Park in Antwerp. Incidentally it first housed the sculptures of Thomas Schütte, once exhibited in Galerij Joost De Clercq.[28] With projects for the Museum Boijmans Van Beuningen (1997) in Rotterdam and Whitechapel Gallery in London (2009), Robbrecht en Daem already prove that their exhibition architecture is also suited to permanent and large scale museum projects.

However, it is Marie-José Van Hee who, with ModeNatie (1999) was the first and currently the only one amongst them, who has also been able to create her vision of exhibition and museum architecture in her own country. A museum for an applied form of art, fashion, is combined with the Flanders Fashion Institute and the Fashion Academy (Mode-Academie). As Kristiaan Borret noted, her design can be read as a critical comment on the museum's commercialisation at the end of the 20th century.[29] The bookshop and bistro are purposefully located on the street side, and thus not removed from the city, much less used to liven up the museum's interior. The atrium she incorporated in the building block is not a generic shopping mall. The complexity of the building and the programme is not concealed anywhere, and paraded even less as a gimmick. The architecture disintegrates into an ambiguous stairwell where the user must cautiously find his or her way. Van Hee proves that an idiosyncratic and present architecture can still be sufficiently reserved to initiate an equivalent and intense dialogue between art and architecture. This need for dialogue, in which one's own voice can always be heard and distinguished without being overpowering, is something that ties Kieckens, Robbrecht en Daem and Van Hee - and perhaps also an entire generation together.

1. Paul Robbrecht, 'A conversation, November 1997. Farshid Moussavi and Paul Robbrecht', in *Werk in Architectuur. Paul Robbrecht and Hilde Daem, Steven Jacobs* (Ghent: Ludion, 1998): 145.

2. Christian Kieckens in conversation with Peter Swinnen, in Raymond Balau et al., *Christian Kieckens: Zoeken, Denken, Bouwen* (Ghent: Ludion, 2001): 12.

3. For further information about the development of an architectural culture in Belgium see the contributions in this book by Sofie De Caigny and Katrien Vandermarliere, and by Sven Sterken.

4. Wouter Davidts, *Museumarchitectuur van Centre Pompidou tot Tate Modern: verschuivingen in het artistieke begrip van openbaarheid en hun impact op het programma van het museum voor hedendaagse kunst* (Ph.D. diss., Ghent: Ghent University Faculty of Engineering, 2003): xii.

5. Gérard Monnier, *L'art et ses institutions en France. De la Révolution à nos jours* (Paris: Editions Gallimard, 1995): 366, as quoted in Davidts, *Museumarchitectuur van Centre Pompidou tot Tate Modern*, 227.

6. Koen Brams, 'Wat zegt u de tentoonstelling Dear ICC?', *De Witte Raaf* 114 (March-April, 2005).

7. Marc Dubois, 'Nieuw museum zonder verzameling in Antwerpen', *Wonen/TABK* 8 (1985): 3.

8. Paraphrased from Steven Jacobs, 'Een schrijn in het dorp. Stéphane Beels ontwerp voor het Raveel-museum', *De Witte Raaf* 63 (September-October, 1996).

9. See in particular: Bart Cassiman, Paul Robbrecht en Hilde Daem, *De architectuur en het beeld* (Antwerp: deSingel, 1989); Steven Jacobs, *Werk in architectuur. Paul Robbrecht en Hilde Daem*, (Ghent: Ludion, 1998); Franz König, Maarten Delbeke, Stefan Devoldere, and Iwan Strauven, *Pacing through Architecture* (Brussels: Bozar books, 2008).

10. Jan Hoet, et al., *Museum Zoekt Museum: Projecten Voor Een Autonoom Museum Van Hedendaagse Kunst in Confrontatie Met Opties En Realisaties In Binnen- En Buitenland* (Ghent: City Museum of Contemporary Art, 1983).

11. Exhibition in MVHK on 5 April – 4 May 1986, see Marc Dubois, 'Jan Hoet en de architectuur', text published online, 2014, 3: http://www.marcdubois.be/cms/resources/jan-hoet-tekst-met-beelden-1.pdf last consulted 11/10/2015.

12. Jacobs, *Werk in Architectuur*, 17.

13. Jacobs, *Werk in Architectuur*, 49.

14. See for example: Paul Robbrecht, 'De gewijzigde betekenis van het Rationalisme in de hedendaagse Architectuur', *Het Gewad* 4 (1981): 7-8.

15. Bekaert, 'S.M.A.K. Over de aangeboren angst voor architectuur', *in Collected essays Part 7*, by Geert Bekaert, eds. Christophe Van Gerrewey and Mil De Kooning (Ghent: WZW, 2009): 473-482.

16. See Marc Dubois, 'Een galerie-woning. Paul Robbrecht and Hilde Daem: verbouwing galerie Hufkens', *Archis* 2 (1993): 56; and Jacobs, *Werk in Architectuur*, 41.

17. Raymond Balau, 'Displacement. Interview with Paul Robbrecht', in Jacobs, *Werk in Architectuur*, 32.

18. Jacobs, *Werk in Architectuur*, 107.

19. Kieckens in conversation with Swinnen, in Balau et al., *Christian Kieckens*, 15.

20. Raymond Balau, 'Gebouw K', in Balau et al., *Christian Kieckens*, 99.

21. Paul Robbrecht, 'De plaats van de kunst. Raadgevingen en uitspraken, verwijten', in Jacobs, *Werk in Architectuur*, 16.

22. Maarten Delbeke, 'Ephemeral principles', in *Pacing through Architecture*, Franz König, Maarten Delbeke, Stefan Devoldere, and Iwan Strauven (Brussels: Bozar books, 2008): 186.

23. Kristiaan Borret, 'De juiste afstand', in *Marie-José Van Hee Architect*, André Loeckx, William Mann, and Kristiaan Borret (Ghent: Ludion, 2002): 100.

24. Schubert, Anna Luise, 'Wohnhaus and Praxis', *Arch+* 220 (Summer 2015): 30-33.

25. Paraphrased from Marc Dubois, 'XS in meervoud', in Balau et al., *Christian Kieckens*, 41.

26. Geert Bekaert, 'Als de dood voor architectuur', in *Collected essays Part 5*, by Geert Bekaert, eds. Christophe Van Gerrewey and Mil De Kooning (Ghent: WZW, 2008): 127-128.

27. Bekaert, 'S.M.A.K.', 473-482.

28. Maarten Liefooghe and Stefaan Vervoort, 'Een revelerend gesprek: de figuren van Thomas Schütte in Het Huis van Robbrecht en Daem', *De Witte Raaf* 158, (July-August, 2012).

29. Borret, 'De juiste afstand', 100.

BERNARD BAINES — STEPHANE BEEL — PAUL BELLEMANS — JAN BRUGGEMANS — PETER CORNELIS
JO CREPAIN — WILLEM DE BEUS — PHILIP DECEUNINCK — HENK DE SMET — GIEDO DRIESEN
KLAAS GORIS — PIERRE HEBBELINCK — JEAN MICHEL HUYGE · LUC DE MAESSCHALCK — GEORGES ERIC LANTAIR · PATRICK LEFEBURE
EUGEEN LIEBAUT — GUY MERTENS — KRIS MYS — W J NEUTELINGS — MAURO POPONCINI
PAUL ROBRECHT · HILDE DAEM — FRANK STALS — M JOSE VAN HEE — HUGUES WILQUIN — FRANK WINTERMANS · PAUL WINTERMANS

JONGE ARCHITEKTEN IN BELGIE

TENTOONSTELLING
DE SELEKTIES 85-86-87 VAN DE
STICHTING ARCHITEKTUURMUSEUM

VAN 8 MAART TOT 3 APRIL 1988
OPEN VAN DI TOT ZO VAN 14 TOT 18.30 U.

DESINGEL DESGUINLEI 25 2018 ANTWERPEN

Het Singelseizoen 87-88 kwam tot stand met steun van de Vlaamse Gemeenschap en Nationale Loterij
en heeft als belangrijkste sponsors Agfa-Gevaert, het Gemeentekrediet van België, De Standaard en Swift

Ghostwriters of the Young Flemish Architecture
Marc Dubois, Christian Kieckens and the Architecture Museum Foundation, 1983-1992

Sven Sterken

In the early 1980s there were few opportunities outside private home building for young architects in Flanders. Government authorities and corporate entities selected a designer for reasons which often had little to do with the quality of the architecture; competitions for public sector commissions were a rarity. Buildings were erected without much ambition or debate; architectural critique was virtually extinct. Remarkably enough, it was in this climate of indifference that the seeds of present-day Flemish architectural culture were sown. On the one hand, a new generation of architects entered the limelight; and, on the other, initiatives of all kinds emerged from the cultural and academic milieu to lend this young architecture support.[1] The most ambitious example was the Architecture Museum Foundation (Stichting Architektuurmuseum, hereafter: S/AM). Its mission was 'to provide a medium for anyone who feels drawn by or to the design of his or her environment.'[2] This yielded all kinds of initiatives such as educational trips, debates, exhibitions and the publication of a magazine. In this article we ask how and to what extent the organisation has been able to fulfil its mission in the course of its brief existence (1983-1992).[3]

THE IDEA OF A MUSEUM OF ARCHITECTURE

The impetus for setting up the S/AM was to find a home for the 20th-century architectural archives and furniture that was accumulating in the former Museum of Decorative Arts (now the Design Museum) in Ghent. As it stood the infrastructure was incapable of sustaining the museum's activities in the long term, and so the idea arose to set up a broad, interdisciplinary centre dedicated to design in all its aspects.[4] The central character in this was Lieven Daenens, at that time director of the Museum of Decorative Arts. Also drawn into the initiative were the lecturer at the Sint-Lucas institute, Jos Vanderperren, through his contact with the well known designer Pieter De Bruyne, and Christian Kieckens, one of De Bruyne's former students. A fellow student of his, Marc Dubois, had been coordinator of the Architectural Study Centre (CAO) at the Sint-Lucas Ghent since 1978. In this capacity he would organise exhibitions, usually in the institute's White Room. It was the actors' shared interest in recent heritage, their conviction of the need to raise greater awareness, and the idea that this was also of value to contemporary practitioners of architecture that provided the basis for the S/AM. The inspiration for this stemmed from the Netherlands. There had been a foundation of the same name in that country since

Jonge architecten, exhibition in deSingel, Antwerp, 1988.
Archive deSingel.

77

1955 and its years of service had been rewarded by the establishment of the Netherlands Architecture Institute in 1988. The design competition with which it was associated garnered attention from far and wide, and gave rise to some fierce polemics over the individuality of Dutch architecture. At around the same time the Deutsches Architektur Museum (DAM) opened in Frankfurt, housed in a 19th-century villa which had been renovated by Oswald Mathias Ungers. Ungers built a plinth around the lower part of the villa along the full width of the plot, making of it a sort of architectural object on display. Inside he built an architectural shrine, as it were, constructed from basic architectural elements such as columns, floors, walls and windows. In canonising the idea that architecture is a discipline unto itself, the DAM became an architectural manifesto that probed the discipline's potential and limitations.

This dual guise of the architecture museum - institute and architectural statement - was what led S/AM to organise an international competition for ideas on the subject of 'Architecture Museum'. The scope was both deliberately broad and vague: 'Design of the spaces which, according to your philosophy, are needed to define a museum of architecture. The spaces should be set out in the environment of your choosing. The design should evoke a vision of architecture and museum.'[5] But the competition was not a success, despite the international interest and high number of participants (76); many of the entries were of an admirable graphic and poetic quality, but few managed to raise the debate beyond the anecdotal, the ironic or the provocative. One entrant, for example, proposed trips to sites of world architecture, another envisioned scaffolds to allow a closer look at some of the town's historic buildings; yet another simply said that the exercise was futile. The jury stated: 'It was our observation that the entries as a whole were sorely lacking the vitality of 'what tomorrow might bring'. And many of the entries offered nothing in the way of a holistic vision: but merely the development of a single aspect, just one part of the total picture.'[6] Though in the end there was no winner, seven entries were retained for their particular facet of the assignment.[7]

YOUNG ARCHITECTS IN FLANDERS

With its next initiative the S/AM took a different approach. As deSingel in Antwerp had decided its exhibition policy (with architecture at its heart) in 1985, it was less a question of where architecture could be exhibited, but more of what there was to be exhibited. The S/AM made a resolute choice for young, Belgian architecture. It set up a cycle of annual exhibitions to shed light on the work and motivations of the latest generation of architects. These events took place in the Museum of Decorative Art in Ghent and a meticulously prepared catalogue was issued with each one. The S/AM lent shape, in other words, to the hope expressed by Geert Bekaert back in 1983, that a sort of architectural awareness might spring up among the youngest Belgian architects despite the inhospitable climate.[8] At that point the S/AM set out to become the voice of that new generation.

The first exhibition in this series, 'The Home as Architectural Typology', made clear that even the most talented designers in Belgium had to stick to the private housing market.[9] On the other hand, this fundamental building assignment was a free haven for experimentation, innovation and identity. The catalogue deliberately avoided listing the five select designers under any kind of 'ism'; on the contrary, the deeply rooted Belgian culture of individualism was the starting point. Nonetheless, Marc Dubois identified one common characteristic, i.e. 'opposition to any great complexity of architectonic form and pursuit of a more rational planning concept and façade composition. The pairing of the concept 'small scale - human scale' with an armoury of architectonic forms led to a comfortable pseudo vernacular style, which they promptly dismissed.'[10] With his 'typological variations' Bernard Baines, for example, illustrated that as one of the historical town's elementary building blocks, the typology of the row house had not yet been exhausted. Then again, the strict geometrical structure of Jan Bruggemans' own home was the logical consequence of an architectural and personal *credo*: 'What can I omit to allow greater possibility?' And Eugeen Liebaut rebuilt his labourer's cottage in Aalst along the same lines: he kept nothing but the skeleton and employed autonomous elements such as stairs, a slope and a curved wall to structure the internal space. The exhibition also premiered Jo Crepain's De Wachter house; in a nod to the classic Roman villa, he organised sleeping, eating and being together in three 'temples' around a shared patio. Every bit as imposing was the De Mol villa by Robbrecht en Daem, in which the rediscovery of Palladio's legacy influenced the interaction between the façades and the landscape.

The idea was intentionally expanded in the next exhibition. 'Young Architects in Belgium' exhibited a representative selection of the early work of 13 designers.[11] This time, amidst all the diversity, Marc Dubois identified a common attitude: on the one hand, 'the desire to create something, to actually build something', and on the other, 'a tremendous professional sobriety'.[12] He thought that these young architects were characterised by 'the drive to throw themselves wholly into every little project - even if what they earned bore little relation to the effort they put into it, to take the time to invest in

Cover De woning als architectuurtypologie. Marc Dubois, ed, De Woning als architectuurtypologie, Stichting Architektuurmuseum (Ghent: 1985).

'Jonge Architecten in België', exhibition in Designmuseum, 1986. Work by Stéphane Beel in the foreground. APA archive Marc Dubois.

themselves with a view to achieving greater intellectual maturity and so merit the title of architect.'[13] Although most of the projects were again houses, the diversity was even greater, if possible, than the year before. The influence of Mario Botta trickled through in a compact brick house by Jan Bruggemans, while Frank and Paul Winterman presented a 30m long, beam-shaped volume which placed two perfectly mirrored family dwellings together. The cluster-shaped family home designed by Paul Bellemans was set in a glass-house for reasons of energy consumption, and in the best post-modern tradition visitors were fooled by its façade, that of a temple. This theatrical gesture contrasted with the architectural acupuncture of Robbrecht en Daem architecten; their Mys house literally evolved into an exercise in 'living with architecture' because it was still occupied while the work was being done. It was also intriguing how Marie-José Van Hee assigned an electrical transformer box and a family dwelling a logical place in the historical fabric of Ghent. It was exceptional for an architect to have their first piece of work immediately published. This was also true for Stéphane Beel, whose Van Peel home in Zoersel was also exhibited. With an ease bordering on negligence Beel adopted the clear idiom of modernism here, only without its functionalist basis: 'A shape can take many programmes. Function and programme can take strength from shape, in the way that form strengthens content in poetry. It is the relationship, not the shape, which is important.'[14] This sort of modesty was not for Willem Jan Neutelings: his exuberant villa in Brasschaat was a juxta-position of submarine, Italian palace and post-war petrol station. The projects by Beel and Neutelings marked a clear point of transition; later Bekaert correctly identified the two villas as 'foundlings that set the scene for a new generation of Young Gods, who trod forth into the world of architecture without a care.'[15]

S/AM continued in the same vein and organised an exhibition of young Flemish architects again in 1987.[16] This time it was no longer about the family home, but the idea that architects can be all-round designers who feel at home in a variety of media, scales and programmes. For example, the selection contained urban development plans for the

Cover: Jonge Architecten in België, Stichting Architektuur-museum (Gent: 1985).

Patria site in the heart of Leuven (Mauro Poponcini), two social housing estates for the WISH 85 competition (Giedo Driesen and Frank Stals), traffic-calming colour schemes (!) for the Leopold II tunnel in Brussels (Patrick Lefebure in association with Pieter Claerhout), minimalist interiors for the Style retail chain (Peter Cornelis), temporary tribunes for the Papal Visit of 1985 and even a design for a carpet (both Mauro Poponcini). But that did not mean, said Christian Kieckens in the catalogue, that these designers had disavowed architecture. On the contrary, 'the architectural space always provides inspiration and background.'[17] Another common theme had already come to the fore: 'the inner power and intensity to express architecture (...). The search for identity, recognisability, working with constant values, etc.'.[18] The layout of a pharmacy by Klaas Goris, for example, showed, through accurate detail, not just great craftsmanship, but how detail plays a role in the totality of the architectural space.

The three S/AM exhibitions on young architecture in Belgium did not go unnoticed. For example, in September 1987 the Dutch architectural magazine *Archis* devoted a special edition to Belgium. S/AM produced a map for the occasion showing Belgian architectural production since 1970, based on 150 projects. Another important moment was the reprise of the three 'Young Architects' exhibitions in deSingel in 1988.[19] Not only was this the biggest overview of recent Belgian architecture in years, but the preview became a memorable moment when Jo Crepain, on the initiative of S/AM, used an introductory speech as a ruse to read out an open letter addressed to the policymakers.[20] The actual reason for this was the award of the design contract for the mail sorting office and the courthouse extension in Antwerp to one and the same architect without any form of competition. The signatories were aghast at how unfair this seemed; if one architect is no more expensive than another (because the fees are set by law), why didn't the government simply choose the best? Or were there other reasons afoot? And if so, what were they? This much 'political impropriety' was more than the signatories said they could bear: 'we can no longer accept a Belgium (...) saddled with urbanus syndrome, or government ministers who operate systematically to make our people and culture appear ridiculous.' The letter also said that, unlike neighbouring countries with an active building policy, Belgium found itself 'in a dark recess full of intrigue, corruption and triviality.' For this reason the signatories made three demands: a freeze and review of government contracts in progress, the appointment of a Flemish Government Architect (in line with the Dutch example), and proper application of the fee scales by the various government authorities.

S/AM took advantage of this momentum to crack open another symbolic case, namely that of the Belgian pavilion for the world exhibition in Seville (1992). Outraged by the triteness of the proposed design (an inverted diamond), it demanded – and obtained – that the contract be awarded on the basis of a competition. As S/AM duly noted, the winning architects of this competition were all under the age of 40; it thus proved to be an ideal way to offer opportunities to young talent, and showed that 'an intelligent design has nothing to do with the size of an architectural firm, or references based on trade volume or turnover.'[21] For this reason the 1990 edition of 'Young Architects (in Flanders)' featured three of the competition entries.[22] The winning design by Driesen-Meersman-Thomaes portrayed Belgium as an 'ethereal structure of delicate balances in which phenomena thrive in peace' and consisted of a uniform, closed box in which heterogeneous architectural elements are stacked (escalator, containers, a wooden shed, an industrial lift and staircase). The proposal from Frank Delmulle was conceived as a series of experiences; the visitor arrived in a cool 'cave' from which an escalator took them up to the actual exhibition areas. Xaveer De Geyter divided the area into four quadrants, each with its own programme (garden, square, theatre, exhibition) through which visitors could choose their own path. The designs were more about experience scenarios, and making them possible, than about organising spaces, shapes or programmes. De Geyter's suburban villas in Mariakerke and Brasschaat, which premiered here - and became instant icons among students of architecture - followed similar principles; they transformed suburban living into a metropolitan experience in miniature, and one that cautioned against the fake pastoral idyll of the popular farm-style houses. The 1990 edition of 'Young Architects' made it clear that a generation was on its way that would self-confidently set its own rules and strike out on a path of its own. By Flemish standards, the exhibition was a huge success, not just for the massive turnout (6,000 visitors) but also for its therapeutic effect: it dispensed with the idea that architecturally speaking, Flanders was a developing country.

THE S/AM MAGAZINE

The evolution of Flemish discourse on architecture is easy to trace in the pages of the S/AM magazine. Initially it began as a heterogeneous information sheet that covered events and activities at home and abroad. The first edition (1983/01), for example, contained a description of the work of Álvaro Siza, an article by Ungers on the DAM in Frankfurt, a discussion of two sofas by Mario Botta, and a piece on Mallet-Stevens' recently protected Noailles villa. It wasn't long before it established a few preferred lines of content and subject, among them the publication of early home-grown work. The paper also gave plenty of space to interior and furniture design, which, Kieckens wrote, received less attention, if that were possible, than architecture because 'a certain hush envelops the realm of interiors. Theirs is a world that lurks behind closed doors.'[23] In 1987 a special edition entitled 'Efemere beelden' [Ephemeral Images] (S/AM 1987/01) was published on the subject of minimalist store interiors in Brussels and Antwerp. In the context of its 'Young Interior Designers' exhibition that S/AM organised in 1988, the S/AM also dedicated special editions to the work of Claire Bataille and Paul Ibens (S/AM 1988/02) and recent store interiors by the likes of Pascal Van der Kelen, Vincent Van Duysen and Dirk De Meyer (S/AM 1988/03).[24]

Another common thread running through the back issues of the S/AM is the announcement and discussion of architectural competitions, one of its bones of contention. Competitions were seen as the ideal way to depoliticise government commissions and improve the quality of public architecture; this is because they obliged the authorities to give precise specifications, gave young architects the opportunity to take on more sizeable commissions, and helped increase public interest and support of architecture.

Belgian pavilion Sevilla 1992.
Photo from exhibition catalogue.

First page from S/AM 1983/01.
Exhibition of Álvaro Siza,
Design Museum Gent.

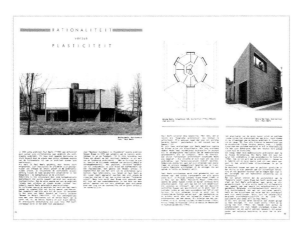

S/AM 1986/02, p 4-5.
Projects by architect
Paul Neefs.

Cover, Theme issue on
BAC-headquarters Brugge by
Stéphane Beel, S/AM 1992/01.

The validity of this position was reinforced by successful examples, such as the well-known WISH competition (1984-87) for social housing. To stimulate the private sector too, a special edition was produced under the title 'Bouwen voor het geldwezen' [Building for Finance] (*S/AM* 1987/3). It resulted from the decision of the BACOB savings bank to award design of its regional offices in Mechelen and Bruges under a multiple contract. To curry more publicity for this initiative the S/AM published not only the winning designs (by Georges Baines and Stéphane Beel respectively) but those of the other nominees.[25] Later too, important competitions such as those for a passenger terminal in Zeebrugge (*S/AM* 1989/03), the Oostkamp cultural centre (*S/AM* 1990/2-3) and the urban design scheme for Hoog-Kortrijk (*S/AM* 1992/02), were given extensive coverage. The best illustration of how painfully these competitions came about can be found in the torrent of opinion pieces published by Marc Dubois in the S/AM, and other media over the government's lame (non-existent?) architectural policy. Prestigious projects such as the international exhibition halls at the Flanders Expo in Ghent, the Museum of Modern Art (now SMAK) and the new Flemish administration's imitation gothic *Markiesgebouw* next to Brussels Cathedral, became tragicomic characters in pieces which Dubois presented under 'The Belgian saga continues'.

In the course of its ten-year existence the magazine gradually acquired a more monographic character. For example, in 1986 a full edition was devoted to architecture in Rome in the 20th century (*S/AM* 1986/03), whereas the last edition of 1988 presented the early work of a trio of as yet unknown architects, i.e. Jan Maenhout, Jef Van Oevelen and William Lievens (*S/AM* 1988/04). Despite S/AM's focus on present-day architectural culture, it did devote plenty of space to recent and unknown heritage. For example, it dedicated an edition to the so-called 'Turnhout School', paying special attention to Paul Neefs, who was seen as a link between modernist ideals and their influence in the work of Stéphane Beel and others (*S/AM*, 1986/02). Then again, ensuing special editions provided the basis for a later rediscovery of Juliaan Lampens (*S/AM* 1987/02) and Jacques Dupuis (*S/AM* 1989/01-02). The design of the magazine reflected and supported this evolution towards a more monographic scheme. The meticulous cutting and pasting that was so typical of the early issues made way for a restrained, professional layout which allowed

plenty of room for plans and illustrations. In 1990 the magazine was published in a format which was almost square and employed significantly more negative space; with this, the magazine's evolution to a monographic series became sealed in its design, and this was at its most apparent in the edition dedicated to Beel's recently opened BAC headquarters in Bruges (*S/AM*, 1992/01).

FLANDERS AT VENICE: AN (ANTI) CLIMAX

We could use the S/AM magazine's evolution from a makeshift rag to a polished magazine as a metaphor for the cultural shift it helped bring about. In the early 1990s architecture gradually became respectable in Flanders, particularly once the young Flemish government had realised its utility in shaping a regional identity. For example, the then minister of Culture, Patrick Dewael, appointed S/AM as curator of the Flemish entry to the 1991 Architecture biennale[26], but not before Marc Dubois, through the intercession of Francesco Dal Co (the curator of this prestigious event), came up with the proposal himself. Originally, through a combination of apathy and administrative carelessness, there were no plans whatsoever for Belgian participation in the 1991 architecture biennale. Thanks to a simple but ingenious plan by Christian Kieckens, i.e. a system of continuous 'display counters' in bare pine, the chambers of the Belgian pavilion were fitted with an expanse of neutral surfaces on which a variety of architectural takes came to stand opposite and alongside each other. It would be difficult to conceive of a better metaphor for architectural culture in Flanders; as Marc Dubois noted in the catalogue, there was no reason to make grand statements: 'Ever since the Art Nouveau period at the turn of the century, Belgium, including Flanders, has failed to make any real contribution to the development of European Architecture. (...) To many people, the small country sandwiched between the Netherlands and France represents a void on the architectural map of Europe.'[27] The curators therefore thought it better to let the architecture speak for itself and, to that end, to give the designers all the space they needed. As it turned out, this was a good move: even the ever critical Geert Bekaert praised the diverse, but well-conceived selection. In addition to the Van Roosmalen house designed by bOb Van Reeth, the Villa M by Stéphane Beel and De Geyter's car-on-the-roof villa in Brasschaat, there was a display of the final design for the Belgian pavilion in Seville (Driessen-Meersman-Thomaes). Luc Deleu's 'Antwerp Your Next Cruise Stop' was displayed as a mobile bridge over the river Scheldt. And there were first showings too, including Beel's Raveel Museum and Van Reeth's design for the KBC Bank headquarters in Brussels (not realized). In these two designs Bekaert saw the antipodes of the prevailing Belgian architectural culture: on the one hand, the government's growing belief in architecture and, on the other, the dereliction of the private sector, which remained loyal to the large, established architectural firms. Nevertheless, he concluded, 'from all this there was a glow of modest but persuasive vitality, a rare naturalness and authenticity. At the fun fair, which the Venice Biennale surely is, it was a relief.'[28] But this highpoint, after years of effort, was quick to devolve into a Pyrrhic victory for the S/AM. The hope 'that the invitation to Venice would signify the beginning of more funds to enable the Foundation's further development' was in vain; grant applications to the Architectural Order and the National Lottery were turned down.[29] In 1993, members received a letter containing the message that the ten-year jubilee would not be a cause for celebration and that the S/AM magazine would by necessity have to close down.[30]

THE LEGACY OF THE S/AM

After S/AM disappeared from the scene several of its initiatives were further developed by other actors. In 1994 deSingel, for example, organised the exhibition 'Mein Erstes Haus - recent work by young Flemish architects'.[31] The focus on the house allows us to draw a comparison with the first exhibition in the *Young Architects* series, and illustrates how radically the context had changed in ten years. For Kieckens, who was part of the team of curators (along with Marc Dubois and Katrien Vandermarliere, architectural curator at deSingel), it was an occasion to underline the importance of exhibitions like these: 'For many young architects the opportunity to show their work - often a first house - means both mutual confrontation and the introduction of their ideas to the outside world. An event like this always gives the outside world the opportunity to reflect upon and discuss new directions and visions within contemporary architecture.'[32] The same idea lay behind the first Architectural Yearbook, which provided an overview of production between 1990 and 1993. This was one of the first policy instruments developed for architecture at the Ministry of Culture. Its focus was not solely on designers. Besides the more academic essays, it also contained a summary of recent publications and exhibitions, and so gave an idea of what those outside of the professional context were actually saying and thinking about architecture. That had been what the S/AM was all about, not defending the ideological, deontological or professional interests of architects, but creating a favourable context for architecture. By hammering home the need for a culture of debate, research and publication, the S/AM created the blueprint for Flan-

ders' present day architectural organisations.[33] But the S/AM was more than a beh
ind the scenes player; it has been alleged, for example, that the organisation merely
propagated the good taste of minimalism and that as a result it presented only a selective
picture. Looking back at the 'Young Architects' exhibition of 1989, for example, Willem
Jan Neutelings commented: 'This set the tone for Flanders as a self-professed, hot spring
of Good Taste, wrested from the happy chaos of the 'Belgique à Papa' and guided by the
Young Turks of Flemish Minimalism. (...) On that day in Ghent a suffocating blanket fell
over Flanders. For twenty years now, since that day, our region has been under the iron
rule of Minimalism and its Good Taste.'[34] This type of criticism misinterprets the role of
figures like Marc Dubois and Christian Kieckens. Neither were neutral observers or critics
of architecture, nor were they curators with clear cut, artistic agendas. It might be more
accurate to describe them as the *ghostwriters* of this early Flemish architecture: in close
collaboration they achieved through actions, pictures and words those ideas which their
colleagues sought to express through buildings.

The rhetorical question as to whether the Architecture Museum Foundation was a
utopian dream or a necessity - in allusion to the title of the 1983 memorandum of
incorporation - is still topical today.[35] The need for cultural architectural associations is no
longer in doubt; they are crucial actors in the creation and preservation of a broad social
and political base for architecture. But the chief aim of the S/AM, i.e. the foundation of a
museum of architecture, may well have remained utopian; no Ungers-style building ever
materialised in Flanders. The Architecture Institute Flanders (VAi), which was founded
in 2001, did assume some of the tasks that might be appropriate for a museum (such
as organising the Flemish participation in Venice Biennale, publishing the Architectural
Yearbook, marking out a publications policy), but was housed in the building of the
deSingel Arts Centre. That said, in its early years the VAi created strong visibility through
its own website and initiatives like Architecture Day. When in 2003 the VAi was also given
responsibility for architectural archives through the foundation of the Centre for Flemish
Architectural Archives, it was again decided to apply a network solution to the issue of
archives, rather than argue the case for a central depot with a museum-style organisation.
But perhaps this sort of 'virtual presence' and the current network of smaller architectural
organisations and exhibition spaces (and their mutual, stop-go constellations) is a better
metaphor for the spatial reality of the Flemish 'nebular city' than any architectural statement could ever pretend to be.

[1]   In addition to the S/AM, Ghent also had *Architectuur als Buur* (which
      mainly promoted the local architectural scene since 1988), the heritage
      association *Interbellum* (which focused on modernist architecture
      since 1980), the monographic publications in the series *Vlees & Beton*
      (published by the Architecture & Urban Development research group
      of the University of Ghent) and the Centre for Architectural Studies

(CAO) at the Saint-Lucas Institute, which organised exhibitions and
issued a newsletter.

[2]   *Bulletin of the S/AM* 0 (1983): 1 (hereinafter *S/AM*).

[3]   This article paints the history of the Architecture Museum Foundation
      for the first time and offers a character sketch of the organisation rath-
      er than an exhaustive portrait. It is based on the publications of S/AM,

contemporary press clippings and the association's archives, which are kept at the Architectural Archives of the Province of Antwerp (APA). I would like to thank Marc Dubois for his comments and additions to earlier versions of this article.

4   On the foundation of the S/AM, see also Monique Bucquoye, 'Een museum voor bouwmeesters', Knack (Ghent edition), 10 August, 1983, 11 12.

5   The majority of the 76 actual entries were from Belgium (44) and the Netherlands (18). The jury was made up of Thijs Asselbergs (young architect and publicist), Wim Quist (Netherlands Chief Government Architect 1974-79), Paul Robbrecht and bOb Van Reeth. The initiative gave rise to an exhibition (Architektuurmusea, Centrum voor Kunst en Cultuur van de Sint-Pieterabdij, 2-18 March, 1984 and a publication (Christian Kieckens (ed.), Architektuurmusea, (Gent: Stichting Architektuur Museum, 1984)). For a full overview of the entries, see S/AM 2 (1984): 3-4.

6   Kieckens, Architektuurmusea, 23.

7   The seven recognitions were for the following teams: Van Gheluwe/ Azou, Wim Cuyvers, Stefan Cuyvers, Camile Van Steegeren/Maaren van der Hulst, Geert Driesen, Manceliescu/Opreanu/Ardeleau/Clit, Office for Post-Metropolitan Architecture.

8   Geert Bekaert, 'Wie over architectuur wil spreken, sta op en zwijge ...', in Vlees en Beton 75, 'Geert Bekaert. Verzamelde Opstellen, deel 4 – De Kromme Weg. 1981-1985', eds. Christophe van Gerrewey and Mil de Kooning, (Gent: WZW Editions&Productions, 2008): 305-331.

9   De woning als architectuurtypologie, 07-30 June, 1985, Museum of Decorative Art, Ghent. The catalogue was published as Marc Dubois, ed., De woning als architectuurtypologie (Gent: Stichting Architektuur Museum, 1985).

10 Dubois, De woning als architectuurtypologie, 6.

11 'Young Architects in Belgium', Museum of Decorative Art, Ghent, 13 December, 1986 – 15 February, 1987. The exhibition was shown later that year at Galerie Westersingel, Rotterdam (forerunner of the NAi) and at the TU Delft Faculty of Architecture. The catalogue was published as Christian Kieckens (ed.), Jonge Architekten in België (Gent: Stichting Architektuur Museum, 1986).

12 Kieckens, Jonge Architekten in België, 6.

13 Ibid., 6.

14 Jonge Architecten in België, 1986, 23.

15 Geert Bekaert, Hedendaagse architectuur in België (Tielt: Lannoo, 1996): 193.

16 'Young architects (in Belgium)', Museum of Decorative Art, Ghent, 19 December, 1987 – 28 February, 1988.

17 Kieckens, Jonge Architekten in België, 19.

18 Ibid., 35.

19 Young Architects in Belgium, deSingel, Antwerp, 8 March – 3 April, 1988.

20 'Open letter to ministers De Wael, D'Hondt, Geens, Olivier, and anyone else who becomes involved in building and renovation at one point or another', archive of S/AM, APA. The letter was signed by Bernard Baines, Peter Cornelis, Willem De Beus, Henk De Smet, Klaas Goris, Jean-Michel Huyghe, Georges-Eric Lantair, Eugeen Liebaut, Kris Mys, Mauro Poponcini, Stephane Beel, Jo Crepain, Philips Deceuninck, Giedo Driesen, Pierre Hebbelinck, Luc de Maesschalk, Patrick Lefebure, Guy Mertens, Willem-Jan Neutelings, Frank Stals, Paul Wintermans, Jan Bruggemans, Marc Dubois, Christian Kieckens, Paul Bellemans.

Shortly before this Francis Strauven had complained about the lack of transparency in the award of government contracts in Archis: 'De negatie van een eigen bouwcultuur', Archis 9 (1987): 12-17.

21 Jonge architecten (in Vlaanderen) (Gent: Stichting Architektuur Museum, 1990): 9. The five selected projects (2nd and 3rd prize ex aequo) were first published in Marc Dubois, 'Van Diamant tot Kubus', S/AM 1 (1990): 11 13.

22 Young architects (in Flanders), Museum of Decorative Art, 14 December, 1990 – 17 February, 1991. The exhibition was then also shown in De Brakke Grond in Amsterdam, 4-26 May, 1991. It featured work by Wim Cuyvers and Dirk De Meyer, Johan Decoker, Xaveer De Geyter, Lieven Dejaeghere, Frank Delmulle, Martine De Maeseneer, Henk De Smet and Paul Vermeulen, Driesen-Meersman-Thomaes, Klaas Goris and Kris Van Zeebroeck. The catalogue was published as Jonge architecten (in Vlaanderen) (Gent: Stichting Architektuur Museum, 1990).

23 Christian Kieckens (ed.), Jonge Interieur Ontwerpers (Gent: Stichting Architektuur Museum, 1988): 6.

24 Young Interior Designers, Museum of Decorative Art, Ghent, 16 December, 1988 – 19 February, 1989. The catalogue was published as Christian Kieckens (ed.), Jonge Interieur Ontwerpers (Gent: Stichting Architektuur Museum, 1988).

25 Christian Kieckens, 'Competition for branch of BAC Savings Bank in Mechelen', S/AM 2 (1987): 12-20. The other laureates were Frank and Paul Wintermans, and Henk De Smet. On the competition for the provincial headquarters in Bruges: 'Architectuurwedstrijd Gewestelijke Zetel BAC te Brugge', S/AM 1988/01, 6-9. Beel's commissioned design was published in S/AM 1 (1992).

26 Architetti della Fiandra was held in the Belgian Pavilion in the Giardini, Venice and ran from 8 September, 1991 to 6 October, 1991. The catalogue was published as Marc Dubois, Christian Kieckens (ed.), Architetti della Fiandra (Gent: Stichting Architektuur Museum, 1991).

27 Dubois and Kieckens, Architetti della Fiandra, 20.

28 Geert Bekaert, 'Architetti della Fiandra', Ons Erfdeel 2 (1992): 206.

29 Marc Dubois, 'Architetti della Fiandra', S/AM 1 (1991): 5.

30 Letter to the members of the Architecture Museum Foundation, 19 April, 1993, 2p., Archive S/AM, APA.

31 Mein Erstes Haus – Recent werk van jonge Vlamingen, deSingel, 27 January – 6 March, 1994. The accompanying catalogue was published as Katrien Vandermarliere, Mein Erstes Haus – Recent werk van jonge Vlamingen (Antwerpen: deSingel, 1994).

32 Vandermarliere, Mein Erstes Haus, 10.

33 On the place and meaning of cultural architecture organisations in Flanders, see Sven Sterken and Els Vervloesem, 'Bij de wissel van de wacht. Een status questionis van de recente beleidsinitiatieven inzake architectuur', in Jaarboek Architectuur Vlaanderen 04-05 (Antwerpen: Vlaams Architectuur instituut, 2006): 11-25.

34 Willem-Jan Neutelings, 'Maximalisme. Het einde van het Minimalisme en de goede smaak', A+ 204 (2007): 82-91. This is an abridged version of the speech marking the occasion of the Charles Vermeersch Chair, University of Ghent, 9 October, 2007. Neutelings refers here to the preview of the 1989 exhibit.

35 'De Stichting Architektuur Museum: Utopie of noodzaak', S/AM 0 (1983): 1.

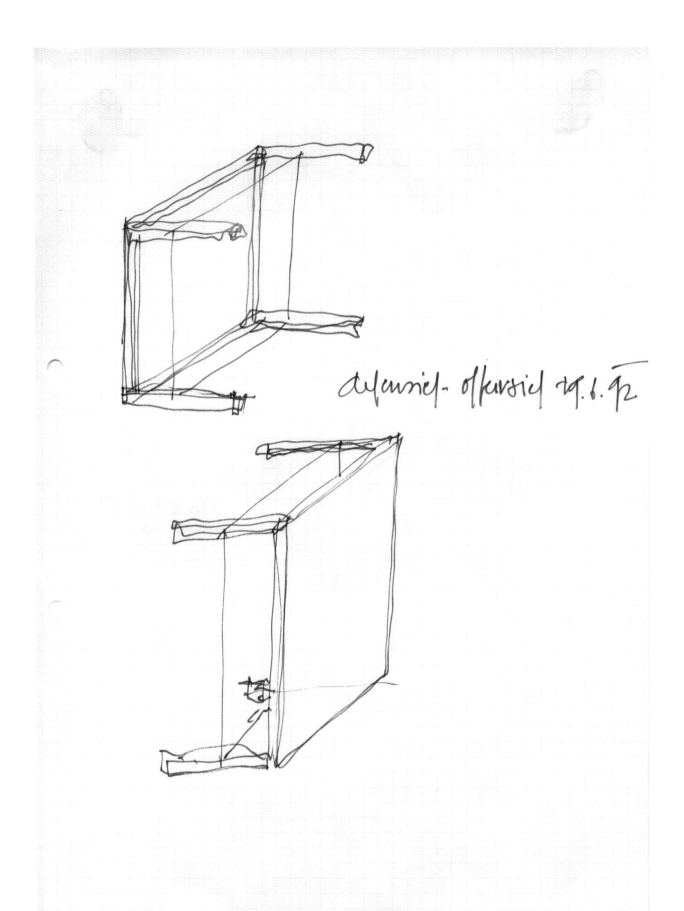

defensief - offensief 29.6.92

Fredie Floré

The Architectural Practice as Breeding Ground for Interior and Furniture Design

Many of the last century's pioneers in furniture and interior design, trained or worked as architects.[1] There are numerous examples: Henry Van de Velde, Mies van der Rohe, Gerrit Rietveld, Marcel Breuer and Alvar Aalto, to name but a few. These designers harboured diverse ambitions.[2] Some strove for the accomplishment of a *Gesamtkunstwerk*. Some responded to the existing market supply, to prevailing taste, or to housing culture; whereas others viewed the interior as the ideal space for the architectural experiment, or regarded design as an integral aspect of an individual way of thinking, conceptualisation or representation.[3] Pragmatic reasons also played a role with some frequency. A paucity of building projects naturally stimulated architects' interest in smaller scale projects, or those with a more explicit temporary character.

We also find a mix of these ambitions and motives among a number of Flemish architects from the 20th century. Architectural historian and critic Marc Dubois has mapped the oeuvre of several key figures since the late 1970s. He developed just as distinct an interest in 'historical' figures - including Albert Van huffel and Gaston Eysselinck - as in the accomplishments of his own generation, to include the works of his friend and colleague Christian Kieckens. While design and interior architecture, as well as their history, were fully developing into independent disciplines, especially abroad but also at home, Dubois continued to consistently promote the intrinsic relationships with architecture and architectural history in often richly documented publications and exhibitions.[4] This enabled him to make the ambitions, approaches or perspectives of a selection of remarkable architect-furniture designers from various periods of the 20th century visible and the object of discussion. While the disciplines of product design and interior architecture were gaining independence through, for example, the establishment of separate courses; the architectural practice was and would continue to be a meaningful breeding ground for interior and furniture design.

HISTORICAL KEY FIGURES

The context in which Dubois - a 1974 architect graduate from the Sint-Lucas Faculty of Architecture, Ghent - completed several of his early projects, immediately solidifies his combined interest in architecture and design. Since the late 1970s, he has regularly collaborated with the Ghent Museum of Decorative Arts (now Design museum Ghent) led by the then newly appointed director Lieven Daenens. In 1983, for example, Dubois compiled an exhibition and publication about Albert Van huffel, the architect who designed the Basilica of the Sacred Heart in Koekelberg, Brussels - a monumental art deco building, which is viewed today as one of the Belgian Catholic church's most

Christian Kieckens, Sketch for Defensief – Offensief, 1992.
Personal archive
Christian Kieckens.

significant 20th-century building projects.[5] The Museum of Decorative Arts did not simply organise an exhibition about architecture, Van huffel also designed countless utilitarian objects and interior elements including rugs, furniture, embroidery, light fixtures and silverware, as did several of his contemporaries. In fact, he is a telling example of an architect that viewed his creations as all-encompassing projects. His own 'schooling' constituted the ideal foundation in this respect. Van huffel studied the art of painting, decorative arts and architecture in Ghent, prematurely dropped out of several of these courses, and became proficient in furniture and interior design at a Ghent furniture company.

The tone of Dubois' texts for the catalogue makes it clear that he primarily wanted to rescue Van huffel from oblivion. Van huffel, he asserted, had for far too long been exclusively identified with the Basilica, a project which had up until that point been discussed in an overly isolated manner.[6] Dubois counteracted this with an extensive discussion and contextualisation of his work in its entirety. This operation was possible as the Museum had been able to get its hands on the architect's private archive. The catalogue contains, for example, a description, illustrated with photographs and drawings, of the Bruxelman house in Ghent-Ledeberg (1923-1927). The project illustrates Van huffel's profound interest in crafts and in creating a well-balanced and all-encompassing composition. Architecture, interior and design - including Van huffel's garden design - speak the same design idiom, with a zigzag line as a recurring motif.

The collaboration with the Museum of Decorative Arts resulted in more exhibitions about architect-designers of the past. Five years before the Van huffel project, Dubois was involved in a publication and exhibition about the Flemish modernist 'architect and furniture designer' Gaston Eysselinck, whose work continues to intrigue him to this day.[7] With regard to furniture design, Eysselinck should be positioned in the wake of this generation of architects – Mart Stam, Marcel Breuer, Charlotte Perriand, and so on – who experimented with the concept of mass-produced furniture, generally with the distinct ambition of improving the quality of the everyday living environment, also

Albert Van huffel, dining room of Bruxelman residence, Ghent, 1923-1927.
Collection Design Museum Ghent.

Gaston Eysselinck, Catalogue FRATSTA, 1931.
Collection Design Museum Ghent.

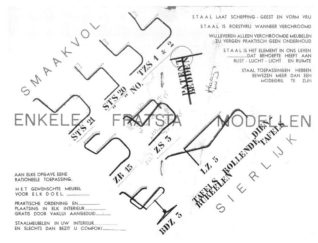

for the lower social classes. Eysselinck perfectly translated this ambition in the tubular furniture he designed for his own house in 1931, but which he, following foreign examples, hoped to commercialise under the name FRATSTA, an abbreviation of Fabriek van RATionele STAalmeubelen (Factory of rational steel furniture). An advertising brochure displays different seating elements in profile - including the I 75 lounger. The furniture items are presented as 'tasteful' and 'decorative' and as a practical and comfortable solution for any interior. The chrome-plated steel is recommended as an outstanding ingredient for 'our life... that needs peace - air- light and space.'[8] The fact Eysselinck's furniture was in no way factory produced, but instead was created with the craftsmanship of a local bicycle maker, merely confirms the great aspirations of the architect.

Eysselinck's own home was inspired by Le Corbusier's 'five points towards a new architecture' and was intended to be a personal contribution to modernist architecture. As Dubois explains, it 'symbolised a new way of life, in which the analysis of the functions and application of the new technique was entirely at the service (sic) of humanity.'[9] The furniture and objects in the house were - analogous to the objects in Le Corbusier's Pavilion de l'Esprit Nouveau (1925) that Eysselinck had also visited - essential to the 'eloquence' of the whole.[10] They explained the architecture and, similar to the objects in the French master's pavilion, represented its most tangible rhetorical dimension.[11]

A number of Eysselinck's steel tubular furniture items are included in the Museum of Decorative Arts' permanent collection and shortly after their first exhibition, were exhibited again, including in 1987 as part of the exhibition: 'Buismeubelen in België. Tijdens het Interbellum', of which both the composition and catalogue were managed by Dubois.[12]

Gaston Eysselinck, interior of Eysselinck house with chaise longue LZ5, Ghent, 1931.
Collection Design Museum Ghent.

CONTEMPORARY DESIGN PRODUCTION

During the 1980s, the Ghent Museum of Decorative Arts also provided a platform for contemporary perspectives on interior and furniture design, including those by architects and the now recognised new professional category of interior architects. In 1983, Dubois and Kieckens founded the Architecture Museum Foundation (S/AM) on the museum's premises with the aim of 'preserving documents related to the development of modern architecture and highlighting the cultural significance of contemporary architecture through exhibitions and publications.' One of the foundation's first activities, besides founding a magazine, was to organise the exhibition *Alvaro Siza en de architectuur in Portugal* in 1983 in the Museum of Decorative Arts. Kieckens was responsible for designing the exhibition.[14] S/AM also devoted attention to interior and furniture design. In the series of monographs that the foundation published in the 1980s, number five is devoted exclusively to fifteen 'young interior designers' including, for example: Ann Buvens, Koen Deprez, Wim De Vos and Vittorio Simoni.[15] Once again the publication accompanied an exhibition in the Museum of Decorative Arts, as did several previous monographs about 'young architects'. Each time the objective was to provide a platform for a new generation of designers. According to the organisers, interior designers in particular needed this, for the simple reason that the vast majority of their work is situated behind closed doors. The exhibition's introduction also

Christian Kieckens (lay-out), pamphlet for exhibition Jonge Interieurontwerpers. The cover shows a shop interior designed by Koen Deprez, Museum voor Sierkunst, Ghent, 16 december 1988 - 19 februari 1989. APA archive S/AM.

Cover of the 1987 catalogue Denk-beelden. Meubelideeën na 1980. Vanfleteren E (ed.) 1987 'Denk-beelden. Meubelideeën na 1980'. Gent: Hoger Architectuurinstituut Sint-Lucas.

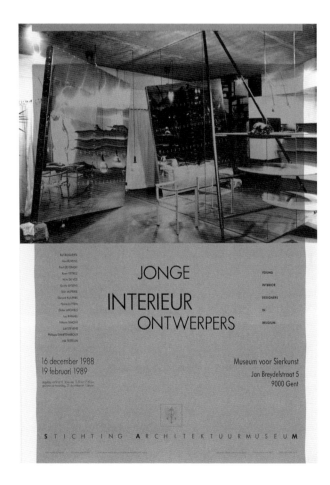

touched upon a second reason: 'Moreover it is virtually impossible in Belgium for these designers to confront their ideas with existing well-established values. Only a few exhibitions about small furniture objects bear sporadic witness to this.'[16] One of these rare exhibitions was 'Denk-beelden. Meubelideeën na 1980', which had been organised the previous year at the Hotel d'Hane Steenhuyse in Ghent on the occasion of the 125th anniversary of Sint-Lucas Ghent.[17] Kieckens was also responsible for designing this event.

Also in 1987, one of the editions of S/AM's quarterly magazine was largely dedicated to furniture design. The issue, with Kieckens as the final editor, combines a variety of contributions, several of which are linked to the phenomenon of the architect-furniture designer. For example, it is noteworthy that the essay by Adolf Loos 'Die Abschaffung der Möbel' (The Abolition of Furniture) from 1924 was reprinted. It states that when designing an interior, modern architects should only concern themselves with built-in furniture elements – which are part of the wall – and not with so-called mobile furniture. 'The production of mobile furniture should be left to the carpenter and the upholsterer,' Loos suggests, 'They make splendid furniture.'[18] As such he displayed his aversion to the fully designed and in his opinion, artificial interiors of for example, architect and contemporary, Josef Hoffman. In S/AM's magazine, the statements by Loos are combined with a reprint of the article 'Space Architecture' from 1934 by the Austrian-American architect Rudolph M. Schindler and photographs of the 'mobile' furniture he designed for Woning Wolfe in Avalon, an interview with interior architect Pieter De Bruyne, graduate of Sint-Lucas in Ghent, a short article (taken from Blueprint) about furniture design by the Japanese fashion designer Rei Kawakubo, and an excerpt from a discussion of the work by the Japanese furniture and product designer Shiru Kuramata. The eclectic collection of texts and images touches on implicitly diverse design issues, not least of which includes the professional profile of the furniture designer.

S/AM's publications and exhibitions about interior design and furniture design of the late 1980s testify to a growing interest in these disciplines as autonomous design practices. This is consistent with developments in the field of education in the previous decades. After the Second World War, several courses in interior architecture were also established in Flanders, and discussions surfaced repeatedly about recognition for the profession.[19] Many young interior architects and furniture designers from the 1980s, however diverse their work, viewed the interior not as a rhetorical component of a larger all-encompassing architectural design, but as a fully-fledged design activity in itself. This was also revealed by the work presented in the Museum of Decorative Arts. That precisely this location could be used for an exhibition about 'young interior architects' was of exceptional added value for the organisers. The catalogue's introduction stated that 'with the most important art nouveau collection in Belgium, for example, the archives and furniture projects by Pieter De Bruyne, the furniture range from the 1930s and the ongoing contemporary acquisitions from the collections of Memphis and Studio Alchimia, among others, this 'house' constituted a fitting entourage for presenting new designs by young people'.[20] Indeed, director Daenens developed an acquisition policy which, unlike that of the past, explicitly focused on recent, 20th-century design production, starting with new design from Italy.[21] However it was predominantly the direct confrontation with history in the museum - via the collection and the building itself - that was viewed as an important advantage in this post-modern era. At that time, just as it does today, the museum occupied the 18th-century Hotel de Coninck, fitted with period rooms, whose dilapidated rear building was largely replaced by a new building by the Ghent architect Willy Verstraete in the early 1990s.

AN ARCHITECTURAL BREEDING GROUND

Parallel to interior architecture and furniture design's increasing autonomy and degree of professionalism, architect-designers continued to make a meaningful contribution to the production of and the debate about interior and design in Flanders. A prime example is Kieckens who, according to Dubois played a vital, pioneering role in the development of S/AM between 1983 and 1992. He also expresses great admiration for Kieckens' highly diverse design production. 'The image of the architect that exclusively designs

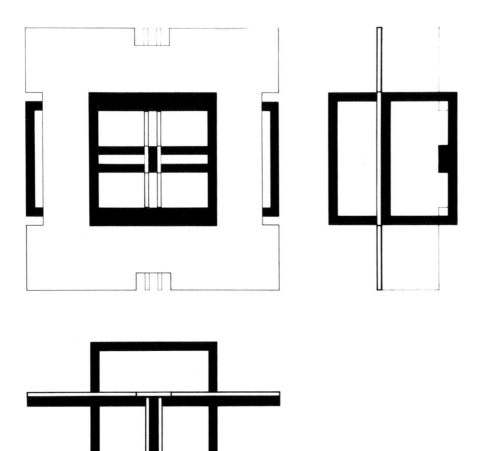

Christian Kieckens, design for a 'table object' in black and white, 1979.
Deetaai Study Group (Christian Kieckens and Jos Vanderperren), CRESCENDO 1, architectuur 1980 (Wezembeek-Oppem: DEETAAI, 1980): 49. Scan APA.

buildings, does not apply here,' he notes. Indeed, Kieckens re-interpreted the figure of the architect-designer through a combination of graphic work, product design, furniture design, exhibitions, developments, architectural projects and urban development proposals. Inspired by the work of Pieter De Bruyne, he developed a profound interest in metrics and spatial relationships such as those that can be found, for example, in baroque architecture. He had already expressed this interest early on. The first edition of *Crescendo*, a publication from 1980 by the DEETAAI working group - consisting of the architect Jos Vanderperren and Kieckens - presented architecture as well as furniture designs by this duo. The designs - houses, a neighbourhood centre, a 'garden structure', tables, a bathroom cabinet, various 'objects' etc. - spoke the same language, inspired by historically-charged geometric structures and ratios, often inscribed in a square or cube.[22] Several furniture items were painted in contrasting colours, reminiscent of the furniture designs by De Bruyne. As such the constituent elements of the tables and other 'objects' were explicitly articulated.

During decades to follow Kieckens, partly inspired by an abiding interest in developments in other cultural disciplines such as visual art, film and music, gradually developed a layered design strategy that was to be a breeding ground for countless large as well

**Christian Kieckens,
Table Onofre, 1988.**
Photo Mirjam Devriendt and Jean-Pierre Stoop.

as several small-scale and temporary projects. 'In fact his attitude is consistent with that of some Italian 'architect-designers' such as Achille Castiglione or Andrea Branzi,' stated Dubois in 2001.[23] One remarkable small-scale design by Kieckens from 1988 is the one-person bistro table Onofre. In this case the emphasis on underlying geometric structures is far less obvious and the paintwork has made room for a subtler play on the types of wood. Onofre is made from American cherrywood and walnut - that engage in such a way that they simultaneously articulate and manipulate the table's basic elements - stand and tabletop. The tabletop is trapezoidal - a clever design that offers the solitary user the possibility of combining eating and reading, and also provides him or her with an open perspective of the interior in which he or she is situated.

Kieckens and Dubois collaborated on exhibitions on several occasions. In 1991, they documented the recent architectural production in Flanders in *Architetti [della Fiandra]*, the Flemish submission in the Belgian pavilion at the Venice Architecture Biennale. The project was an S/AM initiative. Dubois was commissioner of the exhibition.[24] Kieckens was responsible for the exhibition design. Together, they devised the concept for the catalogue and the exhibition. Kieckens designed a number of wooden elements - elongated horizontal plateaus, vertical plates, horizontal reading tablets - that brought additional structure to the pavilion's interior and could serve to bear drawings, photos, room texts, models and books. The exhibition elements did not appear to try and clarify or explain the architecture of the Belgian pavilion – a project by the architect Léon Sneyers from 1907. In the first place the largely symmetrical interior showed itself as an autonomous intervention, which engaged in dialogue with the traditional museum interiors and with the exhibited work of diverse colleagues, including contemporaries Paul Robbrecht en Hilde Daem and Marie-José Van Hee.

The 1990s also saw collaborations involving Dubois and Kieckens in the context of the Interior Biennale in Kortrijk. In 1994, architectural critic Geert Bekaert, former chairman of the Interior Foundation, invited Kieckens to devise a new spatial concept for the fair. Starting from the Interior Foundation's strategic advisor, Andrea Branzi's suggestion to

Christian Kieckens
(exhibition design)
and Marc Dubois (curator),
exhibition Architetti [della
Fiandra] in the Belgian pavilion,
Giardini di Castello,
Venice, 1991.
Photo Christian Kieckens.

introduce a linear structure that would connect all the halls in the complex, Kieckens developed a grid pattern of streets around a central 'rambla' or promenade axis. Two years later, Dubois was commissioner of the Interior Biennale and Kieckens designed a variant of the 'urban' structure for the fair with a central promenade flanked by a series of lit porticoes.

One of the striking secondary projects of the biennale in 1996 was the 'Tafels van de 20ste eeuw' exhibition, with Dubois as curator and Kieckens as the exhibition designer. The installation consisted of a magnified, upside-down table, of which the tabletop's underside formed the exhibition floor. On the floor stood 62 table designs from the 20th century, including the dining table Model 322 D.S.1 by Charles R. Mackintosh (1918), Eileen Gray's side table Model E. 1027 (ca 1926-1929), the coffee table from the Plywood Group by Charles and Ray Eames (1946), the Quaderna table by Superstudio (1970-1971) and the Less table by Jean Nouvel (1994). The collection also included a number of Belgian examples, such as Gustave Serrurier-Bovy's Silex table from 1905 and the dining table 'Homenaje a Eduardo Chillida' by André Verroken (1994) and a design by Paul ibens and Claire Bataille from 1996.[25] While Kieckens derived inspiration for the general structure of the Biennale from patterns of urban development – the rambla, the grid – here he performed a reverse rescaling. The figure of the table constituted the basis for an intervention with architectural panache. This intervention was again an autonomous act of design. However, in contrast to the museum spaces of the Belgian pavilion in Venice, the stately Kortrijk halls required a grander gesture. Kieckens' response, the giant table, was a piece of 'expressive' architecture that was somewhat shamelessly thrust under the elegant wooden rafters. Kieckens applied the motif of the table for a second time a year later in 'Tafel-Landschap', an exhibition about his own work in the deSingel arts centre in Antwerp. Upon arrival, the visitor could step in a large wooden installation from the sloping surface that led to the elongated exhibition gallery. As one ascended the slope, the perception of scale changed. At first it felt as if one was in an interior. A few steps later and the wooden construction revealed itself to be a large table.

Christian Kieckens (exhibition design) and Marc Dubois (curator), Exhibition tables of the 20th century, for the Biennale Interior Design, Kortrijk, 1996. Photo Reiner Lautwein.

**Robbrecht en Daem,
Richter table, 1992.**
Photo Kristien Daem.

The exhibition and accompanying catalogue, de 'TAFEL', related to furniture design and the history of furniture, but the link with architecture was pivotal. In his contribution to the catalogue, Bekaert, referring to Hannah Arendt, explains that the table 'is the ultimate architectural analogy'.[26] The table provides order, makes the civilised world tangible. It can foster togetherness, when used during a meal for example, but it can just as well introduce a spatial divide, as is often the case in a doctor's consultation room or manager's office. In the same catalogue Branzi describes architects' interest in designing furniture and observes a shift from a fascination for the chair among many modernist architects to a fascination for the table among younger generations. In his opinion this development is highly significant and very promising. He believes that tables introduce more complex spatial relationships and facilitate more functions and a greater arsenal of interpersonal relationships than the chair. 'Making a table means building a house,' stated Branzi, 'The table is the model of the house, of the work, of human relationships. It is around the table that the architecture devises itself, as a progressive composite of enclosures, of feeble protection and of diaphragms, extending to the dimension of the city.'[27] In his text in the catalogue Dubois builds on Branzi's insights: 'a table can be regarded as miniaturised architecture.'[28] He subsequently develops a historical-thematic perspective, wherein the idea that the table in the 20th century has not been the subject of any fundamental innovations, but rather has undergone multiple reinterpretations, is key. The text's conclusion significantly addresses 'the table as a metaphor of architecture' and consists of a brief anthology of constructions - including the National Gallery by Mies van der Rohe (1962-1968) and Emil Schubiger's bridge in Val Nalps (1957) - which as a consequence of their design, conjure up associations with the table archetype.

According to Dubois, Kieckens' designs possess 'an architectural undercurrent' also when it comes to small-scale projects.[29] With regard to other architects of his generation the individual conceptual framework also constitutes a fertile breeding ground for interior and furniture projects. For example it is difficult to view the Richter table by Robbrecht en Daem (1992) separated from the intense dialogue that the architects engage in with the visual arts in their architectural projects.[30] The wooden writing desk - finished with a linoleum desktop – was created as a birthday present for the painter Gerhard Richter with whom they, certainly in this period, were regularly in touch. The piece of furniture is a serviceable object, reflecting the architects' perspective on architecture as a utilitarian discipline. The gently sloping, hinged, trapezoidal tabletop, the storage space underneath, the 'back legs' that move slightly backwards form an inviting, stable workstation for the human act of writing or drawing. During the 1990s, architect Marie-José Van Hee also designed furniture, but at first glance seemed to follow the previously cited motto of Adolf Loos. She primarily focused on wall cabinets, built-in furniture. The cabinets often formed a vital component of the architecture and especially of the wall as an architectural element. The front façade of her house in Gh-

Marie-José Van Hee, House Van Hee, Ghent, 1990-1997.
Photo Peter Lorré.

ent (1990-1997) is 'expanded' on the inside with a high, continuous closed wall cabinet with deep window recesses above.[31] As part of the thick wall façade, the cabinets shelter the adjacent, stately living area from the outside world, the city. At the same time they discreetly support life's everyday activities. This interior is averse to any artificiality.

THE BREEDING GROUND MAPPED OUT

Just as several of his fellow contemporary architects, Dubois' interest in interior and design testifies to an unmistakable architectural perspective. He outlined the work of diverse Belgian/Flemish architect-furniture designers from the previous century: from historical figures that honoured the principle of an all-encompassing design project or viewed furniture design as an integral component of their own vision of modernist architecture, to fellow contemporaries who accomplished in some cases a significant number of interior and furniture projects founded on a personal and sometimes multi-disciplinary reference framework. Some of these projects were conceived as inextricable components of architecture, such as the permanent furniture in Van Hee's projects. Others were more stand-alone projects. Just as Robbrecht en Daem or Kieckens designed architectural projects, so too did they design furniture pieces and interiors.

Dubois' reference framework was that of architecture and architectural history, also when it concerned furniture design or other small-scale objects. The nature of his approach, in which a great deal of attention was often devoted to the design qualities of objects, the 'spirit of the times' and the designer's oeuvre, and in which the focus was on a selection of exceptional productions, gradually started to come under pressure with the emancipation of design history – particularly in England – during the last few decades of the 20th century.[32] For example several authors felt that anonymous design, collective aspects of product development, processes related to consumption, appropriation and the creation of social meaning, equally deserved attention. At the same time, the 'classic' art or architectural-historical approach continued to be relevant, especially with regard to the ongoing creation and mediation of a canon of Belgian designers and interior architects. Several of these designers, whose work according to Bekaert was less spectacular and dogmatically inspired than that of their foreign contemporaries, while all the more driven by a fundamental interest in the immediate reality, had long hovered under the radar.[33]

1 Gabriele Lueg, 'From Aalto to Zumthor – *Furniture by Architects*', in Furniture by Architects. From Aalto to Zumthor, eds. Petra Hesse and Gabriele Lueg (Cologne: Verlag Walther König, 2012), 20.

2 Marian Page, *Furniture Designed by Architects* (London: The Architectural Press Ltd., 1983): 7.

3 René Spitz, 'Dreams of life on dentists' chairs or The designer chair and the architect's image,' in *Furniture by Architects. From Aalto to Zumthor*, eds. Petra Hesse and Gabriele Lueg (Cologne: Verlag Walther König, 2012): 82-3.

4 Grace Lees-Maffei, 'Introduction: Professionalization as a Focus in Interior Design History', *Journal of Design History,* 21(1) (2008), 1-18.

5 Marc Dubois, *Albert Van huffel. 1877-1935* (Ghent: Snoeck-Ducaju & Zoon, 1983).

6 Dubois, *Albert Van huffel*, 11.

7 Hervé Demeyer, Marc Dubois and Lieven Daenens, *Gaston Eysselinck architect and furniture designer (1907-1953)*. (Ghent: Snoeck-Ducaju, 1978); Marc Dubois, *Architect Gaston Eysselinck: zijn werk te Oostende 1945-1953: de fatale ontgoocheling*. (Bruges: Province of West Flanders, 1986); Marc Dubois, *Gaston Eysselinck 1930-1931: woning Gent*. (Oostkamp: Stichting Kunstboek, 2003).

8 Marc Dubois, *Buismeubelen in België: Tijdens het interbellum*. (Ghent: Museum of Decorative Arts, 1987): 58.

9 Demeyer, Dubois and Daenens, *Gaston Eysselinck architect and furniture designer*, 17.

10 Alina Payne, *From Ornament to Object. Genealogies of Architectural Modernism* (New Haven/London: Yale University Press, 2012): 5-6.

11 Payne, *From Ornament to Object*, 5-6.

12 Marc Dubois, *Buismeubelen in België. Tijdens het interbellum*. (Ghent: Museum of Decorative Arts, 1987).

13 Francis Strauven, 'Architecture Museum Foundation (S/AM) 1983-1992', in *Repertorium van de architectuur in België van 1830 tot heden*, ed. Anne Van Loo (Antwerp: Mercatorfonds, 2003).

14 Raymond Balau et al., *Christian Kieckens: zoeken, denken, Bouwen*. (Ghent: Ludion, 2001):26, 123-9.

15 Christian Kieckens (ed.), *Jonge interieurontwerpers*. (Ghent: Stichting Architektuurmuseum, 1988).

16 Kieckens, *Jonge interieurontwerpers*, 6.

17 Vanfleteren E (ed.) *Denk-beelden. Meubelideeën na 1980*. (Ghent: St.-Lucas Faculty of Architecture, 1987). Erik Vanfleteren was teacher Furniture Design and Christian Kieckens was assistant.

18 'Die Herstellung die mobielen Möbel überlasse man dem Tischler und dem Tapezierer. Die machen herrliche Möbel.' Adolf Loos, 'Die Abschaffung der Möbel' (The Abolition of Furniture) (1924). *S/AM* 4, no. 4 (1987): 12.

19 Els De Vos, Inge Somers and Bart Eeckhout, 'Three profiles of 'interior architects' in Postwar Flanders: the historic distinction between practitioners with a degree, domestic advisers, and interior decorators.' *Journal of Interior Design* 40, no. 2 (2015): 37-57.

20 Kieckens, *Jonge Interieurontwerpers*, 6.

21 Fredie Floré, 'Blinde vlek in de historiek van het Design museum Gent', *De Witte Raaf* 148 (2010): 13; Javier Gimeno-Martinez and Jasmijn Verlinden, 'From Museum of Decorative Arts to Design Museum: The Case of the Design museum Gent', *Design and Culture* 2, no. 3 (2010): 259-284.

22 Christian Kieckens and Jos Vanderperren, eds., *Crescendo* 1 (Wezembeek-Oppem: DEETAAI, 1980).

23 Balau et al., *Christian Kieckens*, 29.

24 Marc Dubois and Christian Kieckens, eds., *Architetti [della Fiandra]*. (Bruges: die Keure, 1991): 95.

25 Marc Dubois, ed., *de TAFEL*. (Kortrijk: Stichting Interieur vzw, 1996)

26 Dubois, *de TAFEL*, 9.

27 Dubois, *de TAFEL*, 16.

28 Dubois, *de TAFEL*, 23.

29 Balau et al., *Christian Kieckens*, 29.

30 Steven Jacobs, 'Onvergetelijke plaatsen', in *Werk in architectuur: Paul Robbrecht and Hilde Daem*, Steven Jacobs, Paul Robbrecht and Hilde Daem, (Ghent: Ludion, 1998): 6-60.

31 André Loeckx, 'Het derde huis', in: *Marie-José Van Hee. Architect*, André Loeckx, William Mann and Kristiaan Borret (Ghent: Ludion, 2002): 32.

32 Kjetil Fallan, D*esign History. Understanding Theory and Method* (Oxford: Berg Publishers, 2010): 8-10.

33 Geert Bekaert, 'De averechtse metropool', in *Design Made in Belgium 1900-1994* (Kortrijk: Stichting Interieur, 1994): 5-15.

Architecture between Dwelling and Spatial Systematics
The Early Works of the Generation of '74

Caroline Voet

Just like music, architecture alone must determine the themes it wants to express. Determining and defining a theme are architecture's paramount conditions. However, it is crucial that every project has a theme as its foundation. The requirement to thematise architecture consists of nothing less than its extraction from the impasse of pure functionalism. A building without a theme, which is not sustained by an idea, is architecture without thinking.[1]

The architectural discipline supports on the knowledge of the architectural form, which means the history of architectures. This discipline is characterised by repetition and the absence of any representation, she structures places.[2]

Paul Robbrecht and Hilde Daem, Marie-José Van Hee, Christian Kieckens and Marc Dubois continued to collaborate after completing their studies at Sint-Lucas in 1974, not only through the Architecture Museum Foundation (Stichting Architektuurmuseum, hereafter: S/AM), but also on joint architectural projects. Following the collaboration with DEETAI from 1980 to 1983, Christian Kieckens worked with Robbrecht en Daem and Wim Cuyvers between 1984 and 1986. In 1987 Christian Kieckens collaborated with Marc Dubois on a renovation project in Ghent. Beginning in 1990, Marie-José shared office space with Robbrecht en Daem. Since then they regularly developed joint projects. As far as these works are concerned, one could say that there is a certain commonality, stemming from the tone of their shared quest. Van Hee mentions 'a rooting around', 'the hunger' for architecture and spatiality. They desired architecture apart from social context or an all-encompassing functionalism, and sought autonomous foundations for the creation of architectural space. They strove to control the creation of architecture from a specific embedding of historical knowledge within a contemporary discourse, a quest that relied more on the general debate about architectural form that emerged in the 1970s. The language and themes they employ are aligned with a broader international movement that yearned for the autonomy of architecture. Thus architecture involves a reading of the spatiality, of its staging. From here the generation of 1974 developed its own architectural language, the seeds of which can be seen in their early work. This text departs from this broader context to zoom in on this generation's early work and to expose its roots and evolution.

Sketch Paul Robbrecht. Paul Robbrecht, Hilde Daem, Wim Cuyvers and Christian Kieckens, Reorganisation of De Smet house, Ghent, 1984. Paul Robbrecht (Projects from 1984) in Marc Dubois, ed., De Woning als architectuurtypologie (Ghent: Stichting Architektuurmuseum, 1985): 55. APA archive S/AM.

Since Heidegger offered architects a new meaning for place in *Bauen Wohnen Denken* (Heidegger, 1954), architectural theorists sought more in-depth ways of describing and implementing the architectural manifestation of house and city based on this phenomenological idea. In the 1970s, this appeared to be a balancing act between reinterpreting history and anticipating new social issues. 'What then, must we demand from architectural space in order that man can still call himself human', was the key question that Christian Norberg-Schulz put forward in 1971.[3] He was responding to what he described as a common 'naive realism' in the 1960s, which would dominate the discourse on architectural form, either disguised as the study of 'architectural perception', or as three-dimensional geometry. In both cases the issue of space as a dimension of human existence was evaded, resulting in the concept of space being viewed as outdated or even superficial. He also criticised architecture that as a 'chaotic form' would like to connect with contemporary disintegration and the speed of communication, production and mobility. Architecture characterised by total freedom could not exist according to Norberg-Schulz. Architecture had a major responsibility: the facilitation of the imagination as an ambiguous, complex but structured space, the provision of a human existential foothold. Thus architecture could not be volatile or mobile, but rather was characterised by slowness. In this regard he specifically referred to a stable system of places, capable of being bound to history via their slow progression.

SUBLIMATIONS FROM THE BAROQUE AS FOUNDATIONS FOR AN EXISTENTIAL SPACE

In their early work both Paul Robbrecht and Christian Kieckens strove to make architecture a place with which history can forge a connection. It was Venturi who showed them how this could be achieved.[4] Venturi analysed history in a distinctively architectural manner and demonstrated that it could also be directly used in the actual design process. Paul Robbrecht remembered that at Sint-Lucas he had only attended three of Hoppenbrouwers' lessons; nevertheless, it was these lessons that introduced him to Venturi and Wittkower's perspective. Hoppenbrouwers presented Wittkower's *Architecture in the Age of Humanism* not as a stand-alone approach, but from the perspective of the impact this book had on the school that Alison and Peter Smithson had built in Hunstanton in 1950. Robbrecht was inspired by this specific link between history and contemporary interpretations. He was impressed by the approach and audacity of the symmetry in this building, something that was not done at that time.[5] Captivated, he left for Italy with a scholarship in 1979, as Godecharle competition laureate, to study Palladio and the Baroque. Palladio and Borromini explicitly filter through in Robbrecht's early work. A good example of this can be found in a project that was devised at the same time as his Italian journey: The De Mol villa in Kortrijk (1981-1983), one of the first houses by Robbrecht en Daem. Like a diorama ensconced in the surrounding landscape, the house plays push and pull with symmetry and asymmetry, as the result of 'shifts and transformations in the floor plan'.[6] Paul Robbrecht talked about keeping nature and artefact within strict confines as a way of building tension between the two. The house is envisaged as a hinge on a strip of landscape, with a directional change at its centre.

**Robbrecht en Daem,
Villa De Mol.**
Kortrijk, 1981-1983.

See also '3x3 projects', 144-147.

The façades are conceived as lenses, focussed on the landscape, framing sections of the surrounding panorama. Corners and cornices serve as brickwork frames, layering the whole in terms of line, surface and volume.

The country house appears as a sort of deconstructed abstraction of Palladio's Villa Malcontenta, seen through the eyes of Colin Rowe.[7] Similarly, they are symmetrical, rectangular boxes, directed towards the landscape through frames and loggias. Rowe demonstrated that the floor plans use a similar modular grid, based upon the golden ratio and square, expressed with the proportions 2 and 1 consecutively. We see the same process at work in the De Mol villa, only here the rear wall also rotates to reso-nate with the central axis. A series of five porticoes, with five minute perforations are positioned asymmetrically above them in the rear wall. The ensemble folds inwards, shifting away from the basic symmetry meticulously composed of rows of windows, porticoes and loggias. On top, there is a cornice with a pronounced curve. All the Palladian ingredients are unmistakeably present, but are emphatically juxtaposed with one other, thereby spectacularly enhancing the effect.

As the next Godecharle competition laureate, Christian Kieckens also set off for Bohemen in 1981 to study the baroque churches of Giovanni Santini and in 1982 he studied Borromini in Rome. More than Paul Robbrecht, he believed that this architec-ture was founded upon an underlying geometrical system. This approach was heavily influenced by artist, designer and architect Pieter De Bruyne (1931-1987). Kieckens was a diligent student of De Bruyne's study of Egyptian ratios through measurement and analytical drawings. Introducing his own work in the 1990 *S/AM* catalogue, he began with a treatment of the spatial blueprint for the Cheops pyramid from 1983. He used it to illustrate an example of the spatial dimension: a criterion for relationships between plan, apothem's cross-section, diagonal cross-section, and the actual size of the side faces.[8] Delving deeper into De Bruyne's analyses, Kieckens began a 'study of the constant and metamorphosis in the Borrominian space'.[9] Although Kieckens' own research between 1982 and 1985 led him to uncover Borromini's essential spatial systematic of 'tre et uno assieme', De Bruyne was already familiar with geometric analyses of the Baroque from a few early studies within his milieu at Sint-Lucas Brus-sels. In a 1976 publication of A+, Kieckens discovered an article by Jos Vanderperren and José Kennes, students and later colleague and assistant to Pieter de Bruyne at Sint-Lucas Brussels, about the systematic, spatial world of Guarino Guarini, a study based on their 1974 thesis.[10] In this, several of Guarini's buildings were reduced to a Renaissance plan, usually the Greek cross, and from there elaborated into a baroque model of circles demonstrating the origins of the convex and concave movement in the walls. They describe Guarini's spatial stratification as 'mutually connected centres (nodal cells), the basis for interpenetrating centralised fields'. This idea of architecture as a systematic of dynamic proportional fields, they say, was adopted from Christian Norberg-Schulz's *Existence, Space and Architecture*.[11] In this book Norberg-Schulz also made frequent reference to the Baroque. He borrowed the concept of the 'field' or 'campo' from Paolo Portoghesi's *Borromini, architettura come linguaggio* published in 1967.[12] But Norberg-Schulz did not introduce field as a mere spatial systematic. He used the term to describe his concept of existential space: a coherent and meaningful, stable concept of space that each of us develops, necessary to the manifestation of our existence. This was distinct from *perceptual space*, which he described as more egocentric and as a constant succession of variations later reconstructed to form a meaningful whole. Through existential space he was aiming at spatial schemata, the composition of more invariable elements, universal elementary structures (archetypes) or socially and culturally conditioned structures.[13] Whether the space was architectural or expressive it was the manifestation of human existential space; Norberg-Schulz sought to approximate the relationship between the two. This brought a new level of meaning to the use of ratios. Norberg-Schulz defined several elements of architectonic space: the central place or node, the enclosure, which synthesises inside and outside, path and axis, and domain and district.[14] He would refer to Borromini for this integrated whole or 'field' forms, saying that the architectonic field had taken on a new meaning: Borromini's spaces were all synthesising totalities from which any distillation of individual units was impossible. Typically, these integrated architectonic fields would involve overlapping spaces that were centralised and longitudinally enclosed. The curved walls have their own centres, and so in themselves constitute interpenetrating centralising fields. No monotonous repetition here, but systematic alterations in direction and density. The dynamic zones of interference between fields were for movement, for example entrances.[15] Norberg-Schulz referred to Christoph Dientzenhofer and Balthazar Neumann for the transformation of solid walls in their buildings into systems of columns and suffused membranes. Guarini was proposed as an example in which interfering zones were made into extensive dynamic patterns.[16] The belief that architecture could evoke an existential dimension through a spatial systematic like a dynamic field, not by virtue of symbolism but through the space itself, was a potent attraction for the generation of 1974. Control of these spatial systems, in drawings and in detail, for them defined the architect's craft.

Just before the Borromini analysis, in 1980, Christian Kieckens joined the DEETAAI working group, a design collective founded in 1976 by Jos Vanderperren, 'a systematic analysis of their own design and the performance that is triggered by this design'.[17] In 1981 their 'The House between the History and Now', project, a submission for the 'Shinkenchiku Residential Design Competition '80 (The Japan Architect, Tokyo) was awarded an honourable mention. Using an art nouveau house by Paul Cauchie as the basis they proposed a new plan typology for the row house. Using a superimposition of the plan and façade they strove to convey the exclusively aesthetic qualities of the façade in what they considered everyday plan organisation. The depth of the house was made equal to the height of the façade and six façade elements were projected into the plan: cellar window, two side windows and a balcony, four circular elements, the circular window and lock, wall graffiti and roof termination were reworked on one or several levels into new elements of the plan such as floor termination, columns,

Christian Kieckens and Jos Vanderperren (DEETAAI), **The house between the history and now.** Shinkenchiku Residential Design Competition '80, The Japan Architect, Tokyo, February 1981.

See also '3x3 projects', 154-155.

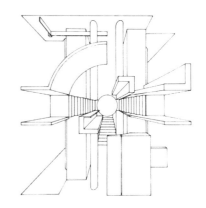

cupboard volumes, views, floor and attic mirrors, etc. Jos Vanderperren described DEETAAI's motives for anchoring the building's history in a new way from the perspective of the designers' geometric thinking:

> The newly introduced elements, arising from the geometrical wall pattern and projected in the new plan, reinforce the constant values contained in the historic work and are also a plea for the creation of designs bound to tradition, history and cosmos. The simplified tantric motif refers to history's everlasting continuity (…) The 'ma' character indicates a time-space relationship in the design. The integration and reintroduction of existing elements is a reference to the coexistence of the past and present.[18]

ARCHITECTURE AS AN INSIDE WITHIN AN OUTSIDE: THE AMBIGUOUS WALL

Just like Robbrecht and Kieckens, in her early work Marie-José Van Hee attempted to create architecture as a place with which history can connect. Although her quest for an understanding of historical examples departed from the same point, she distanced herself from the more abstract spatial systematic. As such, she related more closely to Norberg-Schulz' idea of an architecture stemming from experience and slowness. For her, architecture primarily involved creating a place from the boundaries of a human existence, in all its mundane and earthly affairs. To do so she sought an origin dating further back in history than the Baroque, as is clear from the thesis she produced at Sint-Lucas in 1974 'Beschouwingen omtrent tuinen in de Middeleeuwen tot in de tijd van Lodewijk XIV' (Reflections on gardens in the Middle Ages up to the period of Louis XIV), in which she conducted research into 'creating gardens'.[19] In addition to the garden itself, she aimed to encompass the residents who experienced them, in order to try and penetrate an existential core idea. What possessed these people to construct a garden? How did they use them? What forms did they take? What boundaries applied and what elements were characteristic? In this way she described the life of the Carthusian monks and the monastery gardens, which lay enclosed in the space of the monastery, and how the first gardens planted on castle grounds were herb gardens located close to the lady of the castle's dwelling, thereby facilitating her cultivation of medicinal herbs. She analysed the more recent medieval gardens as a place where beauty was characterised by a multiplicity of symbolisms, but above all it was a place where the noble lady and gentleman could receive their guests on turf benches of wood or stone.

Unlike Paul Robbrecht and Christian Kieckens, she did not appear to believe in architecture founded on Renaissance or Baroque design systems. Van Hee disregarded this and linked it to an illusion of order or the fictitious. When she referred to the labyrinthine lines in the floors of the early medieval cathedrals in Chartres, Bayeux and Reims, she did not do so with regard to the spatial pattern, as Venturi did. She was more fascinated by the approach adopted by the horticulturalist Sir Frank Crisp who, in the early

Fragment from: Guillaume de Lorris, Le Château de Jalousie - Le Roman de la rose, manuscrit Harley, 1490.
Marie-José Van Hee, 'Beschouwingen omtrent tuinen in de middeleeuwen tot in de tijd van Lodewijk XIX' (Thesis, Hoger Instituut Sint-Lucas Ghent, 1973-1974): 22.

20th century considered the lines as 'the symbolic display of the labyrinthine creases of sins which beset humanity'.[20] She approached the Renaissance as a time rife with excesses and man's desire to become more acquainted with nature by subjecting it to 'the illusion of order': symmetry, proportions and size, as elements conditional for beauty.[21] She strove to go beyond the illusion and returned to Giovanni Boccaccio's 14th-century *The Decameron*, in which he depicted the main castles surrounding Florence from the perspectives of various characters. Thus Van Hee focused on, for example, the point where the main characters beheld the garden's splendour after having rested in a loggia that overlooked the courtyard and the ensemble bedecked with ivy and seasonal flowers.[22] The baroque garden was therefore approached from men's pursuit of superiority, or as Huizinga referred to in his *Homo Ludens*, as 'a vision of the consciously exaggerated, deliberately intimidating, the familiar fiction so inherent to the Baroque'.[23]

In her work, Van Hee had already developed an architecture that intensely exploited the liveability and perception from within, in which the garden played a different role each time. Nevertheless this search for the authenticity of perception and liveability in her early works was characterised by a certain severity and monumentalism. In the Derks - Lowie house in Ghent (1983-1986) the garden plays a prominent role, as an external city room, that is shaped through the dialogue between layered façades with colonnades and garden walls. The design is symmetrically organised around a central axis that guides the eye from the inside to the outside, from the fireplace towards the garden to an open garden house as gallery at the back. It is the elementary details of the building's components that stand out. Columns and walls follow the same plane, without any decoration so that they appear as an abstraction of themselves. Two steps are exactly aligned with the slender columns. Next to the stone walls with their hardened skin, the fine rhythmic profiles of the windows and frames provide a contrasting, softer materiality. All of this is complimented with the layout of the pavement and the symmetrical green flowerbeds.

Consequently Van Hee had another take on Venturi, whereby the systematic served perception. In *Complexity and Contradiction*, Venturi definitively changed the way in which the wall was viewed as a boundary. He responded in his own way to the dialectic between form and concept and to the alternating meanings that arose as a consequence. The fact that an architectural form could act as a bearer of meaning and a bringer of meaning (signified and signifier), just as with language, led to ambiguity as a necessary characteristic of architecture's complexity and contradiction, for according to Venturi, architecture was form *and* substance, abstract *and* specific, texture *and* material, whereas its meaning originated from its internal characteristics and specific context.[24]

The architectural approach from inside, the design of the interior from within, is important in this respect. Architecture is an enclosure that communicates with its environment. Venturi proposed that:

> … designing from the outside in, as well as from the inside out, creates necessary tensions, which help make architecture. Since the inside is different from the outside, the wall – the point of change – becomes an architectural event. Architecture occurs at the meeting of interior and exterior forces of use and space. These interior and environmental forces are both general and particular, generic and circumstantial. (…) Architecture as the wall between inside and outside becomes the spatial record of its reconciliation and its drama.[25]

Just as Venturi described the phenomenon of the wall, so too did he address the problem of the opening, in this way drawing attention to the dilemma of 'dual' wall structures as surrounding surface, which was shaped both from within and without.[26]

This was far removed from the open, flowing architectural fields of the 1920s, in which the boundary between inside and outside evaporated and thus became transparent or infinite. Once again this boundary was brought back to the realm of the finite, and constituted the reason for developing a layering of encasings and frameworks between inside and outside. The relationship between the interior and exterior and all its spatial elements - wall, colonnade, portico, window, loggia, gallery etc. - became a fully-fledged theme in the design process.

In Christian Kieckens' early work with DEETAAI the wall was afforded the status of a geometric surface, supporting, intersecting and criss-crossing. As such it was not so much the spatial experience that presented him with design themes; he was more driven by the way in which his designs were 'read' by the user. The influence of deconstructivism is evident here. Just like Eisenman, Kieckens wanted to strip the space of functional preconceptions, an in this way to confront people with essential spatial meanings. It was through The Japan Architect journal that Kieckens was introduced to the work of for example Kisho Kurokawa and Arata Isozaki, who worked with the theme of the 'ma' concept as a space that was intertwined with time, an 'in-between space', a grey zone. Kieckens was particularly interested in the work of the deconstructivist architect

Hiromi Fujii. Just like in the Baroque, each architectural element was autonomously expressed as a spatial entity but in an abstract manner, apart from the structure. In deconstructivist architecture, the baroque elements that work on the boundary between lightness and weight, through their convex and concave interweaving performance, are dematerialised, as it were, in their abstraction. As a result the cohesion between the parts and the whole were achieved differently: more from a composition of heterogeneous fragments. Hiromi Fujii combined this spatial approach with a methodology of transformation processes, in which the cube always formed the basis that was subsequently scaled and rotated. Christian Kieckens' fascination for Hiromi Fujii's work resulted in a more detailed exploration of the latter, inspiring the exhibition he organised with DEETAAI in twelve architectural institutions in Belgium and The Netherlands in 1981.[27] The contrast between baroque and deconstructivism is significant, and yet DEETAAI succeeded in combining them by stripping them down to their spatial systematic. In DEETAAI's work, which consists of a collection of furniture items as well as renovation projects, we see an obvious interplay between architecture and interior, whereby the furniture was released from 'scale' and was stripped back to 'size', built according to a well-defined system of ratios. In order to highlight this inter-action, Christian Kieckens began with a quote by Norberg-Schulz:

> Architecture protects furniture and furniture protects things that are found in the core of the core. This is how man is able to experience his environment as meaningful.

As for the constructive detail, the same techniques were used in a spatial intervention, which can be seen in the series of drawings for a furniture item with mirrors from 1980 Furthermore, Christian Kieckens proposed reading as a dual view:

> By excluding scale or by introducing a second scale, one is confronted with a constant questioning of the dual 'view': of inside out and/or outside in.

> The interrelationship resulting from the dual view consists of the exchange between volume/space, such as furniture/interior, architecture/environment, earth/cosmos, etc. By entering the space man becomes a binding element between these concepts; he becomes the midpoint between these poles. The experience of the volume, simultaneously from the inside as well as the outside, - finding oneself at the centre - makes it possible to open new dimensions: the interior as a cloak for man and furniture, architecture as a cloak for man and the interior.[29]

In an interpretation of the work, Jozef Victoir proposed that DEETAAI wanted to penetrate 'the essence of architecture'. Using 'contemporary structo-design elements' the designers strove to create an environment which, in relation to the past and through simultaneously experiencing the interior and exterior spaces, would allow penetration of 'I' with the 'other', namely the community: 'Indeed it is true that a sort of tyranny of the form appears in these

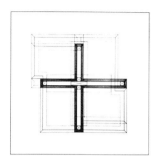

designs, which as such may result in misinterpretations. Nevertheless, this aspect is merely a mask. Or better still, it signifies an invitation to acquire, via a trusted design relationship, a deeper understanding of the essence of the design theme.'[30]

In Marie-José Van Hee's Derks - Lowie house we see a similar geometric building plan. The square house is organised from a central double cross that encases a staircase and storage space. Symmetry dominates the floor plan as in a Palladian villa. The central stairs on the central axis lead to the upper floors, each one to the left and right on the same landings, porticoes and rooms, without a clear destination. Windows are positioned to emphasise the monumentalism. The rooms are formed by recesses and cabinets, while subtle frames are applied to the external façades and the ceiling as reliefs. Here the play of layering arises from the autonomy of the abstract form. Yet the very same subtle relief surfaces and frames on the outside, symmetrical here, ensure that the house on the corner plot integrates seamlessly with the urban fabric. The staircase is not only central as an abstract figure, but orchestrates the movement in the house as a succession of passing through, ascending and entering.

Equally in the work of Robbrecht en Daem, classic architectural elements such as a gallery or colonnade were added to restructure existing spaces from within. This can be seen in a series of renovation projects between 1980-1985, made public in collaboration with Christian Kieckens and Wim Cuyvers. In this way spatial elements are deployed differently as a design principle: based more on a synthesising spatial effect. What's important is the place they make, the perspective they create, and the movement they promote:

> The gallery is as much a window as a passageway, it is a scene for family life, a filter between inside and out, a mirror between the real and ideal, and a frame or a boundary, as well as an unveiling.

That's what they had in mind with the Desmedt house from 1985, to achieve a new cohesion between the different components of the house through the employ of three colonnades, which act as spatial bonds. Their objective was not to define the functions of the different living areas, but rather to introduce a passage that was dynamically inhabitable. The orderliness of the colonnades was evocative of the simple window arrangement in the façade. Robbrecht viewed it as a 'meaningful breach' of the space, a spatial intervention such as 'disruption and synthesis'.[32] Similarly, extensions were arranged using galleries and colonnades in Van Hee's work. Vinken - Van Hee house in Passendale, 1985-1990) as well as that of Robbrecht en Daem - Kieckens - Cuyvers Extension of the Stes house, 1985).

It was through the concept of 'meaningful breach' that the original house was primarily served by the Stes house's arrangement. Van Hee used the arrangement to serve the layering between the house and the garden. The architectural elements from the Latin building tradition were applied in accordance with their relationship with the unbuilt space: the villa with the landscape, the arcade with the square, the roof terrace with the sky, the balcony with the view of the street.[33] With a similar tactility, Van Hee applied this in her new projects. Van Hee - Coppens' house and workplace from 1990-1993 are like a horizontal composition of pleated screen walls and galleries around an inner garden and several cores such as a hearth or a kitchen. The layering between the interior and exterior evokes the dynamic spatial superimposition such as those found in the houses of Frank Lloyd Wright or Mies van der Rohe; however, here the walls lose a greater degree of clarity. As a boundary between the interior and exterior they are

Paul Robbrecht, Hilde Daem, Wim Cuyvers and Christian Kieckens, Extension of Stes – Robbrecht house, Gent – Mariekerke, 1985.
Paul Robbrecht (Projects from 1984) in Marc Dubois, ed., De Woning als architectuur-typologie (Ghent: Stichting Architektuurmuseum, 1985): 52-53. APA archive S/AM.

Marie-José Van Hee, Extension of Vinken - Van Hee house, Passendale, 1985-1990.
Photo Daniël Libens.

See also '3x3 projects', p138-139.

constructed from consecutive layers of wall sections with windows that are subdivided in a vertically rhythmic fashion, via colonnades. This means they are consistently tied to galleries and overhanging frames. Between this layering the movement through the dwelling and its gardens is staged in disparate styles. Composed as an enfilade, the living areas progress one after another, enabling one to gradually pass through them. Two stairwells make it possible to circulate through the house in different ways. The hearth situated at the end of the living room, like an intimate fireside lounge, is positioned a little higher, a difference in height that is also repeated in the garden. A third exterior staircase connects a gallery downstairs with terraces and galleries upstairs.

THEMATISATION AS FOUNDATION FOR ARCHITECTURAL DESIGN

The generation of 1974's design research into form and spatiality is emphatically manifested as a response to participation architecture on the one hand, 'architecture with no architect', and a functionalist approach in which the complexity of the building programme was used to develop new potentials on the other hand.[34] In the Flemish architecture landscape they saw this as a quest: the creation of architecture focused on the pursuit of the essence of the architectonic form and space. In doing so they strove for a layering of meanings, or an understanding of the relationship between the architectural form and the meanings they could convey. In an introduction to Kieckens' work, Marc Dubois wrote of 'thematisation as salvation'[35].

In 1984 the first *S/AM* monograph appeared with the topic 'Architecture museums'.[36] Architecture was displayed as a theme in itself in the most direct manner. Unger's Architecture museum in Frankfurt took centre stage with the theme of incorporation, referring to the 'house in house' principle of a new modular structure around an existing villa, the merging of history and topicality. Devoting attention to the ever changing relationship between inside and outside through the successive architectural elements discussed as layered mantles: trellis work, modular structure, wall - steel, concrete, plaster, stone - filigree, openings, profiling and solid element.[37] The accompanying quote by Ungers is clear: 'Architecture that does not derive its themes from itself is like a painting that aims to be nothing more than a photographic reproduction. Only architecture itself can be the theme and content of architecture.'[38] In the introduction

'Efemeer versus tijdloos' (Ephemeral versus timeless) Christian Kieckens reflected on the history of the architecture museum and returned to Villa Hadriana (114-135) as one of the first of its kind, as an 'outdoor' museum of different architectures, a collection of stone travel memories of other cultures.[39] This was followed, as a statement and reference to Hadrianus, by a theoretical project by Robbrecht en Daem, 'Klein Openluchtmuseum voor Architecturen' (Small Outdoor Museum for Architectures).[40] It is a confrontation of 'distinctive architectural identities reduced to an area of 40 by 40 metres'.[41] In the various lithos, sketches and drawings, as well as finger exercises, we see different references including to the English baroque architect Hawksmoor, with whom Paul Robbrecht became familiar via Venturi. Here too the influence of Palladio and Aldo Rossi dominates, and yet we already begin to see a more personal interpretation. Robbrecht spoke here of the influence of work by artist friends such as Thomas Schütte's 'Pezzi', architectural models, which as works of art were in possession of their own independence. It enabled him to formulate a distinct position on the confrontation he was developing:

> The game of attraction and repulsion affects their autonomy, their personality becomes enforceable and consequently they become usable objects. In addition to the succouring of autonomy, from the distance they assume with regard to life, they become comfortable products, engaged in life itself. At that moment a building becomes part of an urban inevitability, a museum space. Each organism is an epicentre of an architectural force field, the overlapping and interference of this force field is the urban space.[42]

What Robbrecht was examining here is the presence of architecture, as Kahn did in his drawings for The Dominican Motherhouse.[43] Robbrecht was impressed by the confrontation between the larger sculpted volumes in Kahn's design. What's more, he must have studied the plans for this project himself, their mutual relationship between an

Robbrecht en Daem,
Small Open-air Museum for
Architectures.
Architektuur Musea, Exhibition
Sint-Pietersabdij, Ghent, Stichting
Architektuurmuseum, 1984.
Photo Marc Dubois,
APA archive S/AM.

interior surrounding another interior, meticulously drawn in charcoal by Kahn.[44] Kahn described the drawing as it is read by the architect: 'Open before us is the architect's plan. Next to it a sheet of music; the architect fleetingly reads his composition as a structure of elements and spaces in their light. The musician reads with the same overallness.'[45]

Christian Kieckens took thematisation further by not only relating it to his designs but also to language. Thus in Tschumi's deconstructivism with foundations by Deleuze or Baudrillard, he found ways of generating design principles based on word analyses and reinterpretations. What Kieckens created as a result was not only architecture but a framework of thoughts in which architecture and language nourished one another. When he presented his own work in the *S/AM* theme number in 1990, he provided the reader at the same time with a series of quotes and a summary of the themes that underlay his architecture. Along with his work they form what he refers to as a 'STOA': passages that can be read through the themes thus acting as 'highly diverse subjective affinities and interspaces'. By 'reading' he means 'observing with the body and the memory, with the body's memory', as Roland Barthes wrote in 1977. 'This is why architecture can be read.'[46] It is a matrix of references that range from William Forsythe's ballet creations to the polyphonic music by Perotin, from the speed of Milan to Manel Esclusa's night photography, from the illusion of the Baroque to the inertia of Vienna's coffee culture.[47]

Following the collaboration with DEETAAI and Robbrecht, Daem and Cuyvers, we see a distinct methodology and design idiom emerge that made the link between the Baroque and deconstructivism in a completely different way. Their designs wished to convey the dynamic of their own transformation process as a series of clues. However, unlike Hiromi Fujii, it was no longer a deconstruction, but rather a synthesis of spatial figures from which a various rhythmic could exist simultaneously. Marc Dubois referred to it as rather subtle references that allowed the accumulated historic references to re-emerge via the long route of an intense transformation process.[48]

This dynamic is strongly present in a series of ten carpets, which he designed in 1988. The carpets appear to be designed as a single fugal series. He described it as:

> a single conceptual ensemble with the scripture of a plane of perception whose viewpoint and horizon are determined by its extremities and whose eight inter-mediate pieces are cut off. Juxtaposed to the constants of beginning and end, the eight middle parts form the ephemeral: in its entirety the carpet exists only very temporarily, soon each fragment embarks on its own story. As the view from the Piazzetta di San Marco across the Bacino to the Isola di San Maggiore in Venice. The memory and proportion define the static of the perspective, the temporary passages break through in a dynamic fashion. And yet throughout the drawing - perception - each part of the carpet retains a connection with the adjacent one. In their absence they are still present in relation to each other.[49]

Christian Kieckens, Design
of a series of 10 carpets, 1989.
APA archive Christian Kieckens.

Thus Kieckens wanted to incorporate in his work the concept of time (speed), which he believed was an inherent part of the design process, by confronting it with the slowness of the lengthy process of architecture itself. In addition to constant values such as structure, light and proportion that flow from his study of the synthesis of baroque constructions, he searched for impulses from literature, photography and film, music and the visual arts, with which the directness of their expression were diametrically juxtaposed to architecture. He saw potential in these cultural disciplines, with their temporary images, which provide a new, supplementary angle of architecture as a theme. To understand this confrontation of slowness with directness as a layered spatial synthesis, he referred to it as transience, carefully defining the spatial terminology. He used two terms that could be applied in the film industry as well as in literature, music and architecture: 'passage' and 'perspective'. Unlike the static of 'fragment', a term that was often used in deconstructivism, according to Christian Kieckens' passage' possessed a dynamic because it evoked a notion of time: transit, continuity, passage, temporality; a time-space concept that exists between two closely related moments.

> In this sense the term possesses an embodied topicality: where the experience is in the 'now'. Once the passage is over it is already a 'memory'.[50] He positions the term 'perspective' opposite to this: 'it is never fragmentary but always a whole, never in the past but always future-oriented. It also exists between two moments: oneself - now - and infinity. Thus it possesses the notion of perception of the future. In this sense perspective is 'longing'.[51]

Developing a distinctive architectural language with historical building connotations brought with it a new inherently expressive plasticity. Space was not neutral but layered with, as Venturi suggested, several fields of tension as Guarini believed. Similar to his method in the Borromini study, Kieckens often used a series of analyses as a single systematic that dominated the plan, ratio and façade for his designs.[52] The building became a single meta-morphology, in which the solid elements were intended to produce a certain spatial effect. We see this in an extension of an 18th-century dwelling in Ghent, a project from 1989 in association with Marc Dubois. Different volumes arise from the existing architecture, which are linked by subtle rescaling and rotations. Central to this 'geometric volume' is a 'perspectival space' that is projected as an oblique axis from the living room to the garden, to act as a funnel that draws light within. Perpendicular to this axis stands a piece of wall that replaces the existing rear wall as a fine colonnade and simultaneously separates the staircase from the kitchen in the new space. Axonometric projections were developed to achieve this complex situation. This demonstrates how the perpendicular colonnade assumes the dual role of an internal and external façade in different ways. On the one hand from the garden this forms a rear façade for the existing main space, on the other it can also be viewed from the existing house as a front facing façade for the garden and the new space. With the free-standing column in the furthermost corner, Christian Kieckens strove to demarcate surface and volume so that the new, functional part of the building was not

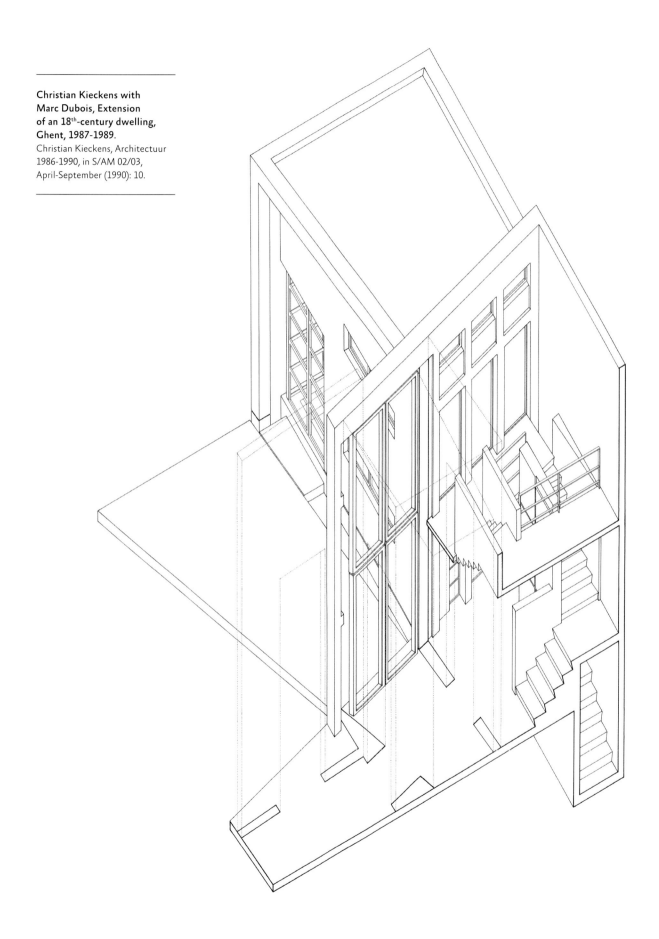

Christian Kieckens with Marc Dubois, Extension of an 18th-century dwelling, Ghent, 1987-1989.
Christian Kieckens, Architectuur 1986-1990, in S/AM 02/03, April-September (1990): 10.

only volume but was also viewed as structure. The symmetrical positioning of the light funnel following an oblique line, and the autonomous clarification of structure and volume are two references to 18th-century architecture, the period during which the existing house with its rococo front façade was constructed.[53]

Nowhere is the plan, façade and interior space so geometrically interconnected as in the initial proposal for a house in Baardegem from 1991. To illustrate this the plans were presented along with their geometric analyses, a systematic that he distilled from his Borromini analyses. The house consists of a main rectangular volume in which a smaller 'winter house' is projected. The main figure is dominated by an axis rotation in the plan that is manifested in the gable roof with a rotated crest. The eastern and western façades have been designed with an oblique cornice, while the northern and southern end façades display an asymmetrical curved roof edge. The circles denoted in the plan determine the ratio of the roof edge's curve. Just as in the previous project the spaces also work in a perspective manner by projecting the axis rotation in various ways in the interior space. The crest's rotation is shadowed by the two adjacent walls, so that the 'winter house' is manifested as a reduced parallel within the rectangular-shaped main space. Between the rectangle and the parallelogram there are two types of intermediate spaces: two functional elements, a kitchen in the east and storage/laundry room in the south, and two enclosed negative spaces that flank the sides: a loggia in the south and a carport in the north. In contrast to the previous project, here we see a more significant anchoring of the spaces within each other.

BEARING A COMMON FOUNDATION

These examples of early work demonstrate the extent to which this generation generated design-defining principles from their study of historical references. Marie-José applied them to establish the relationships between the rooms and between the house and the garden. In doing so she moved closer to the movement and the act itself. In the Van Hee house from 1990-1997 the symmetry and severity is less evident. Despite the monumentality that still governs, it is that of the act of living itself: the living area as a hall with a large central table, with a door, staircase and hearth in the corners.

Christian Kieckens,
initial proposal for House
Van Hover - De Pus,
Baardegem, 1990-1995.

See also '3x3 projects', 158-159.

Robbrecht en Daem, Design
Rückriem Museum, 1993.
Jacobs, Steven (ed.),
Werk in Architectuur.
Paul Robbrecht en Hilde Daem
(Ghent: Ludion, 1998): 39.

To the same extent, the need to explicitly define and disrupt disappear in the later work of Robbrecht en Daem. In the Rückriem Museum, a design in a quarry in Huy from 1993, the building is not a strict architectural design in itself. The overall plan is manifested more as a conglomeration of fused spaces. The garden walls are afforded the same status as the external façades. As a whole they express the enclosure of interior spaces within interior spaces. The façades are characterised by three openings - an aperture, a portico and a window. We recognise a central triangular space, but it does not regulate the whole as a mathematical baroque figure, but is rather embedded in the surrounding open and closed spaces, interwoven with organic views and perspectives.

In Christian Kieckens' work we see a change between the initial and second proposal for the house in Baardegem. No geometric plan is used as a proportional basis. The relationships of the contours are numeric, and in different places the elements' proportion is achieved by the golden ratio. There is no longer a need for building elements to be manifested as autonomous entities, or to build perspectives as literal rooms. Perspectives are created by sequences of frames and views between inside and outside. Structures are present more as housing for spatial effects, and are always manifested in close relationship with the greater whole.

It is with this fluctuating signature with all its layers of meaning that the generation of 1974 brought a blend of Venturi, Wittkower and Norberg-Schulz to Flanders. However it is precisely by casting off their fundamental models, and each other, that these architects each developed their own style with more personal form-defining elements. Whereas the early work still sought innovation and was at times almost reactionary, we see a distinctive design idiom emerge when they let go of this impulse and focus more on the intervention in the space itself, the place and the environment.

Marie-José Van Hee,
House Van Hee,
Ghent, 1990-1997.
Photo David Grandorge.

1 Oswald Mathias Ungers, *Architecture comme thème. Die Thematisierung der Architektur* (Paris: Electa Moniteur, 1983) as quoted in Marc Dubois, 'Het thematiseren als redding', S/AM 02/03 (1990): 5.

2 Paul Robbrecht (Projects from 1984). In Marc Dubois, ed., *De woning als architectuurtypologie* (Gent: Stichting Architektuur Museum, 1985): 48.

3 Christian Norberg-Schulz, *Existence, Space and Architecture* (London: Praeger Publishers, 1971): 114.

4 See also Dirk Somers' article in this book 'Venturi's Discipline'.

5 Paul Robbrecht in conversation with the author, 26 August 2015, Ghent.

6 Robbrecht (Projects from 1984): 48.

7 Colin Rowe, 'The Mathematics of the Ideal Villa: Palladio and Le Corbusier Compared', in *The Mathematics of the Ideal Villa and Other Essays* (Cambridge, MA: MIT Press, 1976): 1-28.

8 Christian Kieckens, 'Stoa', in *S/AM* 02/03, April-September (1990): 9. Here Kieckens refers to the book by Pieter De Bruyne, *Form and Geometry in Ancient-Egyptian Furniture Design* (Ghent: Museum of Decorative Art, 1982).

9 See also the following article in this book: Maarten Delbeke, Belgian Adventures in Baroque.

10 Jos Vanderperren and José Kennes, 'Dossier: Guarino Guarini. Part 1: The Systematic Spatial world of Guarino Guarini', in *A+ 31*, September (1976): 67-97.

11 Vanderperren and Kennes, 'Dossier: Guarino Guarini', 75.

12 Norberg-Schulz, E*xistence, Space and Architecture*, 59, as quoted in Paolo Portoghesi, *Borromini, architettura come linguaggio* (Milan: Electa, 1967): 384.

13 Norberg-Schulz, *Existence, Space and Architecture*, 11.

14 Norberg-Schulz, *Existence, Space and Architecture*, 39-68.

15 Norberg-Schulz, *Existence, Space and Architecture*, 63.

16 Norberg-Schulz, 'Lo spazio nell'archittetura post-guariniana', in V. Viale (ed.). Guarino Guarini e l'internazionalità del barocco. (Torino: Accademia delle Scienze di Torino, 1970): 411-437.

17 Jan Bruggemans, 'Flirt op het raakpunt van heden en verleden.' In the DEETAAI Study Group (Jos Vanderperren, Christian Kieckens), *CRESCENDO 1. architectuur 1980* (Wezenbeek-Oppem: DEETAAI, 1980): 6–7.

18 Jos Vanderperren, 'The house between the history and now', In the DEETAAI Study Group (Jos Vanderperren, Christian Kieckens), *CRESCENDO 1. architectuur 1980* (Wezenbeek-Oppem: DEETAAI, 1980) 76.

19 Marie-José Van Hee, 'Beschouwingen omtrent tuinen in de middeleeuwen tot in de tijd van Lodewijk XIX' (Master Thesis, Hoger Instituut Sint-Lucas Ghent, 1973-1974).

20 Van Hee, 'Beschouwingen omtrent tuinen in de middeleeuwen tot in de tijd van Lodewijk XIX', 17. Here she refers to: Crisp, Sir Frank, *Mediaeval Gardens: 'Flowery Medes' and Other Arrangements of Herbs, Flowers and Shrubs Grown in the Middle Ages: with Some Account of Tudor, Elizabethan and Stuart Gardens* (London: Hohn Lane the Bodley head Ltd, 1924, repr. New York, 1966).

21 Van Hee, 'Beschouwingen omtrent tuinen in de middeleeuwen tot in de tijd van Lodewijk XIX', 18.

22 Van Hee, 'Beschouwingen omtrent tuinen in de middeleeuwen tot in de tijd van Lodewijk XIX'. She refers to Boccaccio Giovanni, *Decamerone* (publisher: Amsterdam: L. J. Veen's uitgeversmaatschappij, 1969).

23 Huizinga, Johan. *Homo Ludens* (Haarlem: H.D. Tjeenk Willink & Zoon, 1939), 178. As cited in: Van Hee, 'Beschouwingen omtrent tuinen in de middeleeuwen tot in de tijd van Lodewijk XIX', 35.

24 Robert Venturi, *Complexity and Contradiction in Architecture* (New York: Museum of Modern Art, 1966): 20.

25 Venturi, *Complexity and Contradiction in Architecture*, 88.

26 Venturi, *Complexity and Contradiction in Architecture*, 68.

27 Hiromi Fujii and Chris Fawcett, Hiromi Fujii: architecture and projects in the '70 – '80 (Brussels: CIAUD-ICASD, 1981).

28 Christian Norberg-Schulz, as quoted by Christian Kieckens in 'Interieur 1980', in the DEETAAI Study Group (Jos Vanderperren, Christian Kieckens), *CRESCENDO 1. architectuur 1980* (Wezenbeek-Oppem: DEETAAI, 1980) 60.

29 Christian Kieckens, 'Interieur 80', In the DEETAAI Study Group (Jos Vanderperren, Christian Kieckens), *CRESCENDO 1. architectuur 1980* (Wezenbeek-Oppem: DEETAAI, 1980) 61-62. Robbrecht (Projects from 1984): 61.

30 Jozef Victoir, 'Inleiding', In the DEETAAI Study Group (Jos Vanderperren, Christian Kieckens), *CRESCENDO 1. architectuur 1980* (Wezenbeek-Oppem: DEETAAI, 1980) 10-11.

31 Robbrecht (Projects from 1984): 52.

32 Robbrecht (Projects from 1984): 54.

33 André Loeckx, 'Het Derde Huis', in *Marie-José Van Hee: Architect* (Ghent: Ludion, 2002): 37.

34 Here Marc Dubois refers to the architect Stéphane Beel. Marc Dubois, 'Het thematiseren als redding': 9.

35 Marc Dubois, 'Stoa', Architecture 1986-1990 Christian Kieckens. 'Het thematiseren als redding', in: *S/AM*, April-September (1990): 9.

36 Kieckens, Christian (ed.), *Architectuurmusea* (Gent: Stichting Architektuurmuseum, 1985).

37 Kieckens, Architectuurmusea: 10.

38 Oswald Mathias Ungers, 'Die Thematisierung der Architectur' (Stuttgart: DVA, 1983): 9, in: *S/AM*, Monography 1: Architecture museums (Ghent: 1984): 1.

39 Oswald Mathias Ungers, 'Die Thematisierung der Architectur' (Stuttgart: DVA, 1983): 9, in: S/AM, Monography 1: Architecture museums (Ghent: 1984): 1.

40 In addition a project follows for a new Art Pavilion in Valenciennes by Philippe Caucheteux, with a triple theme of walls, signs and the times. After this came a report by the International Ideas Competition for a fictional architecture museum in 1983 (jury Thijs Asselbergs, Wim Quist, Paul Robbrecht and bOb Van Reeth). No prize was awarded because the jury was disappointed by the substantive quality of the works.

41 Paul Robbrecht and Hilde Daem, 'Klein Openluchtmuseum voor Architecturen', in Kieckens, Architectuurmusea: 10.

42 Robbrecht en Daem, 'Klein Openluchtmuseum voor Architecturen':12.

43 Paul Robbrecht in conversation with the author, 26 August 2015, Ghent.

44 Michael Merrill, *Louis Kahn: Drawing to find out: The Dominican Motherhouse and the Patient Search for Architecture*, (Zürich: Lars Müller Publishers, 2010): 86.

45 Louis Kahn, 'The Room, the Street, and Human Agreement', in *Louis I. Kahn, Writings, Lectures, Interviews*, ed. Alessandra Latour, (New York: Rizzoli International, 1991): 263.

46 Christian Kieckens, 'Stoa', *S/AM* 02/03 (1990): 10.

47 Kieckens, 'Stoa', 10.

48 Dubois, 'Het thematiseren als redding': 5.

49 Kieckens, 'Stoa', 8.

50 Kieckens, 'Stoa', 8.

51 Kieckens, 'Stoa', 8.

52 He explains this approach using Borromini's *Collegio di Propaganda in Fide*. Christian Kieckens, Lecture 2014x1642, Joker week on 'The Corniche' Ghent University, 2 April 2014.

53 Kieckens, 'Stoa', 11.

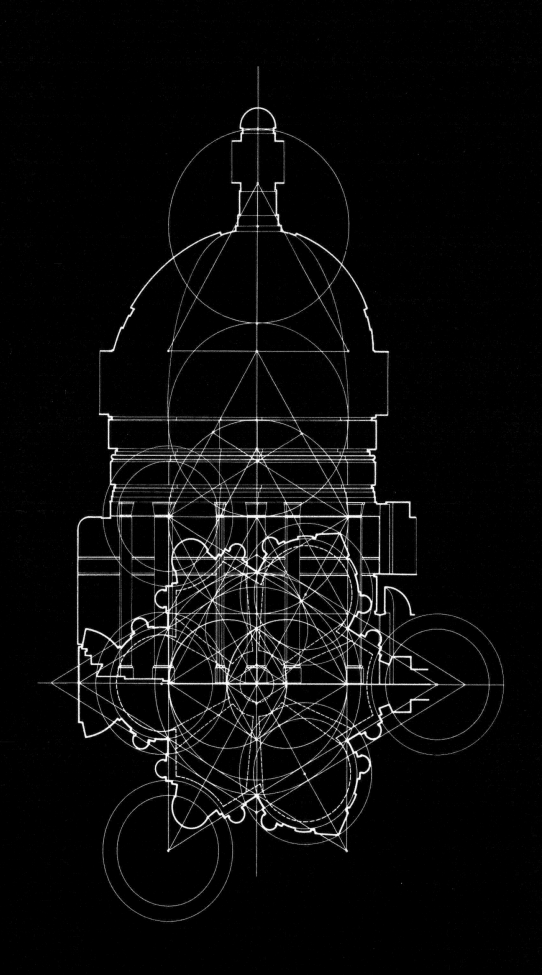

Belgian Adventures in the Baroque

Maarten Delbeke

[FORM IS ONE FUNCTION TOO]

In 1993 Christian Kieckens published the catalogue *[Form is one Function too]* accompanying the exhibition of his work from the period of 1990-93.[1] The catalogue's short introductory essay is followed by two series of geometrical analyses of buildings. First the Cheops pyramid, then four works by baroque architect Francesco Borromini: the church and *cortile of San Carlo alle Quattro Fontane*, the church of *Sant'Ivo alla Sapienza* and the chapel of the *Re Magi* in the *palazzo della Propaganda Fide*, all in Rome. An unrealised project for a house in a country setting is documented next, *inter alia* through a series of four drawings showing how the irregular form of the plan and façades flow from geometric operations on a single oblong. As is the case with the essay, the analyses of the pyramid, and Borromini's work, the illustrations of the unbuilt project are printed on darker and heavier paper than the rest of the catalogue. This gives rise to a separate section, which is introduced by two photos, each having as its theme the painter's performance of copying, mirroring and presentation (one illustrates *Las Meninas*). Quotes from Marcel Proust and Marvin Gaye are given on the last page, expressing the importance of history and the past in informing our understanding of and guiding our actions in the present. In this way bookends of the section illustrate the thinking behind this part as a whole, which is also detailed in the essay. History and the past feed into the present in two ways: by handing down techniques for principles such as order and geometry, and by breaking into the present in the shape of images and citations.

Left:
**Christian Kieckens,
geometric analysis of Francesco Borromini's Sant'Ivo della Sapienza, 1983.**
APA archive Christian Kieckens.

Below:
**Pages from:
Christian Kieckens:
Form is one Function too.
(1993): 8, 14-15.**
Left:
Christian Kieckens, geometric analysis of Francesco Borromini's San Carlo alle Quattro Fontane, 1983.
Christian Kieckens ,
Form is one Function too
(1993): 8.
Right:
**Christian Kieckens,
First proposal for the house in Baardegem (1990).**

See also '3x3 projects', 158-159.

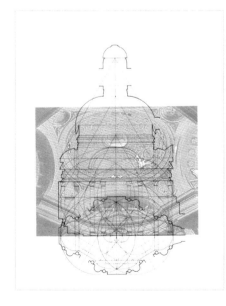

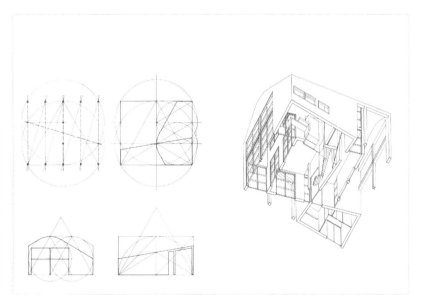

On several occasions Christian Kieckens attributed his interest in the Cheops pyramid to furniture and interior designer, Pieter De Bruyne, who in circa 1974 began his study of Egyptian architecture and furniture through extremely detailed geometric analyses.[2] His geometric analysis of Borromini's work, too, belongs to a tradition of local and international importance. This article seeks to trace that tradition, to reveal how it is picked up by Kieckens' approach to Borromini and entirely redirected. That redirection illuminates the ways in which, like others of his generation, he incorporated his study of the past in his architectural practice. At the same time, an understanding of the tradition on which Kieckens builds brings into sharper focus several themes that are specific to Kieckens' work and that of his contemporaries.

AN ANALYSIS OF THE BAROQUE PERIOD

In *[Form is one Function too]* Kieckens writes that he undertook the study of Borromini in order to understand how Andrea Palladio's method of composing a coherent plan from separate units evolved into Guarino Guarini's three dimensional design system.[3] As Kieckens sees it Borromini's architecture is the missing link in this evolution, because it rests on a deep-seated interaction between separate spatial elements united by the interplay of material structure and light. The analytical drawings of Borromini's buildings reveal geometric operations, which cause plan and section to emerge simultaneously. The drawings are laid over photographs of interior views of the domes to illustrate how the incidence of light adds a certain intangibility to the geometry behind the spatial complexity generating the buildings.

In typewritten notes to the drawings of 1989, partly published in the catalogue, Kieckens refers to a number of illustrations in Paolo Portoghesi's *Borromini. Architettura come linguaggio* (1967).[4] These illustrations are reproductions of design and presentation drawings by Borromini, in which the underlying geometry of the floor plan is suggested by triangles and circles.[5] It were Borromini's own suggestions, which Portoghesi also drew attention to, that Kieckens sought to develop into an in-depth study of the 'metamorphosis' of form present in Borromini's design process.

Kieckens had studied Borromini's work *in situ* in 1982, when the Godecharle Award had earned him an extended stay in Rome. A year before, the very same award had sent him on an educational trip to Bohemia.[6] For that trip Kieckens based his studies on Christian Norberg-Schulz's *Kilian Ignaz Dientzenhofer e il barocco boemo* (1968). In doing so, he took one of the first thorough explorations of the Middle European Baroque as his guide. But Norberg-Schulz's ideas about the Baroque Period had already enjoyed a warm reception in Belgium well before Kieckens' trip.

In the unpublished book *[IMG_barok]* (2009/10), Kieckens wrote that an exhibition curated by De Bruyne in St. Peter's Abbey in Ghent had displayed analytical drawings of baroque buildings. They brought him face-to-face with the system of baroque architecture for the first time, and provided the inspiration for his further studies.[7]

These analytical drawings were probably the work of Jos Vanderperren and José Kennes, originally produced for their joint thesis at Sint-Lucas Brussels, *The systematic spatial world of Guarino Guarini* (1974), under the supervision of De Bruyne. An abridged and adapted version of the work was published in issue 31 of A+, the Belgian architectural magazine, in 1976.[8]

De Bruyne must have guided the choice of subject and its execution. The main references for the thesis are the book entitled *Nel mondo magico di Guarino Guarini* by Mario Passanti (1963), a compilation of surveys and analytical drawings of Guarini's works, and the writings of Christian Norberg-Schulz. Vanderperren and Kennes probably got these works from De Bruyne's private library.[9] No doubt Norberg-Schulz was prominent because of the prodigious interest that De Bruyne had taken in his work since one of his Sint-Lucas students, Raf De Saeger, had brought it to his attention.[10] This interest was fruitful in many respects, because, among other things, it brought De Bruyne, and through him Vanderperren and Kennes, into contact with the international reception and historiography of the Baroque Era, to which Paolo Portoghesi, Bruno Zevi and Robert Venturi also contributed.

BAROQUE AND GEOMETRY

In addition to the studies that Norberg-Schulz dedicated specifically to Guarini, Vanderperren and Kennes rely chiefly on his *Existence, space & architecture* (1971). As is the case in Norberg-Schulz's other work, the Baroque plays a crucial role in this book.[11] In his discussion of spatial constellations, the author borrows the notion of 'field' from Portoghesi's aforementioned monograph on *Borromini*, an entity which 'consist[s] of forces which ought to be balanced in a state of dynamic equilibrium.'[12] Norberg-Schulz

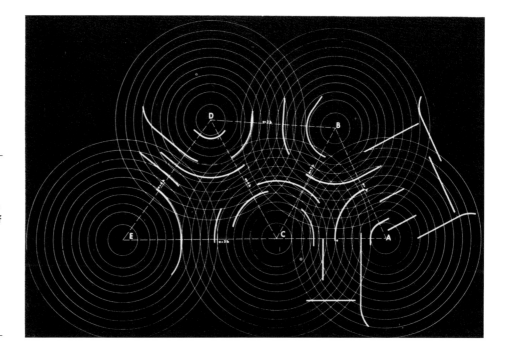

Casa Andreis by Paolo Portoghesi and Vittorio Gigliotti. The drawings present the project as a composition of interlocking concentric circles, where certain segments and intersections are materialised.
Norberg-Schulz, Christian, Existence Space & Architecture (New York: Books That Matter, 1971): 67.

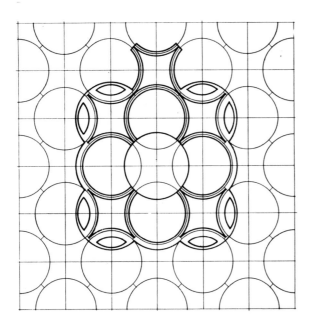
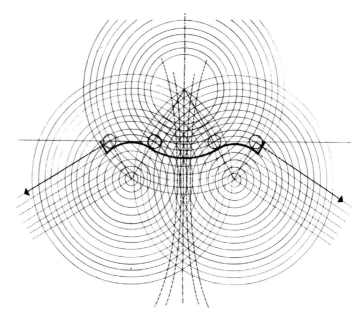

uses this concept to investigate how units such as modules, paths or spaces, relate to a whole. In the process, he takes a lengthy look at the Baroque. The author stresses that Sigfried Giedion was the first to describe late baroque space as one of the 'constituent facts' of modernism, by showing how baroque synthesises separate elements into a whole, yet the elements do not entirely lose their individuality: 'Borromini's and Guarini's wish for integration expresses a new psychological synthesis which unifies traditionally distinct characters.'[13] Modernism has scarcely added anything to this approach, says Norberg-Schulz; on the contrary, it has integrated the 'field' to such an extent that its boundaries have dissolved. He refers to Venturi's *Complexity and Contradiction* to stress the importance of buildings' interiority in relation to the field, and illustrates this quality through the *Casa Andreis* by Paolo Portoghesi and Vittorio Gigliotti. Through the designers' drawings the project is presented as a composition of interlocking concentric circles, in which certain segments and intersecting lines take shape. By including these diagrams in the same series of illustrations as the presentation of the 'spatial field' in the façade of the San Carlo in Portoghesi's *Borromini*, Norberg-Schulz suggests a direct analogy between the historical analysis of the baroque church and the design of the modern house.[14] Beside Borromini's analysis is a reproduction of Norberg-Schulz's own diagram of the 'spatial system' used in Guarini's *San Filippo Casale* church.[15]

In the dialogue between Norberg-Schulz and Portoghesi, baroque buildings emerge as the object of graphic analysis.[16] This analysis covers two related themes: the spatial system used for buildings, and the relationship of units or elements to the whole. The underlying geometry suggests a system, which can be put in place to resolve contemporary architectural problems.

Norberg-Schulz's own scheme of the 'spatial system' of Guarini's San Filippo Casale church. Norberg-Schulz, Christian, Existence Space & Architecture (New York: Books That Matter, 1971): 63.

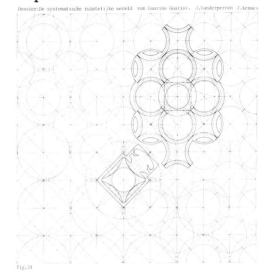

APLUS

31
architektuur
stedebouw
design
september 1976

Scheme showing Guarini's universal design system, on the cover of the A+ that presents the research of Vanderperren and Kennes.
A+ 31 September 1976.

These themes are also right at the heart of the treatment by Vanderperren and Kennes. As the title suggests, the authors set out to uncover a 'system'. The example is Guarini's *San Lorenzo* in Turin (1668-87), a building, which according to the authors arises from a series of geometrical operations starting from the central figure in the floor pattern. As we have said, the authors make explicit reference to Norberg-Schulz, Portoghesi and Passanti. However, compared to their work, fundamental shifts can be observed. Influenced by the metabletic reflections of Jan Hendrik Van den Berg and Jacques Claes, whose *De dingen en hun ruimte* (1970) treated the Baroque as 'a moment in which matter and things become different and are seen differently', the authors place the geometry of the *San Lorenzo* in the religious and scientific context of the 17th century and Guarini's philosophy.[17] The Baroque is rehistoricised and Guarini's work is treated as an historical artefact. From this placement in context the authors posit the importance of specific architectural elements such as the *serliana* (a theme which is central to Passanti's analysis), of the symbolism of light, and of processes such as 'transformation' and metamorphosis, which they associate with contemporary religious and scientific developments. Moreover, influenced by De Bruyne's interest in geometry and Passanti's geometric analyses of Guarini's work, the diagrams of Norberg-Schulz and Portoghesi, which are schematic representations of spatial fields of force, transform into geometric and mathematical design systems based on size, number and proportion.[18] This change can be seen in the way that Vanderperren and Kennes develop Norberg-Schulz's diagram with the 'spatial system' in Guarini's San Filippo Casale and extrapolate it to create a Superstudio-like network which not only generates architectural forms, but regulates the relationships between Guarini's buildings, and between buildings and the town.[19] In the final chapter of the thesis the authors link this interpretation (including the reference to *casa Andreis*) directly to Herman Hertzberger and Aldo van Eyck's concern with relating the individual element to the complex whole.[20] The authors are not primarily concerned with 'spatiality', but with the relationship of order and system to social and cultural context. In this area the thesis frequently quotes Gaston Bachelard's *Poétique de l'espace*, by citing statements such as, 'Ce n'est pas seulement par une géométrie bien ajustée qu'on peut décrire un coffre.'[21] In other words, geometry is just one of the means by which architecture's place in reality can be better understood, albeit an important one.

HISTORICAL ANALYSIS AND DESIGN SYSTEM

The diagram of Guarini's universal design system adorns the cover of the A+ edition in which the study by Vanderperren and Kennes is published. The article on Guarini is paired with a section entitled 'Projects'. The introductory essay by Pieter De Bruyne is about the state of architectural education and advocates an approach, which combines interest in pure form, to be understood as 'spatial creations on various scales', which is linked to 'content', or in other words 'societal needs'. This idea ties in closely with Robert Venturi's *Complexity and contradiction in architecture* (1966), which consists of one section on 'form' and another on 'programme'.[22] And, as is the case with Venturi, the antagonist here is 'spontaneous' or 'do-it-yourself-architecture'[23], and the remedy a renewed interest in 'art historical architecture', where a full analysis of form and meaning can reveal the relationship between the two. De Bruyne's essay is followed by several comprehensively described projects by recent graduates. These also stress how the study of historical architecture can offer a foothold for the present: 'There will always be an unseen structure at the basis of every improvisation and its organisation. This is why we are partial to *barocca* architecture.'[24]

De Bruyne's essay in A+ is one of several published iterations of the epilogue he wrote in his capacity as thesis supervisor to Vanderperren and Kennes.[25] This 'proto-essay' emphasised, more than later articles, the need for 'theory', a systematic approach to design, resting on a critical interest in historical architecture. The influence of Norberg-Schulz is clearly present. De Bruyne also explicitly complies with the standpoint of Venturi in *Complexity and contradiction*, and quotes his opening statement: 'Because I am a practicing architect, my ideas on architecture are inevitably a by-product of the criticism which accompanies working, ...'.[26]

In later versions of the text (published in the catalogues accompanying the exhibitions 'Analyse van het kunsthistorisch bouwwerk and Architectuur te Gent: analyses', both in the Museum of Decorative Art in 1978, and quoted extensively in Jos Vanderperren's introduction to the Sint-Lucas contribution of student work to the exhibition 'Dimensies van onze Stedelijke Omgeving' (ICC Antwerp, 1979)), the focus shifts to the historical analysis *per se* and proposals for works to historical buildings, such as Paul Cauchie's own home (1905).[27] Like the A+, the 'analysis' catalogue contains one of Vanderperren's own designs. The house in question is presented as a series of manipulations on a 'building block', a sort of multilayered core. What is striking is that the graphic presentation of a 'functional analysis of the building block' relates closely to Norberg-Schulz's representation of 'fields', only now as an investigation of 'view out' and 'view in'. As happened with Guarini's analysis, Norberg-Schulz's abstract diagram is literally rendered into a geometrical figure that defines the architectural form.

Christian Kieckens contributed to the architectural investigation that developed under the auspices of De Bruyne in the 1974-80 period when, in the late 1970s, he and Vanderperren formed the study group DEETAAI. One significant result of this collaboration is the catalogue CRESCENDO, published in 1980 and containing an introduction by Jan Bruggemans (who had also assisted the publication in A+). The work accompanied an exhibition held at Sint-Lucas in Schaarbeek and in Ghent, and at the Pius X Institute in Antwerp.

There are no historical analyses in the catalogue, but rather a series of projects. Nonetheless, the initial purpose of the work is to present a design system. This, as Bruggemans writes, consists in an 'analysis of [the designers'] own education'[28]: an effort to understand what can be gained from the past to allow architectural design to escape the cheerless circumstances of the moment. Historical analysis is now interiorised as a doorway to the essential properties of architecture.

Compared with the earlier publications this brings two new themes to bear: the furniture piece and the figure of the curve. Furniture emerges as a real architectural element, produced according to the same design principles as the building; the curve is set out in a 'comparative diagram' which confronts the geometry of the Baroque and the Renaissance with Le Corbusier's modulor rule and the 'sectio divina' or golden ratio of the Cheops pyramid.[29] The axial sequence of squares and circles from earlier analyses throws up centrifugal compositions, which find expression primarily in the design of furniture, not buildings.

Jos Vanderperren.
This house is presented as
a series of manipulations
on a 'building block',
a multilayered core.
Personal archive Jos Vanderperren.
Scan APA.

Group Deetaai II
(Christian Kieckens and
Jos Vandenperren). Design
Competition Interieur Bienale
Kortrijk, 1980.
Comparative scheme.
Personal archive Jos Vanderperren.
Scan APA.

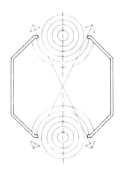

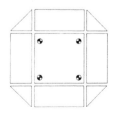

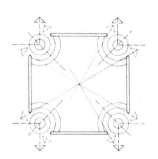

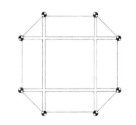

barokschema

renaissanceschema

le modulor
(le corbusier)

sectio divina
(pyramide van cheops)

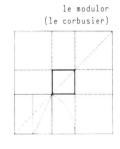

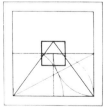

BAROQUE IN BELGIAN ARCHITECTURAL CULTURE AFTER 1990

While still part of DEETAAI, Christian Kieckens designed items such as a *Hommage aan de Boheemse barokarchitectuur* (1981) [Homage to Bohemian Architecture], a piece of furniture which references the work of Kilian Ignaz Dientzenhofer. When DEETAAI disbanded, in 1983, he set up his own practice in architecture and furniture design, where the baroque became a prominent theme. It is at the exhibition '[Form is one function, too]' that the analytical drawings of Cheops and Borromini's work of the early 1980s are displayed for the first time. Compared to the publications of the 1970s and the DEETAAI catalogue, which contain no analyses of baroque architecture, there are several recurrent themes, as well as a few fundamental shifts. This is illustrated by the introductory essay 'Perspective and distance'. It is structured as a sequence of six paragraphs, separated by references. The mention of Heidegger's 'Einräumen' is noteworthy here, and the twin concepts of 'thinking' and 'being' – a reminiscence of reflections on the 'place' of humankind in the world, which is so central to metabletic philosophy. However, Kieckens no longer interprets these concepts in terms of the existential categories of Norberg-Schulz, but rather by using concepts such as perspective and distance, and techniques such as mathematics and sizing. These concepts are in turn related to historical examples (such as Palladio, Borromini, Bernini and Bramante) and, quite explicitly with language. Finally, the references associate these concepts and techniques with a wide range of artistic practices: the perspectivist theory of Albert Dürer, the music of Arvo Pärt, the films of Jean-Luc Godard and the visual art of Bruce Naumann.

Both the references and the line of reasoning indicate how a fundamentally different, but related approach to architecture seems to exist, in opposition to the works previously discussed. The desire for an exhaustive and unified theory of design, in which geometric operations allow the architect to make decisions at every level, is exchanged for an at once more compelling and freer use of geometry. More compelling, because the relatively simple operations of the historical analyses and the initial work of the DEETAAI were exchanged for far more complex figures to underpin layered design operations. Freer, because in actual fact this game of size and geometry no longer claims universality, but uses information specific to the task and seeks points of connection with other historical references, such as Modernism. The analogy to language is meaningful here. This analogy brings the contemporary international debate on architecture in from the cold, and with it the ambition to describe geometrically generated architecture as a bearer of meaning, which is related to all kinds of arts, from Renaissance painting to Minimal Art. Here too, geometry serves to safeguard the autonomy of architecture, but not by saying that architectural design best fulfils its social role when it unfolds in accordance with its own design principles. In Kieckens' approach, geometry suggests links between architecture and other artistic practices, which evade the requirements of functionality and pragmatism, yet at the same time postulate a distinct vision of reality. Baroque is also crucial to this undertaking, no longer as a mere system of architecture, but as an art form, too.[30]

1 [Form is one Function too]. Christian Kieckens architektuur 1990–1993 architecture 1990–1993. Aalst: Christian Kieckens, 1993.

2 Eva Storgaard, 'Pieter De Bruyne (1931–1987). Meubilair, interieurs en gebouwen', in Pieter De Bruyne. Pionier van het postmoderne, eds. Christian Kieckens, Eva Storgaard, [catalogue Design Museum Ghent 7 July – 21 October, 2012], 20–155. (Brussels: ASP, 2012): 66–73.

3 Christian Kieckens, 'Konstante en metamorfose', in [Form is one Function too], 7.

4 Archive Christian Kieckens, 1989.

5 Paolo Portoghesi, Borromini. Architettura come linguaggio (Rome/Milaan: Ugo Bozzi/Electa, 1967) figs IX, XVII and L. The most recent analysis of the geometric figures found in these drawings is by Michael Hill, 'Practical and symbolical geometry in Borromini's San Carlo alle Quattro Fontane', Journal of the Society of Architectural Historians 72, 4 (2013): 555–83.

6 Christian Kieckens, 'Learning from ....', in Pieter De Bruyne, 216–23: 220.

7 Christian Kieckens, [IMG_BAROCK] http://www.christiankieckens.be/downloads/pdf/232.pdf. In Kieckens, 'Learning from ....' 220 the author refers to an exhibition by De Bruyne in St. Peter's Abbey in 1976.

8 Jos Vanderperren, José Kennes, 'Dossier, deel 1. De systematische ruimtelijke wereld van Guarino Guarini.' A+ 31 (September 1976): 67–97.

9 It was Ria Verstappen, librarian at the Design Museum in Ghent, who brought it to my attention that these books were in De Bruyne's collection.

10 Eva Storgaard, 'Vanuit de blauwe kamer. Scandinavische invloeden op Sint-Lucas (1950-1980)', in Tekenen & Betekenen. Opstellen over het architectuurinstituut Sint-Lucas 1862-2012, eds. Rajesh Heyninckx, Yves Schoonjans, Sven Sterken. (Leuven: Leuven University Press/Lipsius, 2012), 110–18: 114–5.

11 Gro Lauvland, 'The 'Recurrence' of the Baroque in Architecture: Giedion and Norberg-Schulz's approaches to constancy and change', in The baroque in architectural culture 1880-1980, eds. Andrew Leach, John Macarthur, Maarten Delbeke, 223–30. (Aldershot: Ashgate, 2015).

12 Christian Norberg-Schulz, Existence, Space & Architecture (London: Studio Vista, 1971, 60.

13 Ibid., 63. The reference to Giedion ibid., 66, f.n. 34.

14 Ibid., with the illustration from Portoghesi, Borromini, 383.

15 Norberg-Schulz, Existence, Space & Architecture, 63.

16 On the importance of the Baroque to the architectural work of Portoghesi, see Sylvia Micheli, 'Between history and design. The baroque legacy in the work of Paolo Portoghesi', in The baroque in architectural culture 1880-1980, eds. Leach, Macarthur, Delbeke, 195–210.

17 Jacques Claes, De dingen en hun ruimte. Metabletische studie van de perspectivische en van de niet-perspectivische ruimte (Antwerp: Nederlandse boekhandel, 1970): 95. Claes's concept of the Baroque ties in closely with that of Heinrich Wölfflin.

18 It should be noted here that the curriculum at Sint-Lucas gave plenty of room for geometry in the lessons of Louis van Mechelen (brother Urbain) and Marc Cole, see Kieckens, 'Learning from ....' In Pieter De Bruyne, 220, and Dirk Van de Perre, Op de grens van twee werelden. Beeld van het architectuuronderwijs van het Sint-Lucasinstituut te Gent in de periode 1919 – 1965/74, (Ghent: Provincial Administra-tion of East Flanders, 2003): 86–87. Van de Perre mentions that in the 1970s van Mechelen discusses the work of Norberg-Schulz and Robert Venturi (published in A+ 26, March 1976).

19 Jos Vanderperren, José Kennes, De systematische ruimtelijke wereld van Guarino Guarini, unpublished thesis at Sint-Lucas Schaarbeek, 1974, 194: 'And so we are gradually coming to suspect that Guarini saw this grid as the ideal design framework on which to build his work.'

20 Ibid., 199-202.

21 Ibid., 105.

22 Jos Vanderperren, José Kennes, 'Dossier, deel 2. Projekten', A+ 31 (September 1976): 101. For the role of this division in the line of reasoning found in Complexity and Contradiction in Architecture, see Maarten Delbeke's, 'Mannerism and Meaning in Robert Venturi's 'Complexity and Contradiction in Architecture', Journal of Architecture 15, 3 (2010): 267–82.

23 Vanderperren, Kennes, 'Dossier, deel 2. Projekten', 98. And so this collective contribution became part of the discussions that dominated the early years of the A+ magazine, see Maarten Delbeke, 'Architecten en kritiek. Bedenkingen bij 200 nummers van A+,' A+ 200 (2006): i-iv.

24 Vanderperren, Kennes, 'Dossier, deel 2. Projekten', 102.

25 Pieter De Bruyne, 'Nawoord' [Epilogue], in Vanderperren, Kennes, De systematische ruimtelijke wereld van Guarino Guarini.

26 The quote is from Robert Venturi, Complexity and Contradiction in Architecture (New York: MoMA, 1966): 18.

27 Pieter De Bruyne, José Kennes, Frank Jennen, Bernard Lefever, Jos Vanderperren, Analyse van het kunsthistorisch bouwwerk. 23 maart – 12 mei 1978, Museum voor Sierkunsten, Gent. Schaarbeek: Higher Sint-Lucas Institute, 1978; Architectuur te Gent: analyses. 24 maart – 7 mei 1978, Museum voor Sierkunst, Gent. Ghent/Schaarbeek: Museum of Decorative Art/Sint-Lukas, 1978; Jos Vanderperren, '10 Brusselse woningen.' In Dimensies van onze Stedelijke Omgeving, 17 november – 23 december 1979. (Antwerp: ICC, 1979): 2.1–2.3.

28 Jan Bruggemans, 'Flirt op het raakpunt van heden en verleden.' In the DEETAAI Study Group (Jos Vanderperren, Christian Kieckens), CRESCENDO 1. architectuur 1980 (Wezenbeek-Oppem: DEETAAI, 1980) 6–7.

29 CRESCENDO 1, 63.

30 In parallel, Bohemian Baroque featured in a Belgian historical architectural study, which was independent of any form of operability. In 1997 Dirk De Meyer obtained his doctorate on the subject of Bohemian Baroque architect Johann Santini Aichel; in the foreword he thanks Kieckens for the 'inspirational travel advice', in whose footsteps he undertook the opening strides of the study, see Dirk De Meyer, 'Dank.' [Thanks] In Johann Santini Aichel. Architectuur en ambiguïteit, Ph.D. diss., TU Eindhoven, 1997, 2 vols., supervised by Prof. Gerard Van Zeijl.

3x3 Projects

Early Projects by Marie-José Van Hee,
Robbrecht en Daem and Christian Kieckens

Marie-José Van Hee,
House Derks - Lowie

Ghent, 1983-1986.

Photo Michiel Hendryckx. Plans and section Marie-José Van Hee.

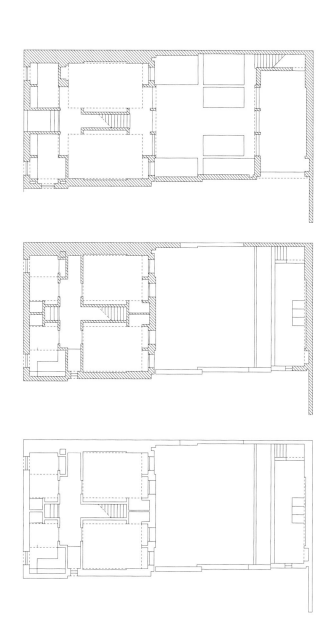

Photo Michiel Hendryckx.

Photo Michiel Hendryckx .

Photo Peter Lorré.

Marie-José Van Hee,
House, office and warehouse
Van Hee - Coppens

Deinze, 1990-1993.

Photos from top to bottom: Crispijn van Sas, Michiel Hendryckx , Peter Lorré, Peter Lorré. Plans and façades Marie-José Van Hee.

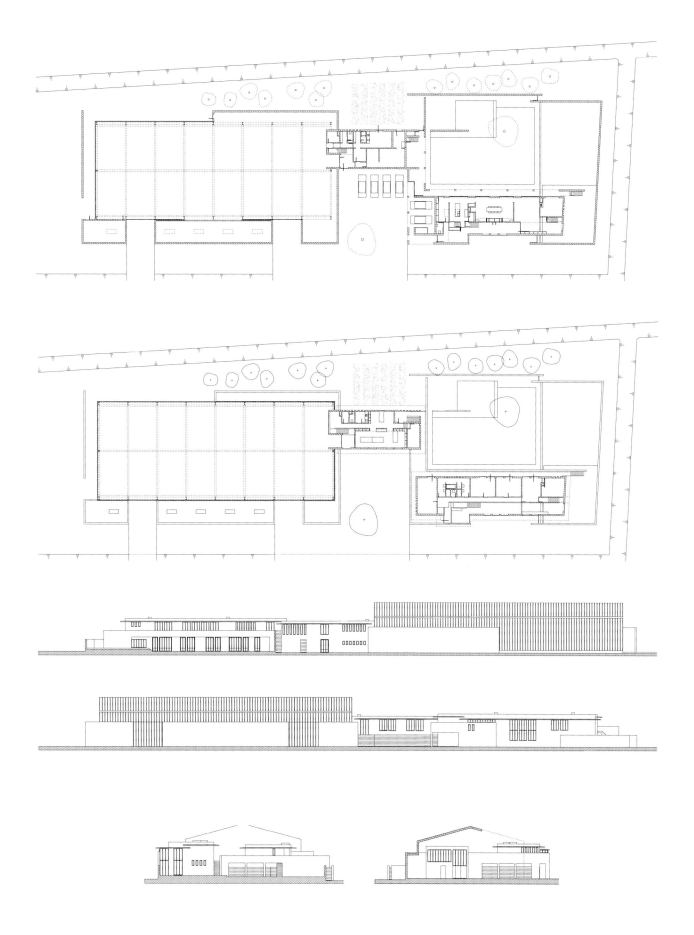

Marie-José Van Hee,
House Van Hee

Ghent, 1990-1997.

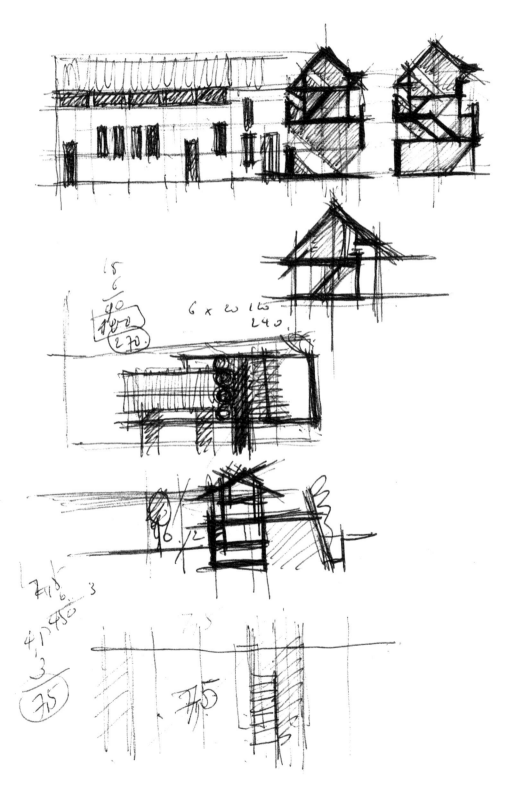

Sketch Marie-José Van Hee, 1990.

Photos above: David Grandorge, photo below: Michiel Hendryckx.

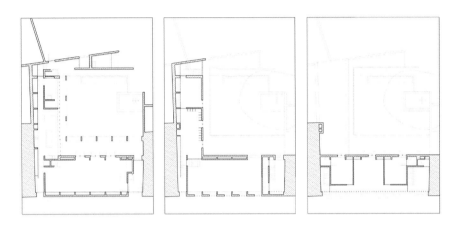

Plans Marie-José Van Hee architecten.
Photo Kristien Daem.

Sections Marie-José Van Hee architecten.
Photo Peter Lorré.

Robbrecht en Daem,
Villa De Mol

Kortrijk, 1981-1983.

Photo and plan Robbrecht en Daem, scanned by APA.

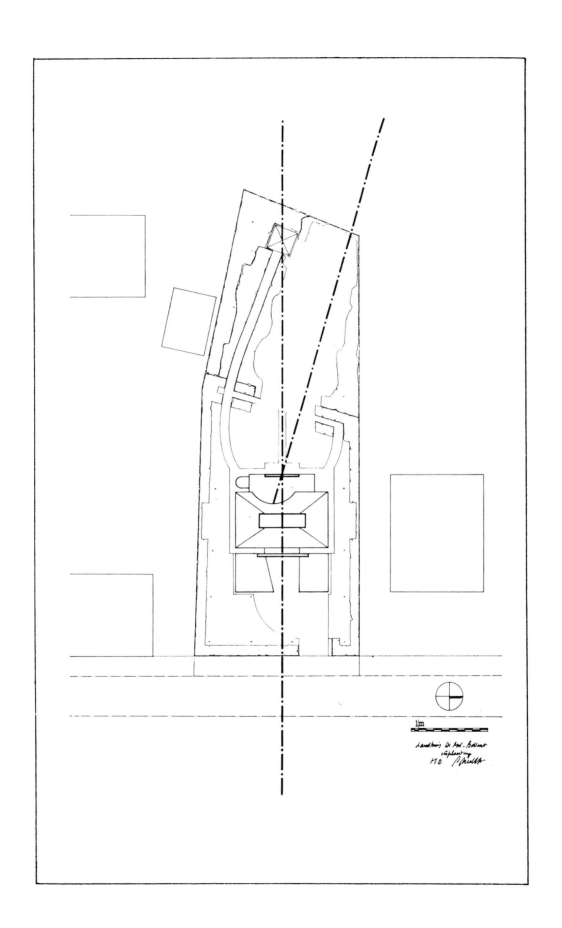

1m

Landhuis De And - Bollaert
inplanting
H.O.

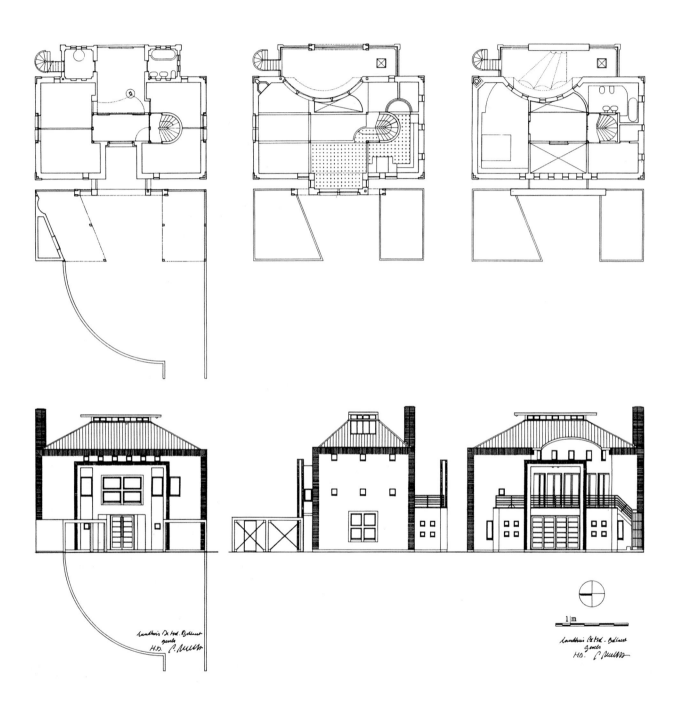

Photos, plans and sections Robbrecht en Daem, scanned by APA.

Robbrecht en Daem,
Floor for a Sculpture, Wall for Painting

Scenography, de Appel arts centre, Amsterdam, 1987.

René Daniëls, *Without title*, 1987.

Philippe Van Snick, *Without title*, 1987.

Cristina Iglesias, *Without title*, 1987.

Isa Genzken, *Without title*, 1987.

Cristina Iglesias, *Without title*, 1987.
Photos Edo Kuipers, de Appel arts centre, Amsterdam.

Robbrecht en Daem,
Bank Building
Kerksken, 1988.

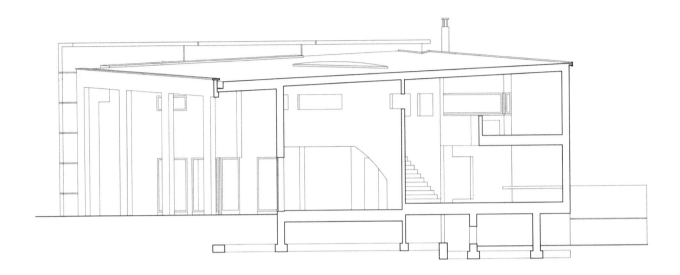

Plans and section Robbrecht en Daem.
Photo Kristien Daem.

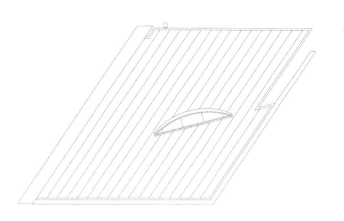

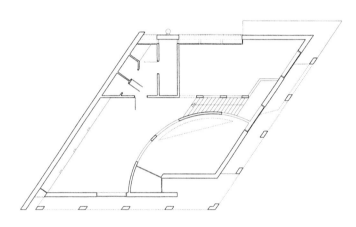

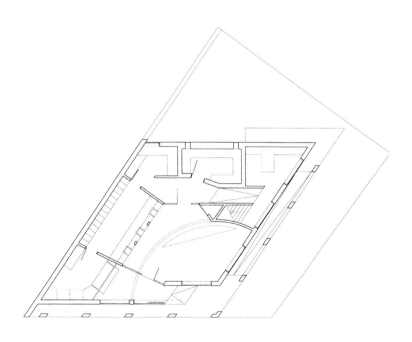

Photos Kristien Daem.

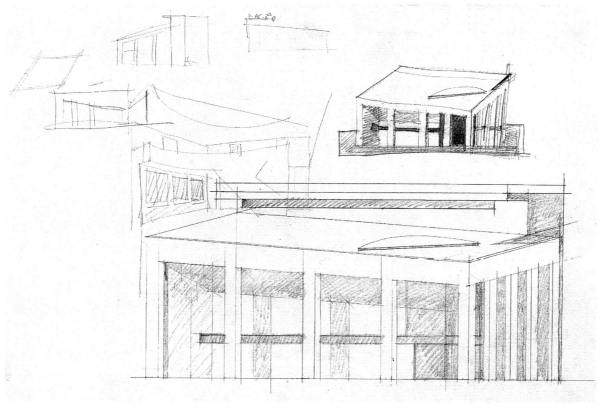

Sketch Paul Robbrecht, 1988.

Christian Kieckens and Jos Vanderperren (DEETAAI), The House between the History and Now
Shinkenchiku Residential Design Competition '80,
The Japan Architect, Tokyo, February 1981.

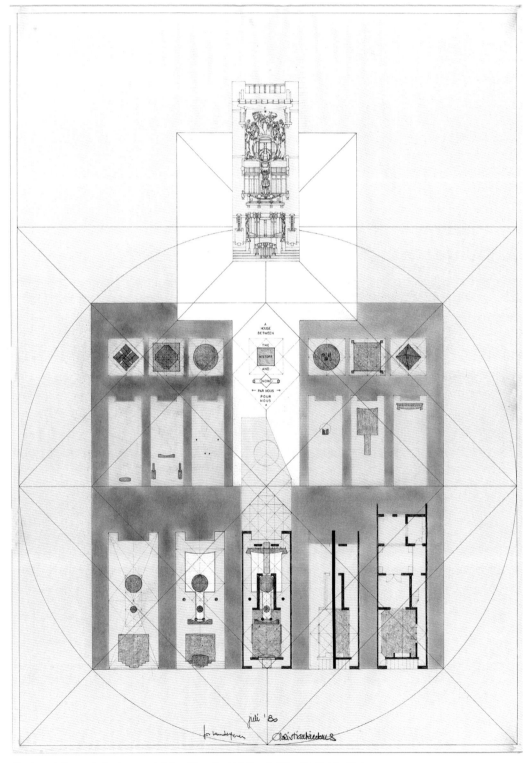

Development of a new plan typology, as a rebuilding of House Cauchie in Brussels. APA archive Christian Kieckens.

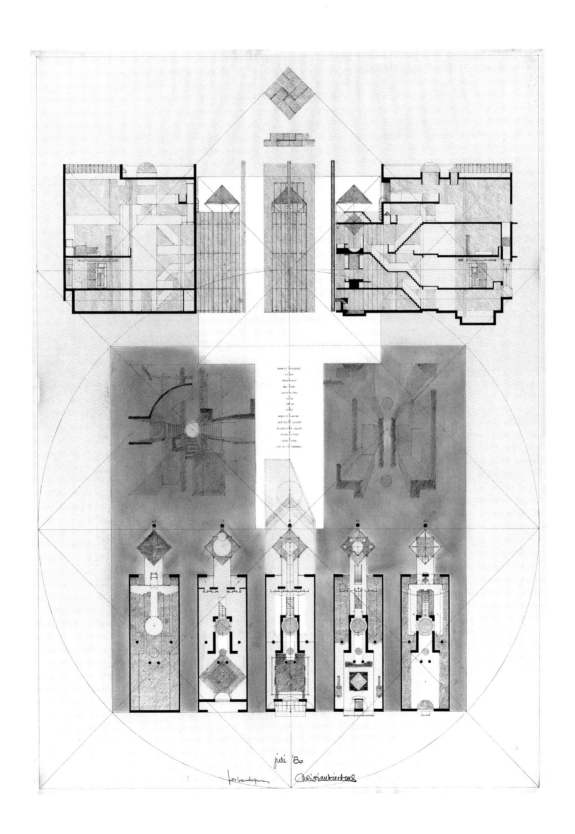

**Christian Kieckens and Jos Vanderperren (DEETAAI),
spatial structure developped as a rescaling of a furniture piece,
for the Design Biennale Interieur Kortrijk**
Competition, 1980.

Model photos spatial structure.
Personal archive Jos Vanderperren.

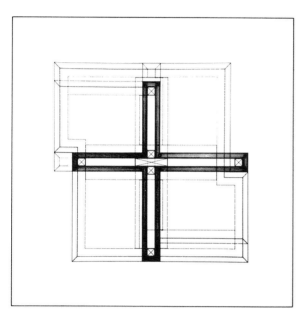

Central furniture piece from 1979, details.

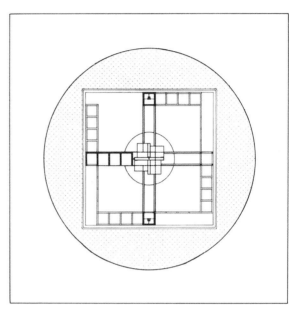

Plan spatial structure.

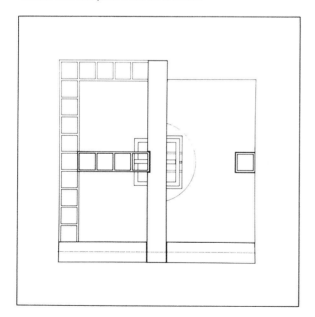

Front view spatial structure.

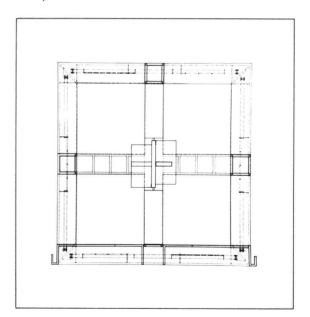

Vertical section spatial structure.

Deetaai Study Group (Christian Kieckens and Jos Vanderperren),
CRESCENDO 1, architectuur 1980 (Wezembeek-Oppem: DEETAAI, 1980):
64-67. Scan APA.

Christian Kieckens,
House Van Hover - De Pus

Baardegem, 1990-1995.

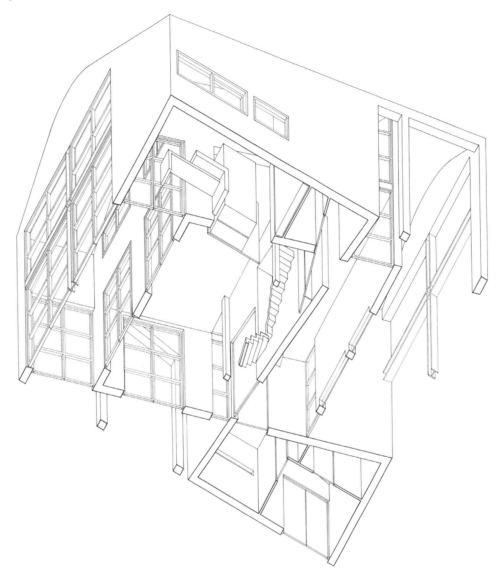

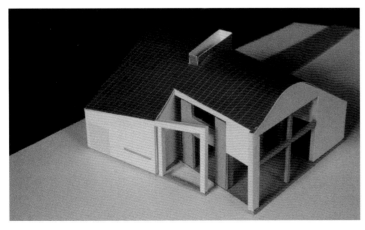

**Isometric view and model,
project proposal May 1990.**
Photo model and drawings
APA archive Christian Kieckens.

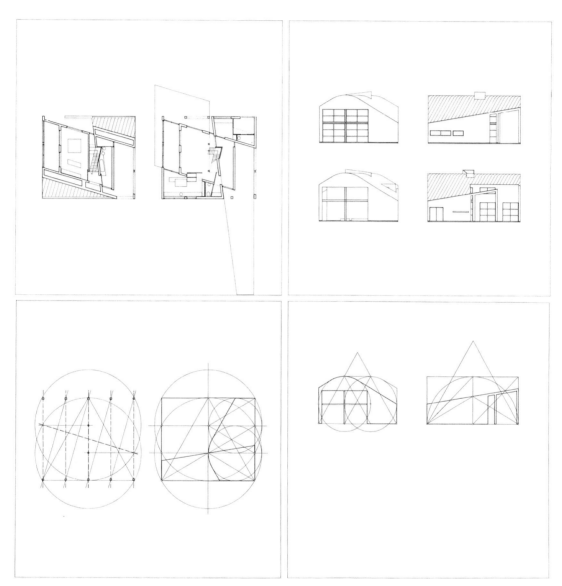

Project proposal May 1990.

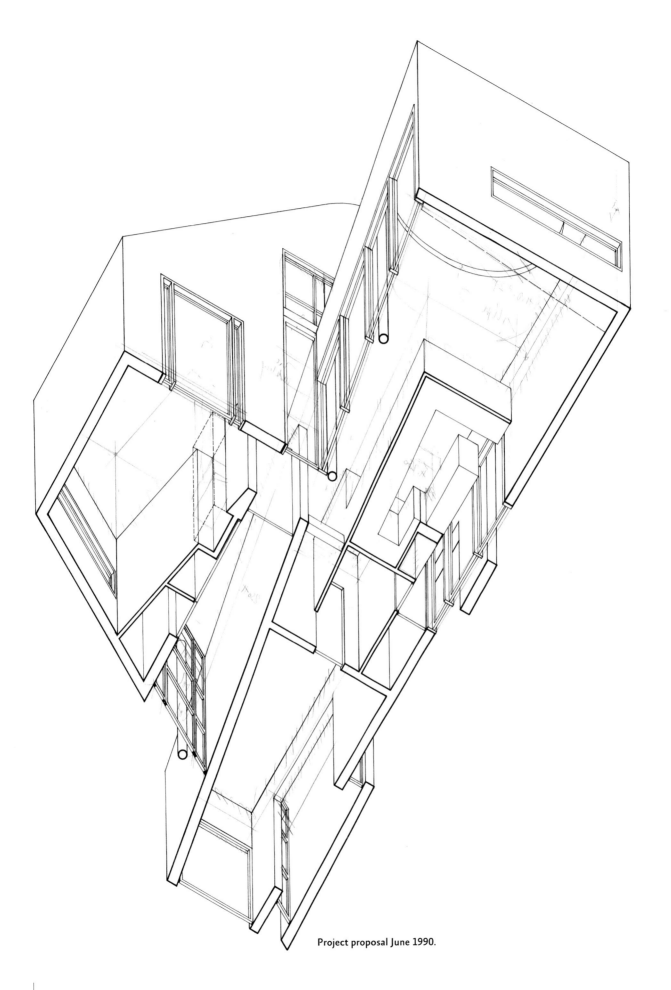

Project proposal June 1990.

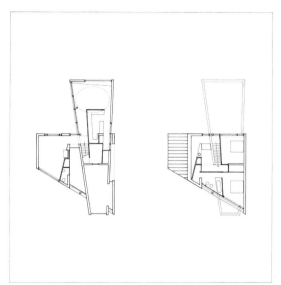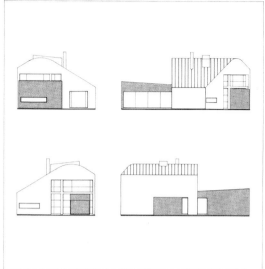

Project proposal June 1990.

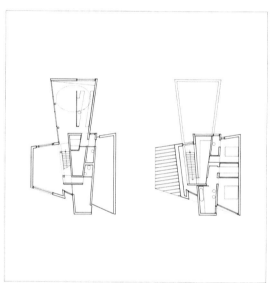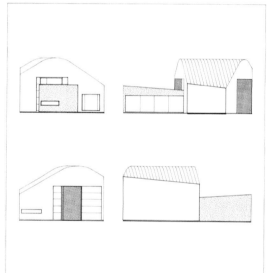

Project proposal August 1990.

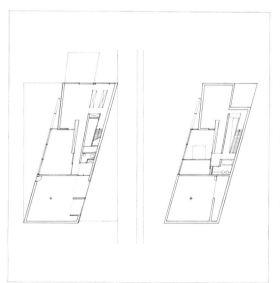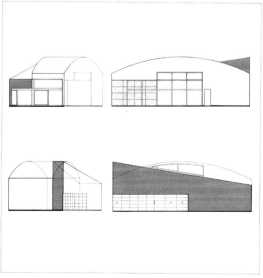

Project proposal October 1990.

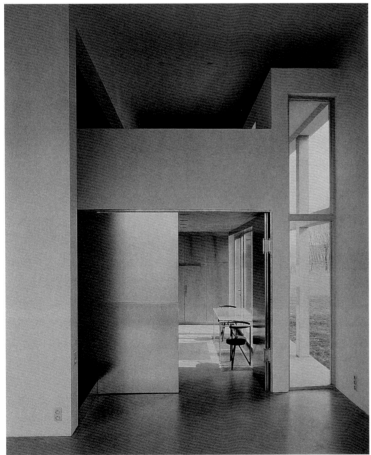

Photos Reiner Lautwein.

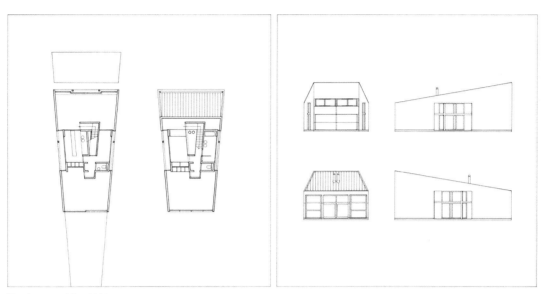

Final project May 1991.

Christian Kieckens, sketch explaining
the proportions of plan and façade, 2015.
The plan proportion is 7 - 10 – 18.
The front and back façade both have
a circumference of 28 metres.
- front façade 7 x 7 metres.
- back façade 4 x 10 metres.

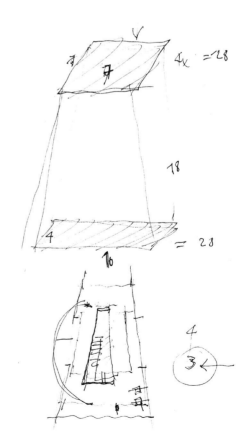

Hybrids
in the Fields

William Mann

It takes barely more than an hour to drive from the tower-house by the dunes to the hut in the hills - from Dutch Zeeuws-Vlaanderen to the edge of Wallonia, from one sparsely populated expanse to another. The tower-house sits within a rectangular enclosure of tall trees, amidst an overgrown orchard and beside an old barn. Both the farm plot and the road that lead to it are elevated slightly above the drained marshland around. The faceted concrete of the tower ripples with the marks of the wooden boards that held it when liquid. Like the stumpy church towers that mark the successive advances of land into the sea, it reads as an isolated stronghold. It is lodged amongst the apple trees by its low, branching plinth in black-stained wood and glass. A bay window hangs off its first floor, a delicate, open structure, the joinery in counterpoint to the mass of concrete. From the roof terrace, through a gap in the trees, the North Sea is a distant haze above the ridge of sand. The stream of ships blinking across the horizon is the only clue that I am close to the dense urban heart of Europe.

At the other end of the route, the hut is reached from the garden of an unobtrusive 1950s house, down a sharply descending track, through the slender trunks and dappled light of a beech wood. Sitting on a zigzag path of sawn boards, the hut is hive-like, a stack of wooden blocks. Lifted on a deck above the leaves of the forest floor, and sheltered under a mossy

Marie-José Van Hee architecten, House in Zuidzande, 2006-2011.
Jaarboek Architectuur Vlaanderen N°10, 2012: 54.
Photo David Grandorge.

Robbrecht en Daem architecten, Woodland Cabin, Ronse, 2001-2002.
Photo Kristien Daem.

horizontal canopy, the blocks curve in a blur of overlapping facets, forming a pair of inter-secting cones: two rooms, one with a cast iron stove, the other with a bed. It is an elemental shelter, distilled to the basics of repose, with a single material deployed with deceptively calm richness.

Both tower and hut carve vivid spaces of personal detachment from scraps of untouched land. They are sited and constructed with a deft touch, and manage to be at the same time both engagingly naturalistic and convincingly architectonic. They evoke an idea of inhab-iting the land – building intense, persuasive fictions. Make no mistake, this is a generation of architects who have grasped and mastered the pastoral.

Between these two points, crossing through East Flanders, there is little call for the pastoral sensibility. Halfway from polder to hill, the engine strains to the first gentle incline, and I divert towards the glass stumps and stone spires of Ghent. Lodged between two of these spires, just a stone's throw from the old cloister where Marie-José, Christian, Paul and Hilde studied, is an upturned ark of wood and glass shingles, the new Market hall. It is a forceful excavation in the mineral landscape of cobbles and towers, a scrap of meadow beneath the stones, a hovering presence that divides and links the squares around. Leaving this scattered centre, I consult my map with nervous frequency in order to navigate the labyrinth of multiple confluences, extravagant meanders and winding streets. Here, woven into the fabric of the city, are the town-houses on the streets of Plume and Pigs (Pluimstraat en Varkensstraat, red.), compact, austere and luminous. Along the sweeping cut lined in tall plane trees, the sober, classical apartment block, on whose balcony screens the leaves and branches appear as watery reflections; at the threshold to its courtyard, its delicate cornice becomes a heavy, punctuated window to the sky.

Robbrecht en Daem with Marie-José Van Hee, Market Hall, Ghent, 1996-2012.
Photo Marc De Blieck.

Marie-José Van Hee, House Van Hee, Ghent, 1990-2000.
Photo David Grandorge.

These buildings both work with and play with the conventions of city life. The Market hall is an ambiguous figure of the civic, both vacant and overdetermined. In the houses and apartments, a distilled vocabulary of walls and windows is woven into a rich tapestry of streets and courts, shared rooms and private cells, an elusive mix of the Calvinist and the Burgundian: materially austere, spatially rich and lushly verdant. This is a generation of city-builders, too. Tiens....

Just where the city starts to dissolve into its hinterland, lies the practice shared by Paul, Hilde and Marie-José. Barely visible amidst the workers' cottages turned bohemian family houses, the rare slab blocks, the remains of factories and the park on the vestiges of the ramparts, it is a wood-framed hangar whose roof has been broken open. This artfully dismantled shed concentrates many identities in a single room. A two-storey office wing in wood and glass sits under this large roof, beside undergrowth from the forest and a pool surrounded by reeds; as I look out through the ruins of industry, the city seems uncertainly poised between formation and dissolution. In an emblematic choice, this is where these architects have selected to work. This 'rurban' condition, between the rural and urban, and outside the comforts of the pastoral or urban genres, has called each of the three practices to make work of great resourcefulness, nuance and clarity.

Ghent sits at the tangled confluence of Leie and Schelde, at the invisible border between sand and clay, and at the crossroads of Calais-Köln and Rotterdam-Paris. It is neither central nor peripheral, neither dense nor dispersed; rather it is at the heart of a fertile in-between territory in which small scale but intensive agriculture, and specialised industry occupy the gaps in the dense web of infrastructures.

I head out of the city towards the afternoon sun. Here, the patchwork character of the landscape is particularly intense, where the two rivers run close together, separated by a shallow spit. I pass strung-out villages, stands of poplars, glasshouses and sheds, scraps of woodland and the occasional moated farm. Following the ruler-straight Schipdonk canal and its regiment of trees into Deinze, I come to the depot of Van Hee Industriebouw. Where its neighbours sit in an impoverished land-scape of pre-cast concrete and tarmac, it is instead framed by a small copse of alder and a wall overtaken by ivy. It is set behind a narrow drainage ditch, from which emerge grasses, reeds and a willow. To the rear, fruit trees and a glass house are scattered across the space between ditch and wall, opposite a field of maize. The compound reads as a broken series of one-storey walls, with taller volumes behind. It is a chain of smaller rooms, bound together in larger assemblies, which are in turn aggregated in depot and house, joined by the office. Most of the walls to the canal are blind, in a pale lime render; a couple have high level windows; a cluster of three two-storey windows, a composed cut, opens up the house towards the canal.

The grouping of volumes gives house and depot a kind of equilibrium, either side of the central entrance forecourt; it also builds each as a layered set of enclosures, of walled rooms within walled courts within planted screens. Office and house form two sides of an enclosed garden, and are linked by a ground floor colonnade. The depot is lined in the warm tones of plywood, with concrete block walls stepping in and out of its steel frame at low level. The first floor office looks out through its joinery screens, through porches at either end to the depot and garden. The house is a simple linear arrangement of well-proportioned rooms, with the two-storey hall on the canal side illuminated by the three grand windows. The walled garden unfolds opposite the colonnade between a lily pond to a dense bed of shrubs and flowers.

There is a lot of architecture here, perhaps a surplus, even. There is a studied syntax of classical rhythms and enervated gothic verticals; there are echoes of medieval halls which are the focus for life as well as an access to the surrounding rooms, of the pinwheel movements of Arts and Crafts houses, or of the exaggerated horizontality of the modernist house. At the same time, this house-depot is deeply elemental, its two main parts a pair of contrasting dialogues between masonry and carpentry. The austere constructional language underpins a kaleidoscopically rich array of light effects. This is a work of both architectural purity and down-to-earth convenience. Like an unfolded and stretched courtyard farm, work is incorporated as a natural part of the household. The co-existence of its parts is eased and enriched by transitions that are not abrupt contrasts but are themselves rooms. It is a sophisticated work of architecture as landscape, deftly handling the relations of engineered landscape, cultivation, industry and untamed nature.

Skirting this concatenation of villages, I navigate along the edge of fields, past scattered houses, meandering ditches and a gin distillery; past the tall silos of agricultural suppli-

Marie-José Van Hee, House, Office and Warehouse, Deinze, 1990. Paul Deroose landscape architect. View from across the Schipdonk Canal.
Photo Kristien Daem.

Marie-José Van Hee, House, Office and Warehouse, Deinze, 1990. The hall of the house.
Photo Michiel Hendryckx.

ers and tight-packed but random terrace houses on the highway, beside the ornamental gardens of the bungalows and the clump of woodland, until at the edge of Astene, behind a thick hedgerow of hawthorn, a long row of glasshouses appears.

Entering the forecourt, the laboratory building is straight ahead, presenting a sloping gable of prefabricated concrete panels beneath a crisp cornice of zinc and steel, and atop a plinth of rough shuttered concrete. Above, to the left, the wall is eroded, and the cut is lined in timber boarding, meeting the warm orangey brown of the plywood ceiling. The entrance is to the right, beside the glasshouse, through a line of slender steel columns which hold the tall roof. In the ground floor laboratories and the first floor offices, the windows are like horizontal slashes, looking out over the surrounding fields through this colonnade of steel. The dynamic slant of the plywood ceiling hovers above the offices, relieved by the sharp puncture of the rooflight over the stair.

The building is lab, office, caretaker's flat and barn, and its mixed quality is felt in the quiet juxtaposition of galvanised steel columns and polished limestone cills, in the wash of crisp zenithal light on the partitions of plywood. Bound to glasshouse and field, Plant Genetics Systems develops and tests hybrid breeds of rapeseed. A by-product of the city's university, it is part of a network of knowledge at the European scale.

From the fields, it reads as an object, a single volume that strains apart from its neighbours; yet it also reads as a phrase in a wider dialogue across the land. Coolly assembled from ordinary mass-produced elements, its slender columns and large canopy match the weightless volumes of the rectangular copses of poplar that scatter the fields and break the horizon. The architects have here achieved an artful equivalence between building and land-

Robbrecht en Daem, Biotechnology building, Astene, 1993. View from the fields.
Photo Kristien Daem.

Robbrecht en Daem, Biotechnology building, Astene, 1993. View from the first floor terrace.
Photo Kristien Daem.

scape, sitting this large facility at the village edge, and speaking calmly but crisply about its hybrid character, between laboratory and farm, between urban and rural, between science and cultivation.

Crossing the narrow spit of land from Leie to Schelde, the land starts to roll, and the road rises past barns and mills, the villages start to detach from each other's tentacular embrace. Joining the broad modern highway, the road displaces the land as the focus of settlement, its lining of warehouses, showrooms and the odd brick-built textile factory echoing the wide fronts along the Schipdonk canal. As the tall gothic tower of Oudenaarde recedes in the mirrors, the large sheds give way to houses. As the road opens out and the wooded hills approach, one of these houses stands out through its abstract quality, monolithic in grey but textured by its bricks, boards and tiles. This house, and the broad glass and concrete works behind it, is the factory of Drukkerij Sanderus,

Christian Kieckens, Printing Factory Sanderus, Oudenaarde, 1996. The production hall.
Photo Reiner Lautwein.

a printworks specialising in custom printing of packaging, serving small producers in Belgium, France and the Netherlands.

The house contains the reception and meeting rooms on the ground floor, and the caretaker's house on the first. The factory is organised in a series of linear strips, alternating between one and two storeys, bracketing the eaves of the house in its stepped form. The management offices are formed by large wood-framed glazed screens dividing up the front block, facing out to the highway or into the factory. The production hall is an expansive horizontal space with an orderly array of presses. Its sinewy precast concrete beams carry a flat roof of profiled steel sheet, with a storey-high glazed lantern running down its centre. The beams bear on in-situ concrete cross-walls, which form cellular storage and office spaces either side of the hall. On the first floor, part of this rhythm of stepping volumes, the canteen looks out over the roofs to wooded hills on either side.

Christian Kieckens, Printing Factory Sanderus, Oudenaarde, 1996. View from across the highway. Photo Reiner Lautwein.

Large horizontal panes of clear and diffusing glass, the pale joinery and splashes of inky blue glass and the polished concrete floors accept and distort the play of light through the open cells of the concrete structure. Its scale frequently surprises, fusing generosity and intimacy in a fabric of rhythms as calm and satisfying as the quiet hum of the presses that filters through the building. These luminous, transparent spaces draw together the scale of the individual and of the machine, and articulate the flat hierarchy of this century-old family firm. Although its retention was expedient, the house expresses the personal scale of the business. Drawn into the measure and abstraction of the factory, it suggests a package folded and assembled from the flat sheets behind.

Continuing after my diversions, I return to the comforting conventions of the rural idyll; the sun drops as the horizon lifts towards Ronse, the uplands and the woodland cabin, and I leave behind the Flemish valley's patchwork of agriculture and industry, of horticulture and settlement.

This mixed landscape seems to provoke ambivalence among many who care about spatial development in the Flemish region. The low-rise nature of most construction, the strung out villages which blur into one another in the blink of an inattentive motorist's eye, the haphazard juxtaposition of different uses: none of these are qualities that fit with the internationally prevalent ideal of the compact city. From this urban perspective, the mixed landscape is an aberration; for pastoral romantics, it is an abomination. Yet, coming as I do from a city that takes twice as long to cross as this region, and from a culture where sentiment elevates landscape to a picture of itself, I am intrigued by the apparent contrasts and hidden interdependencies of this landscape.

This landscape is neither fully rural nor urban, but rather 'rurban', a hybrid of the two. This has deep historical roots, evident in 16th-century visitors' description of Flanders as a single continuous city. Here, agricultural development and urban growth worked symbiotically: night soil from the cities was distributed to the land, and used to fertilise the production of vegetables in a crop rotation that eliminated fallow periods. Textile production was passed out in 'piece work' from the cities to the outlying villages, where inhabitants would work both the land and the loom, and production could escape the control of the urban guilds. This interweaving of agriculture and industry is far from unknown in other parts of Europe, such as Baden-Wurttemburg, the Po Valley and England's Black Country, making them some of the continent's most economically resilient regions. These might not be cities in the conventional sense, but they are arguably a form of city.

As the buildings in Deinze, Astene and Oudenaarde demonstrate, this 'rurban' territorial condition generates hybrids of familiar building types: house-depots, laboratory-barns, factories-with-houses. These buildings present challenges of scale, siting, organisation, structure and finish, to which there are no conventional responses. Complex interdependencies between neighbouring conditions demand precise, practical responses. Perhaps because of the challenges of these conditions, few of the regions mentioned above have produced remarkable buildings; such buildings might be considered questions of production or of branding, brutally simplified or over-frothed. In these three buildings, cultivated clients have entrusted their small patch of land and their spatial conundrums to the region's nimblest spirits.

Each of these buildings can best be understood as elongated versions of the simple farmstead – combining the small rooms of the house and the large volume of the stable around a yard, joining living and working on a single site. Each architect has found a way to articulate large and small, industrial and domestic as structuring principles, whether through the walled garden, the colonnade or the stepping roof. Mass-produced materials and raw finishes have been deployed throughout, but abstract economy is brought to energetic life by the daylight and sun that the architects invite in, across, through these raw shells.

In other words, when the familiar genres of 'the rural' and 'the urban' cannot be applied, it creates a condition of uncertainty but also of great opportunity. In pastoral conditions, narratives of purity and simplicity, of private possession and hard-maintained leisure seem hardwired into our dreams. In urban conditions, design is codified to mitigate conflict, and gestures of the collective or civic risk to be but hopeful rememberings. The tower house, the woodland cabin, the Market hall, the townhouses and urban housing are all exceptional works by highly accomplished architects, drawing on and refining centuries of professional and creative reflection on these conditions. At first sight, the claims on our attention of the house and depot in Deinze, the laboratories in Astene and the factory in Oudenaarde are less obvious.

But look again, as these buildings show this generation of architects in all their expressive range and practical sophistication - with only a little tradition, convention or fashion to lean on. They are mostly just guided by their empathy, curiosity and invention. Pastoral poets and city-builders they may be, they are also makers who support the culture of making, in all its glorious impurity.

Eireen Schreurs
Mechthild Stuhlmacher | # A Dutch Perspective
Craftsmanship and Continuity

A visit to Marie-José's house in Ghent, which must have been sometime in the autumn of 1999 or 2000, constituted an initial, impressive introduction to the work of the generation of 1974. The reason for my visit and her extraordinary hospitality was an article that I wanted to write for the journal *OASE*. Now, as I reread the piece, it is as though I am sitting at the table once more, in this impressively sensuous space between inside and outside, behind the 'third façade'*, as she called it.

Over the next few years, I encountered a younger generation of Flemish architects through my editorial work for the architectural yearbook. These encounters resulted in cherished contacts and collaborations, especially with regard to education. As part of the 'Interiors' chair at TU in Delft, to which colleague Eireen Schreurs and myself are connected, the input of noAarchitecten, Architects de vylder vinck taillieu, Ono and Bovenbouw and others is considered to be a profoundly enriching experience. Vice versa, in recent years, many of our Delft students head for Flanders and work for these practices.

The editors of this book asked us to re-examine the work of the generation of 1974 from our perspective as Dutch, practising architects and teachers. Perhaps certain features would stand out for us that might be too self-evident for colleagues in their own country to be included at all.

The question formed the rationale for two of the most entertaining road trips through the Flemish autumn landscape, to new projects and cherished buildings that we had visited before. The discussions and email conversations that followed our journeys are provided below.

Mechthild Stuhlmacher, January 2016

**Marie-José Van Hee,
House and practice
in Opwijk, 2005-2011.**
Photo Eireen Schreurs.

* 'Living behind the Third Façade', OASE 55, see www.oasejournal.nl

Dear M,

What better place to have concluded our little trip yesterday than on a building site? That is where it must ultimately happen, where the endless deliberations draw to a close and where the plan takes shape. It was wonderful to roam around the site with the smell of cement and the promise of a remarkable project in the making. Casually musing on the choices and the mastery involved, we were stunned at how architects de vylder vinck taillieu transform the architecture of the Saint Wivina convent in Dilbeek into an indisputable set of rules, exceptions, axioms and candid 'odd bits'. We were in agreement: the Flemish attitude to design is at times quite far removed from ours, but the pleasure and the versatile play with history is both infectious and impressive.

The projects of 'the three' architectural firms that are the protagonists of this book and that we visited in Flanders for this article were the Concert Room in Gaasbeek, the Stadshal (Market Hall) in Ghent, the house in Opwijk and the crematorium in Zemst. They are each notable for their themes, references and sometimes even obsessions. At the same time they also point to a common attitude towards design. We identified a first feature of this shared approach there, on the Wivina building site: the architect's familiarity with his own building history. The Dutch could never imagine building so light-heartedly at a beautiful convent with such an impressive building history. The Nederlandse Monumentenzorg (administration of Dutch heritage conservation) would be simply speechless.

de vylder vinck taillieu architecten, St. Wivina residential care centre under construction, Dilbeek, 2015.
Photo Eireen Schreurs.

Marie-José Van Hee, House and practice in Opwijk, 2005-2011. Window details.
Photo Eireen Schreurs.

Not just the poise, but also the way in which 'the three' use history is remarkable. It may be a theoretical exercise to extricate historical references from their cultural meaning; but 'the three' specifically use the autonomous architectural qualities of historical buildings and the knowledge contained therein. The examples are there for

the taking. The use of daylight in the practice in Marie-José Van Hee's house in Opwijk betrays a clear study of the medieval window, this ingenious construction in which a partition at eye level provides contact with the street and the skylight allows the sun to shine far into the room. The cultural connotations are recognized, for the same high light transports you to an interior by Vermeer, but it also uses his architectural perspective. The frosted bottom part of the window affords the room, which is used for therapeutic sessions, a concentrated atmosphere.

Robbrecht en Daem architecten operate in a completely different way, but also here intensive use is made of architectural insights that are decidedly pre-modern in their multifunctional hall in Gaasbeek: the relatively dark foyer, the thick wooden entrance doors, the skylights in the hall and the church-like attention devoted to the ceiling.

To explain the floor plans, the client who commissioned Christian Kieckens' crematorium directs us to classical examples. However, in addition to the overt cultural connotations it also involves material and spatial insights that are used for the experience of its interiors. The cool terrazzo floor contrasts with the warm skylight; the wooden doors at each point of the compass ensure orientation, and the sunspots that slowly move across the floor add some dynamic variation to this otherwise timeless hall.

You may wonder where this sensibility comes from. Is it part of the training? Is it the historical heritage in Flanders, which flatters itself with the same ease in designing the contemporary landscape? One can only guess. You could also wonder what it offers besides tested spatiality and timeless architecture. Driving through the Flemish countryside, these buildings present us with unexpected connections. They are not bound by their public presence, since the commissions do not lend themselves to that. In Flanders the collective return to history provides the common ground. The Dutch design tradition is built on quite different grounds, with polder grids and an urban development whose tentacles extend to architecture. It brings order to the country to such an extent that quality actually searches out derogations. In the Netherlands history is a distant relative, with whom you speak only of trivial matters. In Flanders, it's your closest friend.

Best wishes, E

Dear E,

How appropriate that you start with the building site. Evidently still the place where everything happens in Flanders, where buildings can become architecture, come alive, or not. Where people wheel and deal and where ultimately all previous design decisions come up again for debate. Before the tender procedure the design process seems, from my own Dutch perspective, incredibly rigid, and you get the impression that Excel documents beat stories and drawings hands down. However, when all the formalities of the procedure and the endless number crunching stop and a contractor is found, a completely different language is spoken.

In Flanders one talks extensively about all the things that have long ceased to be a proper design task in the Netherlands, about profiling, skirting boards, connections and joints; carpenters enjoy the status of a hero in Flanders, and when elements and materials are combined, a distinctive language emerges that constantly harkens back and refers to the past. The building site and the way in which architects deal with it, or better: are forced to deal with it, largely determines the quality and the sense of continuity of architecture in Flanders. And this is expressed in the ease architects address traditional materials and the way they are put together, such as limewash, brick, wood, ceramics and terrazzo. These techniques and materials carry a world of con-notations and references that feel like a rich, collectively supported foundation. The frequent presence of the architect at the building site underlines his traditional role as master builder. In the Netherlands this role has long been interpreted in a completely different way and this has direct consequences for many design and material choices. I also think that this definitely explains a large part of the fundamental differences between Dutch and Flemish architecture.

The hall in Gaasbeek has been built with a reduced palette of materials: red brick painted white here and there, oak, and bronze window frames. Traditional, familiar. Perhaps more aptly termed: timeless. And then applied without a single literal stylistic reference to the past. Encased inside is a feeling of continuity, which forms the archi-tecture's keynote. The history is tangible, but does not have to be named. With Van Hee the references are sometimes a little clearer, but here too they are implicit associations. With Kieckens the forms, symmetrical axes, archways and incidence of light contain very clear references, but here it is the atmosphere that reigns and the way in which the materials are applied in such an unequivocally modern fashion that the associations start to drift, and are no longer literal.

How differently this is conceived in the Netherlands. The deeply-rooted sense of conti-nuity that characterises the generation of 1974 in an exemplary manner has nothing to do with the explicit retro-architecture, which 'the market' increasingly 'demands' in the

Netherlands. And also nothing to do with the ubiquitous occupation with the 'correct' approach to the past, to which many restoration and transformation projects in the Netherlands respond to with steel and glass.

With their seriousness and cultural and historical baggage 'our three' adhere to a select group of architects in Europe that work on a major joint project, I'd like to call 'Weiterbauen'. It is a term that emerged directly or indirectly from the influential chair of Miroslav Šik in Zurich and that is not often expressed literally. The architects trained by Šik, and a separate group of like-minded people in various European countries, regard their work as part of a long, spirited and ever innovative tradition. History lives on in the architecture and is ever the object of new inquiry. It is great to see that through the frequent contacts and congeniality of this group, an enlightened approach to place, culture and history is afforded an ever broader, more interesting and varied foundation. Fortunately, in the meantime ambitious architects of the younger generation have gone to work even on our side of the border to maintain broad, international networks between the Netherlands, Flanders and especially London, a noticeable development that underlines the influence of and interest in the generation of 1974's intellectual legacy.

Best, M

Dear E,

We have already visited the stunning hall in Gaasbeek together twice, with a nine-year gap in between the two visits. On the occasion of the Flemish Architectural Yearbook's presentation in 2006, I had the opportunity of giving a short lecture on what had struck me most as a foreign member of the editorial team, when studying the Flemish architecture of the time. I remember words such as 'precision', 'intensive care' and 'attention to the tangible'. In the Netherlands one would probably describe the qualities that I tried to convey as 'craftsmanship'.

'Craftsmanship' is, without a doubt, an often misused buzzword with a nostalgic undertone. At the same time it is an important term that refers to an architecture defined by a direct link between a spatial idea and the art of building, combining and constructing. The 'artisan' label is traditionally attached to architecture from Alpine countries or Scandinavia, architecture that celebrates the material and manual skills, and that recounts how it was made with every gesture and each detail. But does this meaning of 'artisan' cover the connotation here?

The choice of materials undoubtedly plays a decisive role in Gaasbeek, but is the work of the people who built it readable? Does this architecture involve combining materials, construction, manual skills? When you stand in the room in Gaasbeek, you don't know how the large space was constructed, how the span was achieved, how the bricks remain in place in the ceiling. Evidently this is not what concerns the architects; no didactic story is told. The work of Robbrecht en Daem architecten speaks of a different craft, not the craft of the maker, but that of the designer.

At the time, I gazed from my lectern, charmed perhaps by the only detail in the building that could be called ornamental, the white zigzag edge of the white painted wall on the entrance side touching the ceiling. This is the ventilation system, which conducts its work invisibly, transports air through the series of small apertures in the corner of the room.

Materials are used to paint, or better still: materials are combined as if they are fabrics, wood becomes heavy and brick light, with seams that just may or may not be visible, whether it emerges from a logical construction or not. In fact, the space, its atmosphere and proportion are the only thing that really matters.

When people write about Gaasbeek, they are full of praise for the simple intervention of the ziggurat-shape, which forges the outside and inside into a single whole. Without a doubt, it is a much admired gesture that however, in my opinion, is only brought to life by the precision with which the holes in the brick walls are cut, with which a handful of surfaces are painted white while others are not, and which determines the strikingly

low level of the bookcases' panelling. It is good to see that the room effortlessly hosts concerts and architects' meetings as well as its current (temporary?) function as a living room for a large family with lots of piano-playing grandchildren.

The designer's craftsmanship is also revealed by all the rooms, patios, cupboards and doors in Van Hee's house in Opwijk. It is embodied in the benevolent generosity of the terrazzo floor that forms the sedate basis for the multiform geometries of the rooms with their virtuoso carpentry. The smooth quality of the floor is put into perspective in a relaxed manner by the corresponding, but far coarser concrete outside on the patio. Every single one of the bathrooms and washrooms in the house are spatial gems of light and stone. The heavy concrete beam that traverses the parlour in Opwijk is like a mysterious, sculptural object without weight or purpose. The beam is paraded as a sturdy bearer of paper-thin Christmas lights; the fact that the entire building is resting on it seems to be of secondary importance.

The floor plan in Zemst with its graphic balance also exudes craftsmanship and betrays much of the cultural weight with which Kieckens wanted to imbue his building. The cross-sections demonstrate an architecture that serves light and spatiality. The building also boasts an impressive terrazzo floor, in the same earthy shades as that in Opwijk, but without its outdoor counterpart to bring it into perspective. The way in which the light is directed from above in the various halls and rooms is beautiful and comforting. But it is likewise clear that here Kieckens did not have the opportunity to fully bring his creation on paper to life on the building site. And that in addition to the halls, there are a number of rooms that also lack this inspiration. We note here how indispensable the craft of the designer is to the artisan's craft. In this architecture it appears that one cannot exist without the other.

Best wishes, M

Dear M,

I agree when you write that the 'spatial craftsmanship' in the projects we visited is given priority over the logic of their construction. What the generation of 1974 has in common is a preference for natural materials, and a great command of their properties and cultural 'baggage'. At the same time the materials are 'tamed' in the details in a modernist pursuit of abstraction, until one can paint with the spaces, as you so beautifully phrased it. I reflected on how the craft of creating space actually works.

In Marie-José Van Hee's house in Ghent, which also I visited years ago, there are many examples of details that aim to abstract the materials that comprise them. In Van Hee's living room there is a white object, a staircase, with steps of beige natural stone. The side of the staircase is plastered to the seam, which conceals the thickness of the limestone. The same happens with the wooden cupboard doors in the room. They are painted white, but here too the cross-cut side of the wood is not visible anywhere. Van Hee selected the materials with respect for their 'origin': the slats of the cupboard doors are vertical, as a tree stands, and the stone staircase is obviously a weighty object. At the same time the details of the materials transform the room into coloured planes. The compositions are 'picturesque' collages, with contrast as the main technique: here a window; there a door; here a staircase; there a light section.

The materialisation becomes the deciding factor in the dynamic of the spaces, which are often fairly static. It is logical that the material may not become an object: its thickness, own colour, independent volumetry would only distract. As a consequence the materialisation does not need to be thematised, and Van Hee can use oak in one room and walnut in another, something that most Dutch architects (and far beyond) would never come up with. This is why it is so wonderful to be able to move around in these buildings; that's when you see the interplay between static and dynamic best of all. There is a surprise in store around every corner. From this perspective they are a balancing act between sitting and moving, between classical spatiality and modern details, with everything in between.

Best wishes, E

Dear M,

This is my final contribution to the conversation we have conducted these past few weeks on the bicycle, in the car, at the table, and yesterday at another building site. You described breakfast in a café in Antwerp on a midweek morning opposite someone who was reading Sartre, and how that seemed to you so characteristic of Belgian bourgeois culture. In Flanders there is apparently a cultural (upper?) class, which arrange for the design of their homes, concert halls, galleries, and shops, right down to their furniture. These clients form the layer of humus on which architecture is able to flourish. The collaboration with their architects is based on trust, a shared agenda and mutual respect. We recognised this in clients that we spoke to and who, moreover, we decided, did not all belong to the creative class. They especially valued the open and sometimes lengthy dialogue, and spoke with an almost archaic admiration of 'their' architect. One of them gave the architect a *carte blanche,* imagine! – and is profoundly satisfied with the result.

I have been surprised more often by the natural affinity of Flemish architects with the arts. This is unthinkable in the Dutch engineering tradition, but conceivable at a college of higher education for the arts, where the head and the heart are never far apart. This education in the Beaux Arts or Arts and Crafts tradition is formative, I believe, because I distinguish the same sensibility in the current generation of architects. While in the Netherlands architecture must ultimately serve a social agenda, in Flanders architecture can be absurd, construct its own logic and this is accepted. I recognise this peculiarity, personal expression and tenacity in the work of all three of them.

The artistic education is illustrated by the attention devoted to the process, as an intrinsic part of each project. The last book by Kieckens accurately describes how he develops his designs. He includes probing perspectives and places alternatives side by side. The line drawings of the churches as in the Baroque edition of OASE recount his long-lasting fascination for baroque spatiality: it demonstrates that he regards the process as an independent product. Is it architecture? Art? And then there are the sketches that he and his colleagues produce, which betray the familiarity and direct relationship with this medium. They demonstrate what cannot be explained by functional diagrams: the pursuit of the core of their own distinct architecture.

The fusion of architecture and art is most explicit in Robbrecht en Daem architecten's work and it extensively defines their design practice. The story goes that Paul Robbrecht produces watercolours almost every day that can be read as exercises in colour, composition and form. For a large part his clients come from the arts sector: their practice has designed residences for artists, collectors, pavilions and a number of museums. Not only are they often found in these circles, their architecture also has a specific relationship with the art that it houses: more a dialogue than a modest shelter, and in no way are their projects snowed under by their functional requirements. All the projects convey a relaxed and trusted relationship. Architecture and art converse like neighbours, the dialogue sought in the creative process.

This relationship is less explicit in Van Hee's practice, although she built the ModeNatie, a fashion museum, and collaborated for example on the Hufkens gallery in Brussels. Yet her work also has a distinctly artistic character, as the dictionary describes it: in accordance with the rules of the art. This leaves room for the unusual, the experiment, in understated frameworks that she alone establishes. There is only a general preconceived idea; there is room for development and insight. Here the process appears to be a desired, necessary and lengthy part of the project, also to a remarkable extent for the client.

Best wishes, E.

Rotterdam, 25 October, 2015

Dear E,

I have just returned home from another excursion to Flanders with a group of Delft students, this time to Ghent and the surrounding area. During an evening walk last night, I suddenly acquired a much better understanding of the Market Hall that we had previously visited on a busy and sunny day, and that appeared to us to be large, even a little crude at the time. In the dark, the hall seemed like a great beast with a glistening coat and a warm belly. How wonderful that there was suddenly an openly accessible indoor area in the moist autumn city. The object that appeared something of a mystery during the day and which at first glance seemed to fill and divide spaces, succeeded in connecting the squares as a series of similar rooms. During my second visit, it was already clear that the city had taken ownership of the hall, and the great thing was that this impression endured the following morning in daylight. Some architecture improves when one gets to know it better.

This time the highlight of the trip was our visit to Oudenaarde where we were given a guided tour of the impressive Pamele care centre by noAarchitecten; we were received by the client who was still enthusiastic and involved and warmly recounted the many discussions with his architect, and the references they had visited together. Apparently at the time he went to the Dom Hans van der Laan monastery with the architects of noA, to seek inspiration and to learn from this Dutch monk and architect.

As a result of this shared journey the new care centre at the convent appears totally grounded in its surroundings, and stands proud and familiar at its historical location. What the photos in our excursion guide had depicted as austere and harsh comes across as a warm, rich world for all the senses, framed now by fully grown, lush gardens that seem to be celebrating the summer in the last week of October. The use has softened the building and confirms the decisions made in the design and building process. The dark colours, the abundant use of wood, the concrete and soft limewash form a respectful backdrop. Faces are beautiful in the dimmed light. NoAarchitecten most definitely belong to the group of architects that continue to develop, rejuvenate and expand 'our three's' mental legacy.

We could go on talking for much longer, for many hours in the car, over pints of beer and pots of mussels. Yes please! I hope that we continue our visits to the generation of 1974 and their colleagues. Now that this generation of architects has officially stopped teaching I sincerely hope that they do not stop building and inspiring. We also returned from our trips and discussions enriched, with the feeling that we had learned some fundamental truths.

If I wanted to summarise what the architecture we visited involves, there are three terms that stand out for me most: continuity, rigour and appropriation. These are terms that all the themes we have discussed possess.

Continuity describes character and place and provides an anchor. Rigour involves mastery and balance, precision and meticulous choices. The third relates to generosity, creating frameworks and the ability to accept use and occupancy.

When I first visited Marie-José Van Hee's house in Ghent, I was happy not only to be allowed to walk around it but also to sit down, eat and simply spend time there. In the design of the house she ensured the necessary resistance that her generous patrons sometimes cannot or will not allow her. It came to mind when I visited the noA's monastic building in Oudenaarde, a similar atmosphere reigned there. A rare pleasure. All our terms converge here.

In Gaasbeek too, everything falls into place, the spaces, elements, traces of use and occupancy and the corresponding stories are refined and naturally relate to one another. I am grateful that the client takes the time to act as the host. I would be quite happy to stay here.

noAarchitecten, Pamele care centre, Oudenaarde, 2002-2010.
Photo Eireen Schreurs.

Dirk Somers | Venturi's Discipline

Each generation is shaped by a previous one. Which is why this piece begins a little earlier than 1974. The 1960s was the era in which architecture as a continuum was rediscovered. It was the juncture at which the stable role of design regained its honour and the transience of the function became passé. The early years of this reversal were incredibly turbulent. One could say that it was both an exploratory and a therapeutic period. How could architecture be modern yet retrace the path of its past with such vehemence? How could old principles metamorphose into new ideas? In the great architectural countries such as the US, Japan, Italy and England the wildest experiments to emerge were founded on monumental or historicising ideas about design. The generation of 1974 took root in this extremely rich, fecund soil. It was a time of untold opportunities and very few certainties.

Not entirely free of personal preference, I was struck most by the weight Robert Venturi carried in publications related to this era. Venturi's discourse still resonates today and therefore it is worth exploring it in more detail. In 1966, Robert Venturi published *Complexity and Contradiction in Architecture*: a eulogy to the inconsistency and formal intricacies that architecture was denied by academic functionalism. This was soon followed by the iconographic analyses Learning from Las Vegas and Learning from Levittown, in association with Denise Scott Brown and Steven Izenour.

The common thread in Venturi's explorations is the need for convention. It goes without saying that the complexities and contradictions Venturi describes can only exist by virtue of a significant degree of conformism. This also means that Venturi is not a fan of highly expressionist or sculptural excesses. They reduce architecture to complex uniformity with no room for multi-layering. This desire for conformism - one could say *discipline* - makes Venturi's thinking so timeless and unique.

However general these theoretical considerations are, I am still struck by how impressive the degree of influence Venturi exerted on Belgian architectural culture has been. Venturi's work is invariably situated in the context of modernist dogma and everyday iconography. This means that his oeuvre does great service to historiography that documents the transition from modernity to post-modernity. But this positioning does not explain why Venturi remains so firmly entrenched in the creation of and reflections on architecture to this very day.

You may wonder, without any pretension, whether there is an architectural climate that has been influenced more by Venturi in the past fifty years than that of Flanders. This

Marie-José Van Hee with Robbrecht en Daem architecten, Market Hall, Ghent, 1996-2012.
Photo Marc De Blieck
(© Robbrecht en Daem).

187

assertion sounds non-committal, nevertheless I shall attempt to assemble a number of arguments that will lure us into this bit of bombast. After some reflection I arrive at three motives that one could label as Venturian that are also decisive for the work of the generation of 1974.

Venturi himself provided the first grounds for explaining his enduring relevance. He connects the natural need for complexity to pragmatic facts. Venturi refers to Mies van der Rohe to explain how selective the modernistic design approach is.[1] The work by Mies can only be what it is if it is limited to solving a number of problems. To guarantee the success of the Miesian project the only option is to ignore several pragmatic issues. To Venturi the natural form of architecture's existence is complexity. The ever increasing number of technological and administrative imperatives contribute to the right of an ambiguous, complex architecture to exist. Naturally this argument applies at all times and in all cases, but even more so in a society in which architecture occupies a weak position. In the US and Belgium architecture was marginalised to an even greater extent by the wave of liberalisation following the Second World War. In the Belgian context 'Complexity and Contradiction' should quickly be adopted as a guide for

Robbrecht en Daem with
Marie-José Van Hee,
Hufkens gallery Brussels, 1992.
Cruciform beam structure.
Photo Kristien Daem.

navigating the caprices and lamentations of unpredictable bureaucracy and clients. Other than inventing far-fetched complexities, the contradiction of nature emerges from the murky circumstances that surround the assignment. A very Belgian reading of Venturi legitimises architecture as a play on reality. The solitary Belgian architect arms himself/herself with Venturi and presents himself/herself as a practical strategist that does not address inherent contradictions, but converts them into enthralling designs. I refer to the Belgian architect as solitary here because in the second half of the 20th century there was virtually no professional architectural community to speak of. Due to the absence of any kind of Ombudsman for spatial quality, addressing a large number of matters was not an option. You could argue that the convergence of Venturi's work and the architect's need for self-reliance has led to a kind of regional discipline. The weak position of architecture serves as a basis for its identity as a strategic play on reality.

Paul Robbrecht always positioned architecture in the field of tension between servitude and autonomy. Marie-José Van Hee's perennial pugnacity and the expressive lamentations of Christian Kieckens' did not intend to liberate architecture from its circumstances, but rather to provide the breathing spaced needed to convert these circumstances into thrilling complexities. Naturally, Marc Dubois tried to give shape to a largely absent professional community. It was precisely this minute glimmer of hope in the dark night of the 1980s that illustrates how sparsely populated this society actually was.

Another explanation for Venturi's immanence emerges if you examine matters from an urban perspective. You cannot call that far-fetched. Venturi's interest in urbanisation is obvious in 'Learning from Las Vegas' as well as in his subsequent writings and studies. Venturi's interest in the changing context elevates his discourse beyond the scale of the building. He is clearly searching for a way to re-anchor architecture in the new logic of the city. How does the building hold its own in a city tailored to the car and business? Can architecture be served by the same mainstream phenomena without renouncing its status? We allow America's post-War 'Main Street' and the 'Flemish steenweg' (built-up connecting road) to fraternise for a while with their similar car-oriented, shrill identities. Once again the absence of a professional community is marked in both environments. Urban development seems to have disappeared from the scene, which means that architecture and the city are directly at each other's mercy.

In this kind of biotope formal conventions surface in architecture of their own accord. They take the place of the code that urban development occupies elsewhere. The connections that urban development fails to make are created by the architectural design in its stead. In 'Complexity and Contradiction' Venturi also takes the transformation of the convention as an element of the urban dynamic.[2] Again one could use the term discipline here to indicate how the architect completes the defective context by refining his or her focus when designing architecture. The vacuum created by dysfunctional urban development is repaired by architectural discipline.

**Robbrecht en Daem,
Bank Building
Kerksken, 1988.**
Photo Kristien Daem.

see also '3x3 projects', 150-151.

**Christian Kieckens,
House Van Hover - De Pus
Baardegem, 1990-1995.**
Photo Reiner Lautwein.

see also '3x3 projects', 162-163.

The monumental lobby of the small building occupied by a bank in Kerksken, the spatial staging of Ghent's Market Hall, the wedge between street and landscape represented by the villa in Baardegem are all examples of the way in which architecture steps in where urban development has retreated. In each of these situations a sculptural quality appears that creates order in the midst of an undisciplined urban development.

Finally, I would also like to link Venturi's desire to reconcile high art and low art in architecture to the two previous motives. The term discipline also applies here. Of course Venturi revelled in the introduction of Pop Art to the world's art scene. Once the American street scene was fully absorbed by the pattern of the free market, art also seized onto this condition as a source of inspiration. Venturi viewed this embrace as a carte blanche. His architecture should be just like it. Venturi's ultimate stroke of

**Robbrecht en Daem, House
Mys, Oudenaarde, 1983-1992.**
Photo Kristien Daem.

compositional genius would be to hustle the great Italian mannerists through the vulgarity of America's consumer culture. Lettering, straightened profiling, banal building materials and billboards were part of the complex compositions of his early work.

What passes for Pop Art in Belgium makes use of the local commonplace, rather than the flamboyant iconography of American consumer culture. Marcel Broodthaers, Roger Raveel, Raoul De Keyser and René Heyvaert, all are very disciplined artists that enjoy the frugal manipulation of everyday objects. To this day, art lives to make art that cautiously mixes craftsmanship and familiarity with artistic complexity. Many figurative artists - of whom Luc Tuymans and Michael Borremans are the most reputed - still respect the contours of this discipline.

This well-aimed balance between figuration and abstraction - between the ordinary and the artistic - is so inherent to the generation of 1974. Connecting the ordinary and the extraordinary is clearly manifested in the tautological figures cherished so much by this generation. Heyvaert is not far away when Robbrecht en Daem with Marie-José Van Hee intersect the hollow beams in the Hufkens gallery or when they mount a window in front of the window in Oudenaarde or Rotterdam. They weave together familiar figures in the house and apothecary of Van Backlé - De Feu, by camouflaging a skylight as a terrace table. Later, in the De Causemaecker dwelling, she reincorporates this motif. Christian Kieckens draws a door in the door and a staircase over the staircase in a 19th-century row house in Kortrijk. Laminating and assembling conventional elements is the most visible tactic of converting the ordinary into something extraordinary, of transforming the 'low' into the 'high'.

A great deal has changed in this country since the young Venturi: the architecture community has increasingly professionalized and is now supported by an institutional framework. Urban development is working on a remarkable resurgence under the impulse of urban redevelopment. The gap between high and low art is being reduced by a prosperous middle class.

This broad dynamic has resulted in regular attacks on the discipline of Belgian architecture. Why the service-oriented aspect? Why all that drivel about context? What about that Spartan austerity? When will this country become great, maximalist and virile? Despite these types of charges one can establish with satisfaction that many of the new successes in Flemish architecture are the very testament of this prolific discipline. The charming mix of the ordinary and the artistic in the work of a DVVT or Dierendonck-blancke is to walk across the tightrope that divides high and low art. Agencies such as noAarchitecten and ONO architecture combine the *objet trouvé* (found object) with the new idea in a different way. In Gijs Vanvaerenbergh's work the convention is tastefully reworked into sculpture. Officekgdvs compresses Venturi's complexity into a striking encounter of primary architectural figures. All these agencies discipline their work in a fashion that is in one way or another always reminiscent of the young Venturi.

Today it is increasingly clear how prophetic Venturi was. In the first edition of Complexity and Contradiction Michelucci's motorway church was a sitting target.[3] In Learning from Las Vegas Venturi discusses the arbitrary sculptural nature of a brutalist residence for the elderly by Paul Rudolph.[4] He extends no compassion whatsoever to meaningless expressiveness. What Venturi did not know was that he was only at the very beginning of a great era of meaningless expressiveness. At the time nobody had predicted deconstructivism, the nonsensical pre-packaged culture and the one-trick-pony buildings of the last few decades. However, it is precisely this distaste for the superficial, entrenched expressiveness that binds the current generation of architects to the generation of 1974 and their Venturian discipline.

[1] Robert Venturi, *Complexity and Contradiction in Architecture* (New York: Museum of Modern Art, 1966): 16.

[2] Robert Venturi, *Complexity and Contradiction in Architecture* (New York: Museum of Modern Art, 1966): 38.

[3] Robert Venturi, *Complexity and Contradiction in Architecture* (New York: Museum of Modern Art, 1966): 18.

[4] Robert Venturi, Denise Scott Brown, Steven Izenour, *Learning from Las Vegas* (Cambridge, MA: MIT Press, 1972): 102.

Christian Kieckens, Interieur
Foundation Kortrijk, 1995-1996.
The place and the building.
interventions in a
19th-century residence.
Photo Reiner Lautwein.

Observations

Kristoffel Boghaert is architect and sculptor. He has worked closely with Robbrecht en Daem architecten, and with Christian Kieckens before starting his own office.

Patrick Van Caeckenbergh is an artist. He lives and works in Sint-Kornelis-Horebeke. During his studies in Ghent, he found intellectual and artistic support in the guidance of Paul Robbrecht.

Els Claessens is principal of ectv architects in Ghent and Brussels. She has worked closely with Marie-José Van Hee Architecten and Robbrecht en Daem architecten.

Tania Vandenbussche is principal of ectv architects in Ghent and Brussels. She has worked closely with Marie-José Van Hee Architecten and Robbrecht en Daem architecten.

An Fonteyne is principal of noAarchitecten in Brussels and Bruges. The collaboration with artists forms a central feature of the work of the office.

Pieter D'haeseleer is an architect. He worked for Christian Kieckens.

Hilde Heynen is Professor of Architecture History and Theory at KU Leuven. Along with the figures in this book, she was closely involved in building up an --architectural culture in Flanders.

Francis Strauven is Professor-Emeritus in Architecture History of Ghent University. He has published widely about architecture, and is central to the burgeoning architectural culture of the 1980s and 1990s.

Peter Swinnen is founding partner of 51N4E. He was Flemish Government Architect from 2010-2015, through which he has granted many commissions through the Open Oproep.

Koen Van Synghel is architecture critic, writing on architecture for for example De Standaard. Trained as an architect, he has his own practice focusing on scenography.

Paul Vermeulen is an architect, educator and critic. He is founding partner of DeSmetVermeulen architecten. He won the Flemish Community Prize for Architecture in 2011.

Jacques De Visscher is Professor-Emeritus in Philosophy and Literature of Radboud University (NL) and Sint-Lucas Ghent. He has written extensively on ethics, aesthetics and architecture.

Cristina Iglesias is a Spanish installation artist and sculptor living and working in Torrelodones, Madrid. She collaborated extensively with Robbrecht en Daem.

Tony Fretton founded his internationally known practice in 1982, which combines a strong sensitivity to the site with vernacular and minimalist approaches. He has been in close contact with the architecture scene in Flanders since the 1990s.

Adam Caruso is founding partner of Caruso St John, with a particularly strong reputation in designing projects for the public realm. Their buildings show a striking restraint and awareness of the emotional potential and physical qualities of constructions.

Office Robbrecht en Daem architecten and Marie-José Van Hee Architecten, Ghent.
Photo Fragile, Faculty of Architecture, KU Leuven, Campus Sint-Lucas Ghent.

MOVING - GROWING - TRAVELLING

After working with Christian Kieckens for six years, I ended up with Paul Robbrecht and Hilde Daem via Marie-José Van Hee. The interview in the garden with Paul - at the end of August 1998 - was a mutual exploration of architecture, as well as the painter and sculptor inside each one of us. I was to work on the extension of the Museum Boijmans-Van Beuningen, which at that time was fully in the throes of the design implementation phase.

Robbrecht en Daem architecten rented a few rooms in a middle-class residence on the Kortrijksesteenweg in Ghent along with Marie-José Van Hee Architecten. That year Robbrecht en Daem won the competition for the Concert Hall in Bruges and opened a branch office there. From then on the agency enjoyed steady growth and international recognition. The time of the small practice where everybody knew each other had come to an end. I had moved several times with Christian Kieckens and with Robbrecht en Daem architecten/Marie-José Van Hee Architecten. Taking over a new place, each heralding a new phase, in this case a phase of growth,

or perhaps more fittingly: accommodating that growth. To look back on that era is not nostalgic. It is more a realisation of having had this privilege just before the practice embarked on an era of major growth.

I cherish the journeys with Paul Robbrecht on the way to Rotterdam, to the Boijmans-Van Beuningen, and later to the Veilinghaven in Utrecht and Ruysdaelstraat or Spaarndammerhout in Amsterdam. Five years later an additional chapter was written: the Whitechapel in London. It was these moments, during which I was able to benefit from his abundant knowledge and insights, and a wordless mutual understanding, which ultimately shaped me. In the end I stayed for ten years. 'Moving' and 'always on the road' became a motto.

Henry van De Velde was awarded the Boekentoren project on his 70th birthday. Architecture is a slow discipline; the apprenticeship is long. The works by these four architects have, averse to the issues of the day, become references and fixed beacons. And it is not over by a long shot.

Kristoffel Boghaert, Ghent, September 2015

Living Box, 1980-1984.
Patrick Van Caeckenbergh, *La Ruine Fructueuse. Atlas des Editions* (Tielt: Lannoo, 2012): 18-19.

LIVING BOX

Between 1980 and 1984, I was registered at the Academy in Ghent. To become a sculptor was my goal. From the beginning, the lectures of Paul Robbrecht drew my attention. In a fascinating way, he introduced us to the wonderful world of various architectural and urban problems, both in a historical and contemporary perspective. But also art, philosophy, anthropology, and even music were part of his way of thinking and constructing ideas. He doubted things, lost himself in multiple complex questions and moreover, he let us take part in these doubts. I am very grateful for that.

In the fourth year, we had to present our final art piece to an external jury. I had no idea what to do. Paul told me: 'just show them where you live'. At that time, I was living in a box in an empty factory building. This shelter was the only thing I had worked on during my time at the Academy. In it, I had combined all my knowledge and memories of philosophy, literature and science. I called it Living Box.

Paul sent a photographer to make the right pictures and accompanied and supported me during that time. The jury saw my home as a temporary accommodation for living, study and work, which had become an ever-changing artwork in itself, as a kind of cabinet of curiosities. I graduated with honours. At a certain moment you receive confidence: an insight, an awareness that they had, and I had not yet.

Later on, I decided to study history of architecture in Venice. At that time Umberto Eco, Manfredo Tafuri and Francesco Dal Co were teaching there. Paul Robbrecht wrote a letter of recommendation to the jury who decided over the grant. Paul always defended that sort of hybrid of different creative platforms. But nevertheless I was refused.

Patrick Van Caeckenbergh, Sint-Kornelis-Horebeke, 22 September 2015

Marie-José Van Hee and Paul Robbrecht, gums.
Photo Els Claessens and Tania Vandenbussche.

Our observation dates from some time ago. Back then there was at most a computer for correspondence and plans in an architect's practice. Marie-José and Paul may do things differently today, but at the time that was how a design got started.

José set to work with one base or another, placed a sheet of tracing paper on top and began drawing lines with a thick pencil. One moment with purpose and determination, the next with more misgiving. It went on for hours, sheet upon sheet of tracing paper, thick line over thick line. There was a lot of erasing and rubbing out, with the hand and especially with the kneaded eraser, until everything was black: the tracing paper, hand and eraser. These drawings did not instantly predict the wonderful residences they would become. Perhaps they structured the profusion that filled Marie-José's head.

Paul had the T-square, triangle, well-sharpened pencil and eraser at the ready. Colour was still absent. In an intense flurry of activity, he set a hypothetical plan to paper. Between times he could be seen standing and shuffling about behind the beautiful table. Some erasing went on too; however the spaces did not appear to take shape in the drawing. They might have been visible in Paul's mind before a line was committed to paper.

The birth of a design was an incredibly individual process for both of them, so very different from what we experience, do and teach today. In the current vibrant architectural culture a design is conceived from interaction, consultation and competition. This culture was initiated by the Ghent 5 in the 1980s. A few original, resolute and extremely talented designers were needed to set it in motion.

Els Claessens and Tania Vandenbussche,
Brussels-Ghent, June 2015

Marie-José Van Hee, House in Zuidzande,
folded leaflet produced for the 13th
Biennale di Venezia, 2012

Luxury, calm and voluptuousness. My colleague Philippe Viérin recounts it without hesitation, when I tell him that I have been asked to write something about Marie-José Van Hee. A few years ago, after a meeting with her, he brought a folded sheet of paper to the practice. The paper rustled in its lightness and the way it had been folded made one think of an instruction leaflet for medication. Once it was unfolded, we discovered photographs of the house she built in Zuidzande. The exterior and interior each occupied one side of the sheet, and both worlds merged due to the paper's transparency. The page was cherished and consulted, repeatedly folded up and unfolded, rotated and deciphered. Just as we continue to examine that precious sheet of paper, still discovering things anew, so too do we continue to look to her architecture. The sequence of the spaces, their proportions and ceilings, the characteristic windows that allow the outside in, the chimneys on the roof; composition upon composition, enabling living in the most generous sense.

As apparently simple as it seems, it remains just as troublesome to grasp, even after all these years.

Luxury, calm and voluptuousness. For Van Hee as craftswoman, the architect who has mastered the discipline like no other in order to comprehend the whole, a house belongs just as much to the street as it does to its residents. Viewing the world with this all-encompassing approach is looking for trouble. Naturally, Marie-José Van Hee has known this for a long time, yet she works on relentlessly. Superficiality is not tolerated and what can be improved, must be improved. However, the greatest surprise came during our first encounter. The Flanders Architectural Yearbook was presented in Kortrijk City Hall, our then young agency's first public building. Marie-José Van Hee greeted me, out of nowhere, with a kiss and a wide smile. She literally wrapped her arms around me. The generosity, so typical of her work, and the tangibility of her architecture, were suddenly so unexpectedly close.

An Fonteyne, Brussels, August 2015

Gustave Doré, New Zealander, 1872.
Collection Museum of London.

Where is architecture in Plato's allegory? It is not the fireplace around which everyone has taken a seat, nor the cave as a 'shelter'. It has nothing to do with the perfect fifth 1:2:3, one of Plato's ratios that symbolises the navel of creation. Not the stairs, the structure for ascending skywards, to the opening, with the reward of a different insight, only to tumble down once more.

Architecture is manifested in the attitude of standing up and obeying the compelling tendency to look elsewhere. The interpretation comes after the observation and is the seed from which knowledge is passed on, only then to be understood and valued.

Christian Kieckens uses architecture as a language to offer a message of 'constructed' culture with these interpretations. The intellectual layering and multidisciplinary character of his projects appear to be effortlessly interwoven with personal discoveries, the artistic avant-garde, and an almost ominous urge to structure. I do not know and am not interested in to which 'ism' his oeuvre belongs; it is unique. Just like the image of the New Zealander, originating from a different part of the world, he sits on what remains of London Bridge and draws. In the romantic atmosphere of Gustave Doré, perhaps he is reflecting on a lost society. But we live in the now, and cannot look into the new colonist's mind. By definition, we do know that he looks at things differently. And this point of view seems to me like the most fitting statement for Christian Kieckens' architecture. Baroque! Structure organised in a complex relationship of light and space.

When he stands up, having swept the tattered shreds of eraser from his drawing, we are treated to the vision of the architect who in his peculiarity, looks out upon a society in ruins. There is still so much work to be done.

Pieter D'haeseleer, Ghent, 30 June 2015

F
1
F
2

Portret Christian Kieckens, 1993, cover photo for the catalogue [Form is one Function too] (1993).
Photo Reiner Lautwein.

In the article 'The tall office building artistically considered' (1896) Louis Sullivan advocated a rigorous order of things, namely 'Form always follows function'. Sullivan notes: Whether it be the sweeping eagle in his flight, or the open apple-blossom, the toiling work-horse, the blithe swan, the branching oak, the winding stream at its base, the drifting clouds, over all the coursing sun, form ever follows function, and this is the law'. Where function does not change, form does not change. Almost a hundred years later, in 1993, Christian Kieckens exhibited his work in gallery S65. The overview and the publication are titled 'Form is one function too'. In comparison with Sullivan's bombast Kieckens' premise reads as a whispered afterthought. Something that one perhaps overlooked and whose honour could now be restored. The picture on the book's cover is one of the most intoxicating architectural images the end of the 20th century has ever produced. Standing in the Royal Galleries of Ostend, the architect carries in a model of a house. A reliquary? Or is it a sacrifice? The character's peripheral position suggests a perspective counterweight to the stoa's open colonnade. An enrichment of the public space. The infinite black of a torso, two chained hands, no head. The architect with no face and free of superfluous emotion, emphasising the universal.

After having roamed around for a while, I returned to Belgium in 1997, to embark on architectural practice. But first I had to complete an internship. I flicked through 'Mein Erstes Haus' (deSingel, 1994) and was fascinated by Christian Kieckens' present absence. I was guided to 'Form is one Function too' (F1F2) and saw a picture of the Lynchian gallery that has no equal in architecture. I called the architect. A few days later we would meet for the first time during an interview-like encounter in the Brussels café, A la Mort Subite. I had no idea what Christian Kieckens looked like. I climbed the Warmoesberg, passed the gilded façade, through the heavy oak doors. The architect was sitting there (it was clearly him) at a small bistro table (an Onofre table?), bent over the house speciality, an open face Fromage Blanc sandwich and a glass of Gueuze. We started talking.

Peter Swinnen, Brussels, July 2015

Photo André Loeckx.

MIMESIS: MARIE-JOSÉ VAN HEE AND THE INSCRIPTION OF THE FEMININE IN ARCHITECTURE

Van Hee's work is silent rather than arrogant or pushy. If it forces the onlooker to pay attention, it is because it so masterfully creates an architectural framing which renders the experience of the everyday more intense. Marie-José is indeed not known as an extravert architect, who would develop a specific discourse foregrounding her work. Her aim is to let the works speak for themselves, and her approach as an architect is based on mimesis. Mimesis is a Greek term which was translated into Latin as imitatio. It has to do with forms of similarity. Broadly conceived mimesis refers to a kind of affinity between designer and design, between subject and object, which ensures that the design somehow boils down to a successful translation of all sorts of often contradictory requirements, expectations, needs and constraints into the designed object. Mimesis allows Van Hee to overcome such contradictions in designs which transform functional requirements and constructive necessities into some sublime form.

In her own home the street facade mutates into a very thick, double wall figuring built-in cupboards in the lower half and windows in the upper half. The thick-

ness of the wall thus mediates the transition between public and private, combining the contradictory requirements of providing daylight and ensuring privacy. This pattern of 'doubling' is something Van Hee relies upon quite often, using the double wall to create closets or shortcuts in the circulation, or to overcome differences in floor levels, or to modulate the gaze (facilitating the view from inside to outside, while prohibiting the reverse). Also stairs play an important role. In the ModeNatie for example, the very elaborate stair figures as a kind of hinge around which all the different elements of the program are organised. The stair thus forms a kind of sculpture which ensures the unity of the whole, while still articulating the identity of the parts. This integrating gesture is supported by subtle choices of materials, relying upon textures and colours to make connections or to stress particular aspects. Again and again it is striking how Van Hee succeeds in mimetically framing the unfolding of daily life in such a way that everyday gestures and domestic routines – mounting the stairs, setting the table, feeding the cat – acquire poetic intensity.

Do these mimetic qualities of the work relate to her femininity? It is difficult to evoke gender differences when looking at the work of just one individual. It is also misleading, however, to completely ignore gender when talking about the work of a generation. Statistics unfortunately continue to tell a tale of female under-representation in the professional field, and especially in the higher ranks of that professional field. The 2010 Flanders Architecture Yearbook mentions only 23 women when discussing the work of some 93 architects – and this while for twenty years or longer there have been as many women as men who graduate with a professional degree in architecture. It is indeed clear that more women than men leave the profession at an early stage in their career. Research abroad tells us that there are many reasons for this leaking pipeline, but one of them definitely is the dominance of a masculine culture in the profession. It seems very likely that also Van Hee has been confronted with the effects of an architectural culture which is far from beneficial to women. Recent theories of gender stress the idea of performance and performativity: femininity or masculinity, it is claimed, are not essential parts of the make-up of person (as if one would be 'essentially' woman or man); one's gender rather has to do with the continued repetition of gender performance. Individuals adopt and appropriate their gender identity by repeatedly playing the role of respectively girl or boy (later in life woman or man). Gender thus is a construct rather than an essential and innate characteristic of an individual. Hence one might also play with gender identities: individuals can exaggerate their gender performance, they can install confusion or undermine univalent interpretations. According to Luce Irigaray such mimetic strategies are the best way for women to escape their being determined by masculine domination. Since mimesis (as counterpart of rationality) is often seen as specifically feminine, she thinks women should embrace their mimetic capacities in order to both accept and question what it means to be feminine.

It seems clear to me that Van Hee's work performs mimetic strategies in architecture in Irigaray's sense. Repetition, doubling and theatricality are thus features in her work that contribute to what one might call: the inscription of the feminine in architecture.

Hilde Heynen, Leuven, July 2015

Marc Dubois, 2 into 1 - Villa Stein-de Monzie / Le Corbusier.
The Architectural Review, nr.1079 (1987): 33.

MARC DUBOIS – A PASSION FOR ARCHITECTURE

From the outset, the thing I recognised and valued in Marc Dubois is his passion for architecture. It is this passion that motivates his diverse activities, his pleas for architectural quality, his criticism of the government's ignorance and indifference, as well as his relentless efforts to highlight the innovative work produced by his contemporaries. His passion is most explicit in his publications about the development of modern architecture: about the work of Eysselinck, Van huffel, Hoste and De Koninck, about Snozzi's rationalism and the school of Ticino, the artisanal genius of Scarpa in Venice, the complex simplicity of Siza in Portugal and last but not least, Le Corbusier's purism.

In 1984, he published a penetrating study of Le Corbusier's unexecuted design for the Canneel residence in Brussels[1], and shortly afterwards he surprised readers of the recently founded magazine Archis with a most remarkable article about the Stein-De Monzie villa in Garches.[2] In fact it was a critical supplement to the book by Tim Benton, Les villas parisiennes de Le Corbusier[3], a milestone in the Corbusier study. Using the sketches and writings preserved at the Fondation Le Corbusier, Benton had meticulously traced the origins of Le Corbusier's purist homes. In the chapter on the Stein-de Monzie villa he also establishes that there was a gap among the sketches that were available, so that their correct order was unclear and that the origin of the ABABA grid in the final plan remained a mystery. Marc Dubois filled in this gap signalled by Tim Benton. He revealed a totally unknown sketch by Le Corbusier from 1926, which he had retrieved from the Cooper-Hewitt Museum collection in New York. The sketch unveiled how Le Corbusier conceived the villa concerned for two families as a union of the two homes, one (for the Steins) very similar to the Citrohan-like Guiette house, the other (for De Monzie) closely related

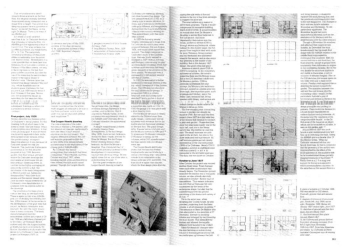

to the symmetrical Planeix house. At the time the implementation plans were developed for the two Guiette and Planeix houses in Rue de Sèvres.

The union of the two types of houses was thus decisive for the Stein-De Monzie villa's structure, not that Le Corbusier united them indifferently. He transformed the floor plans according to the proposed programme (with a shared living room), but retained their sections, and this generated the ABABA grid. Therefore the grid was by no means the basis or starting point for the project, as Colin Rowe claimed in his famous article 'The Mathematics of the Ideal Villa' in 1947; it is a pattern that Le Corbusier only introduced at the end of the design process. In the floor plans and the actual perception of the interior it is merely a fragmentary emerging coordination system through which the purist designs and the space freely evolve. Meanwhile the dual premise of the project remains clearly legible in the façade, it sheds new light on its complex composition.

Benton, who produced a new version of his book in 2007,[4] added an epilogue in which he recognised the fundamental importance of Dubois' article, while he bizarrely enough failed to adapt his analysis from 1984 to reflect the new facts.

But how did Dubois uncover this crucial drawing? At the beginning of 1984, his friend Johan Van Geluwe, the self-appointed director of the Museum of Museums (the M.O.M.), who maintained contacts with virtually all the world's museums, gave him a catalogue of the architecture drawings collection owned by the Cooper Union Museum.[5] Under number 130 he discovered 'First sketches for and photographs of the Villa Stein at Garches', with no illustrations. Intrigued, he enquired about the drawings and received a lovely photo of a sketch from New York, 'purchased in memory of James B. Ford and Peter Cooper Hewitt, 1936.'

Francis Strauven, Winksele, October 2015

[1] Wonen-TABK 18 (1984).

[2] Archis 1 (1985). English version in Architectural Review 1079 (January, 1987).

[3] Philippe Sers, ed., Paris 1984. English version: Yale University Press: New Haven, 1987.

[4] Tim Benton, *Les villas parisiennes de Le Corbusier 1920-1930* (Editions de la Villette: Paris, 2007).

[5] *The Cooper Union Museum Chronicle* 3, no. 4 (September 1962).

Vilhelm Hammershøi, Interior. Strandgade 30, 1901.
Collection Städelscher Museums-Vereins e. V. Städel Museum,
Frankfurt am Main.

THE HOUSE OF HOUSES BY ARCHITECT MARIE-JOSÉ VAN HEE
A SANCTUARY FOR LIGHT, TREE, SPACE, CONTEMPORARY MAN

When she was fifty, Marie-José Van Hee set off on foot to Santiago de Compostela. And what of her house - designed as a sanctuary along the Camino? She left it behind along with a clowder of cats. This writer had the pleasant task of house-sitting. Living in architecture: a discovery! Observing light and time move to the rhythm of the windows, space that unfolds between the rooms across the garden. The main auditorium, the central living area is staggering: an architectural still life with a staircase, cabinet wall topped with high windows, a row of French windows to the garden's corridor, a hearth. Each element has been consciously designed and reads as a word in a poem. A natural white stone floor, the dark stained wood ceiling, steel windows in wooden frames ... Just as poetry wafts between the white and type print of the page, so too does the enigmatic silence in this house of houses illuminate the space.

Van Hee's architecture exudes the traditions that connect Italy with Provence across Great Britain to Scandinavia. Her architectural treasure speaks many languages. Her spirit of kinship with artists such as the Danish painter Vilhelm Hammershøi (1864-1916) is less well-known. A glance at his paintings reveals empty, silenced rooms that afford a view of other rooms through open doors. In her houses Van Hee makes the extreme contours of her house visible and tangible, from wall to wall, floor to ceiling, even if merely to optimise the play on space. Light is also something she shares with Hammershøi, light as a carrier of silence and the process of existential awareness. Except a table and chair, Marie-José Van Hee sweeps her spaces clean to make room for the resident, visitor, guest. As soon as you step inside you feel how the space makes you aware of being – of being here – here between the city and nature. And so the garden, no more than a spot in the city with its water basins, a tree, two walls behind which a kitchen garden lurks – interweaves the house and the gallery with the universe. And this all against the spirit of the times in which living has degenerated into an exchangeable commodity.

Koen Van Synghel, Brussels, July 2015

Renée Heyvaert, Gilbert Heyvaert house.
Photo Jan Mast.

DISCOVERIES

'I was discovered by Marc Dubois.' This is what the witty Willem Jan Neutelings wrote in a reflective article in A+. I think it's a good choice of words: it positions Marc in the vanguard, in the scouting party, conducting the fieldwork propelled by curiosity and a sense of adventure. His historical works are also discoveries. When he talks about them, he sounds like a detective: the intuition, his ready knowledge, his good-natured plan to gain access to somewhere, the excitement of exploring an unknown archive - and lastly, his overt respect for diverse work. Not long ago I visited Léon Stynen's stunning Elsdonck: it was Marc who highlighted this early building in Archis. His case studies led to the comprehensive monographs in whose bibliographies they ended up, many years before, and have enriched our reference framework with predecessors from which the ponderous years of the 1970s had alienated us.

Constructing a reference framework is architectural critique. I cite two pieces by Marc that I believe helped form the self-awareness, the ethics of the newly emerging Belgian architecture if you like. The first, in CAO Sint-Lucas news, concerns a previously overlooked little house in Destelbergen, designed by the artist René Heyvaert for his brother. It describes how practical as well as far-reaching considerations about building and living afford authority to this meagre, very cheap architecture. The second is a good story, in Archis, about a pioneering garden architect, Jean Canneel, and his idol Le Corbusier, whom he asked to produce a design for a house. The design totally satisfied Corbu's Cinq Points but none of Canneel's wishes. Canneel's house was built by his Brussels contemporary Louis-Herman De Koninck: cheap, meticulous, comfortable, a stimulant for Canneel's own creativity, and the most lovable and homely house that modernism produced here. The compassionate aversion to pompous overeagerness, attention to the immediate and what is real, the ability to naturally cause it to endure: the Canneel case is a parable about the might of Belgian architecture.

Paul Vermeulen, Ghent, June 2015

CORPOREALITY

Corporeality is the existential embodiment of time and space. Independent of this concreteness, time and space are nothing more than abstractions. If the practice of architectural designs does not want to lapse into the absurdity of the abstractions, it must remain permanently aware of the original reality of corporelity that forms the basis of and works as a condition for the meaning of all implements, which I use: from the chair on which I sit, the pen with which I write, to the house that I inhabit. All these implements are extensions of my body. If these implements become pure objects, or are reduced to their measurable physicality, they are rendered meaningless, are not even living things. Consequently from this perspective I must see the house first of all as a home. Mere constructions are, like measurable bodies, not homes or chairs and lay beyond the meaningful field of my being-in-the-world. Habitat-architecture starts with designing the dwelling place, in the corporeal self-awareness in and on and around and with all the implements that seem useful to me, such as my clothes - take the relationship that is so evident in French: habitation, habits, habitude, habile and the Latin roots: habitare, habilitas, habitus. In fact successful housewives are the ultimate architects for the other dwellers. It is precisely in housekeeping - the finest symbol of corporelity - in which architecture is made complete as interior art. The study of homely corporelity should not be summarised in the mathematical-physical model, but in the model of images and symbols, metaphors and stories. As Bachelard skilfully put it, there is a 'poétique de l'espace', which indicates that first and foremost we live in - through imaginative images, daydreams and fantasies – in the imaginary. Only after that we do take up the mathematical-physical model, as an auxiliary science, for the infrastructural development. We design just because we are firstly called upon to invoke corporelity (and co-corporelity) affectively and imaginatively in household interiors; because today we risk forgetting and ignoring all this and because we so often lose ourselves in 'l'esprit de la géometrie', I wanted to remind us that: corporelity is the first model for the spatialities in architecture.

Jacques De Visscher, Ghent, May 1987

Excerpt from 'Lijfelijkheid en Ruimtelijkheid' (Corporelity and Spatiality), in *Denk-beelden, Meubelideeën na 1980* (Ideas. Furniture ideas after 1980), exhibition catalogue 125th anniversary Sint-Lucas Ghent, (Ghent: Sint-Lucas Higher Institute of Architecture): 1987, pages 14-15.

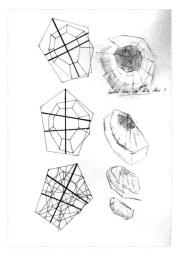

Cristina Iglesias, Sketch for Katoennatie.

MOVEMENT AND TIME

Every project I have collaborated on with Robbrecht en Daem has taught me many things. They helped me connect my discourse with the real while still defending the autonomy of the separate elements.

My work 'Floor for a Sculpture, Wall for a Painting' was my first response to Robbrecht en Daem. In this project, I defended the inclusion of the structural wall of the building as a constitutive part of the sculpture resting on the floor.

In the Katoennatie Building conglomerate, my intervention was asked to bring light into two stories below and along the building. This made me reflect on multiple and simultaneous visions. My effort was aimed at transforming a metaphor into a reality while still keeping a sense of the unreal. The project is based on my thoughts about choreography, movement and time.

In 1997, for the Leopold de Waelplaats, Robbrecht en Daem suggested I think about an artwork in relation to the water, knowing that I was interested in doing some studies on this theme. Here, time was the central issue, and how a passerby or a visitor would approach the Museum, move around and maybe come back. We reflected on how long a visitor to the Museum would dedicate to looking at the paintings and how he/she would find the Deep Fountain once outside. The sequence, the rhythm, the veiling and unveiling of the bottom, the details at close range: all was taken into consideration.

For the 13th International Architecture Biennale in Venice, we used one of my hanging ceilings with a fragment from Stanislaw Lem's text *Solaris*, 'The Dreams'. The story projected shadows over the history of several projects by Robbrecht en Daem. The apparent confusion reflected the complexity of their work.

It has been a pleasure to work with these architects who include art as a part of their design process. Our mutual interests have helped my work develop as well.

Cristina Iglesias, Madrid, October 2015

Robbrecht en Daem with Cristina Iglesias,
Katoen Natie Headquarters.
Photo Kristien Daem.

THE ARCHITECTS VIEWED FROM A NEARBY ISLAND

If I can venture a defining characteristic, it is the productive relation these architects have with their country, region, city and locale: for Robbrecht en Daem and Marie-José Van Hee it is exemplified by their work in the city where they live and know so well. For Christian Kieckens and Marc Dubois it is development of the cultural and intellectual character and intuitions as a whole. It seems that being at ease and occupied in their locale, they were not tempted to create an international identity through rhetoric and restless form making, and were fascinated by the regular practices of Architecture. I was reminded of this when seeing Alvaro Siza speak in London last year, how he talked about architecture in ways that all practitioners do, but at an especially high level. You could understand everything, except this talent. And that is something that could be said for this special concentration of architects.

British architects also work with their locale, but they tend to be critical, ironic and to some extent despairing. In contrast there seems to be a productive understanding among these architects of both emerging possibilities of Flanders in the present moment in time, and its history in the Renaissance and its cultural interchange with Italy. It was Paul Robbrecht who told me of the émigré Italian merchants who commissioned the Madonna of Bruges from the young Michelangelo, and he who also showed how seamlessly the work of artists Isa Genzken and Cristina Iglesias were given a place in the buildings of his and Hilde's practice. In an interview in AR some time ago, Hilde said that they felt closer to British Architecture than Flemish. Thankfully they are not, and their polarity greatly informs British architecture. Their gift, if I can say this, is that from the secureness of their own culture and history they have re-opened an understanding of our own.

Tony Fretton, London, August 2015

Robbrecht en Daem, Concert Hall Bruges.
Photo Kristien Daem.

CONCERT HALL BRUGES

I am a great admirer of the work of Robbrecht en Daem. I appreciate the way that it is so clearly and seriously engaged in the discipline of architecture while at the same time being so formally inventive. The Bruges Concert Hall is not necessarily my favourite of their buildings but it is one that makes me think and go back to. It has very attractive qualities, like the way the project moves heaven and earth to make a bad site good, to rectify mistakes that were made years before the architects became involved in this place. The building's public programme is vigorously deployed so that the hall and its foyers are forced into the public life of the city. There are other aspects of the project I am more ambivalent about like the all-embracing complexity of its red volume which while clearly rhyming with the profile and material of the romantic city centre just a few steps away, is also reminiscent of stealth bomber architecture. But this ambiguity is no bad thing. It is a main ingredient of contemporary Flemish architecture, an important contribution offered up by Robbrecht and Daem, and the others in their extraordinary generation. It is something that they have passed on to their students, or simply through the influence of their work. In my mind I have always grouped the achievements of the Flemish generation of 1950 with their Swiss German contemporaries. Both cohorts picked up the baton offered by Aldo Rossi and Robert Venturi, drawing equally on the lessons of the European city and Main Street America, as a way to make sense of, and to work productively within the difficult territory at the edges of the city. The work of Robbrecht en Daem acknowledges the history of architecture and its place in the city, but it is not involved in the reconstruction of the European city and is not overly concerned with typology, matters that are perhaps not so often compatible with the Flemish sprawl. The work is spatially adventurous and always has a material intensity, and neither is necessarily handled consistently. The concert hall has its little Elizabethan theatre and the more conventional main hall. Immediately adjacent to these are concrete foyer spaces more redolent of motorway flyovers, fine places to enjoy a beer and quote the hard edged paintings of Gerhard Richter.

Adam Caruso, London, June 2015

4 Timelines

These timelines are based on research conducted by Fragile,
Faculty of Architecture, KU Leuven, Campus Sint-Lucas, 2014-2015.

Tutors:	Carl Bourgeois and Caroline Voet
Student team Marie-José Van Hee:	Ghan Oudhuis, Willem Devos, Karel Sucaet and Fran Pieters
Student Team Paul Robbrecht:	Matthias Decleer, Pieter Dossche and Matteo Lampaert
Student Team Christian Kieckens:	Reintje Jacobs, Hannelore Pauwels and Kelly Coomans
Student team Marc Dubois:	Fran Pieters, Eva De Meersman, Annelies De Keersmaecker

Extended by Marie-José Van Hee Architecten, Robbrecht en Daem architecten,
Christiaen Kieckens Architects, Marc Dubois, Caroline Voet, Ghan Oudhuis
and Jins Callebaut.

Christian Kieckens
Timeline

1975-1977
House Kieckens-Troffaes,
Knokke-Heist

1990-1995
House Van Hover-De Pus,
Baardegem

1995-2001
House VM-D,
Oudenburg
with Alvaro Siza

SELECTED PROJECTS

1983-1989
Design of exhibitions for SAM,
Museum voor Sierkunst,
Ghent For S/AM and for
the Design museum

1991
'Architetti (Della Fiandra) /
Architects (From Flanders)',
Venice, Exhibition design,
Belgian Pavilion, Giardini
di Castello, Venezia (IT), curator:
Marc Dubois

1993-1998
Scenography of Interieur
Kortrijk '94-'96-'98 Fairs
at Hallen of Kortrijk

1988
'Woning Mys
in Oudenaarde
(Interventies)'
Group exhibition
'Jonge Architekten
in België'
deSingel, Antwerp

1993
Publication
'Form is one function too'

1996
Publication
'Densities (Downtown Aalst)'
with Peter Downsbrough

EXHIBITIONS & PUBLICATIONS

1951
born

1968
1968 - 1974
Study at Sint-Lucas Ghent

1974
Degree in
architecture
Sint-Lucas
Ghent

1974-1977
Internship architect
Paul Nelis
Internship architect
Achiel Hutsebaut

1983
1983-1992
Co-founder of S/AM
(Stichting Architektuurmuseum
vzw) Graphic design of the
magazineOrganisation of
studytrips and exhibitions

1994
Graphic Design
Architecture Yearbook
Flanders '90-'93

1996
Graphic Design
Architecture Yearbook Flanders
'94-'95

BIOGRAPHY

1980

1993-1996 Professor
Architectural Design at'Academie
van Bouwkunst' Tilburg

1987-1990 Assistent at the HAIR
Institute Antwerp, section Interior Design

1995-1996 Professor Architectural
Design at Institut Saint-Luc Liège

TEACHING

1990-1995 Assistent at the
Henry van de Velde Institute
Antwerp, Architecture Department

1995-1999 Assistent professor
at the Henry van de Velde
Institute and Artesis University
College Antwerp

1980-1990 Professor in Architectural design at the Architecture
Department of Sint-Lucas School of Architecture

AWARDS & RECOGNITION

1981
House Cauchie
Shinkenchiku Residential
Design Competition 80,
Tokyo,
honorable mention

1981
Godecharle Award

1990
'Pari Intervallo', Project for
the Antwerp Quays, 'Stad
aan de Stroom', Antwerp,
Prize Council of Architects
of Flanders

1991
Renovation of the Fondation
pour l'architecture site, Brussels
1st Prize

1969
Publication 'Het lelijkste land
ter wereld' Renaat Braem

1973
Oprichting A+

1983
Competition Carrefour
de l'Europe, Brussels

1985
Start Architecture Program
deSingel, Antwerp

1988
Manifestation Architectuur
als buur, Ghent

1971
'Bouwen in België'
Geert Bekaert
with Francis Strauven

1983
Oprichting Sticht-
ing Architektuur-
museum, Ghent

1986
Art Manifestation
Chambres d'Amis
Initiatief '86, Ghent

1989
Competiton Sea Trade
Centre, Zeebrugge

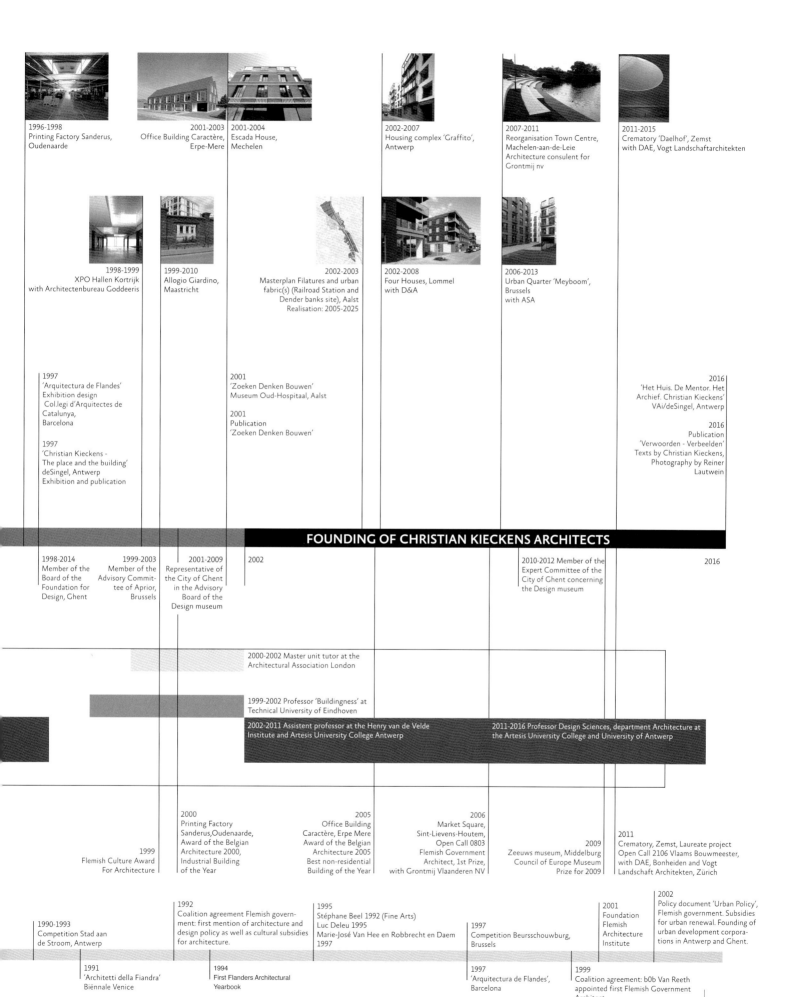

1996-1998
Printing Factory Sanderus,
Oudenaarde

2001-2003
Office Building Caractère,
Erpe-Mere

2001-2004
Escada House,
Mechelen

2002-2007
Housing complex 'Graffito',
Antwerp

2007-2011
Reorganisation Town Centre,
Machelen-aan-de-Leie
Architecture consulent for
Grontmij nv

2011-2015
Crematory 'Daelhof', Zemst
with DAE, Vogt Landschaftarchitekten

1998-1999
XPO Hallen Kortrijk
with Architectenbureau Goddeeris

1999-2010
Allogio Giardino,
Maastricht

2002-2003
Masterplan Filatures and urban
fabric(s) (Railroad Station and
Dender banks site), Aalst
Realisation: 2005-2025

2002-2008
Four Houses, Lommel
with D&A

2006-2013
Urban Quarter 'Meyboom',
Brussels
with ASA

1997
'Arquitectura de Flandes'
Exhibition design
Col.legi d'Arquitectes de
Catalunya,
Barcelona

1997
'Christian Kieckens -
The place and the building'
deSingel, Antwerp
Exhibition and publication

2001
'Zoeken Denken Bouwen'
Museum Oud-Hospitaal, Aalst

2001
Publication
'Zoeken Denken Bouwen'

2016
'Het Huis. De Mentor. Het
Archief. Christian Kieckens'
VAi/deSingel, Antwerp

2016
Publication
'Verwoorden - Verbeelden'
Texts by Christian Kieckens,
Photography by Reiner
Lautwein

FOUNDING OF CHRISTIAN KIECKENS ARCHITECTS

1998-2014
Member of the
Board of the
Foundation for
Design, Ghent

1999-2003
Member of the
Advisory Commit-
tee of Aprior,
Brussels

2001-2009
Representative of
the City of Ghent
in the Advisory
Board of the
Design museum

2002

2010-2012 Member of the
Expert Committee of the
City of Ghent concerning
the Design museum

2016

2000-2002 Master unit tutor at the
Architectural Association London

1999-2002 Professor 'Buildingness' at
Technical University of Eindhoven

2002-2011 Assistent professor at the Henry van de Velde
Institute and Artesis University College Antwerp

2011-2016 Professor Design Sciences, department Architecture at
the Artesis University College and University of Antwerp

1999
Flemish Culture Award
For Architecture

2000
Printing Factory
Sanderus,Oudenaarde,
Award of the Belgian
Architecture 2000,
Industrial Building
of the Year

2005
Office Building
Caractère, Erpe Mere
Award of the Belgian
Architecture 2005
Best non-residential
Building of the Year

2006
Market Square,
Sint-Lievens-Houtem,
Open Call 0803
Flemish Government
Architect, 1st Prize,
with Grontmij Vlaanderen NV

2009
Zeeuws museum, Middelburg
Council of Europe Museum
Prize for 2009

2011
Crematory, Zemst, Laureate project
Open Call 2106 Vlaams Bouwmeester,
with DAE, Bonheiden and Vogt
Landschaft Architekten, Zürich

1990-1993
Competition Stad aan
de Stroom, Antwerp

1992
Coalition agreement Flemish government: first mention of architecture and
design policy as well as cultural subsidies
for architecture.

1995
Stéphane Beel 1992 (Fine Arts)
Luc Deleu 1995
Marie-José Van Hee en Robbrecht en Daem
1997

1997
Competition Beursschouwburg,
Brussels

2001
Foundation
Flemish
Architecture
Institute

2002
Policy document 'Urban Policy',
Flemish government. Subsidies
for urban renewal. Founding of
urban development corporations in Antwerp and Ghent.

1991
'Architetti della Fiandra'
Biënnale Venice

1994
First Flanders Architectural
Yearbook

1997
'Arquitectura de Flandes',
Barcelona

1999
Coalition agreement: b0b Van Reeth
appointed first Flemish Government
Architect.

Robbrecht en Daem architecten
Timeline

1983-1992
House Mys
Oudenaarde,
with Wim Cuyvers,
Marleen Dilissen,
Christian Kieckens

1987
Scenografy 'Floor for
a sculpture, Wall for a
painting'
De Appel, Amsterdam

1988
Bank Branch,
Kerksken

1992-1994
Aue Pavilions-
Documenta IX,
Kassel

1992-2000
Katoen Natie Headquarters,
Antwerp
with Cristina Iglesias

SELECTED PROJECTS

1981-1983
Villa
De Mol, Kortrijk

1986
Scenography
Initiatief 86,
St. Pietersabdij, Ghent

1989-1991
Gallery and Apartment
Meert, Brussels

1993-1997
Canal Houses,
Ghent

EXHIBITIONS
& PUBLICATIONS

1986
'Jonge architecten in
België'
Museum voor
Sierkunst, Ghent

1989
'De Architectuur en het beeld'
Publication and exhibition
deSingel, Antwerp

1991
'Architetti della
Fiandra'
5th International
Architecture
Exhibition,
Venice

HD 1950
born

1975
Degree in Architecture
Stedelijk Hoger Instituut voor Architectuur
en Stedenbouw, Ghent
Degree in Graphic Design
KASK, Ghent

1975
Founding of
Robbrecht en
Daem architecten
with Paul Robbrecht

OWN PRACTICE

PR 1950
born

1969
1969-1974
Study at Sint-Lucas Ghent

1974
Degree in architecture
Sint-Lucas Ghent

Internship architect
Marc Dessauvage

1975
Founding of
Robbrecht
en Daem
architecten
with
Hilde Daem

1980
Member of 'Centro
Palladio' Venice

1989
'Paul Robbrecht Hilde Daem:
De Architectuur en het beeld'

BIOGRAPHY

1978

TEACHING

1992-2015 Professor in Architectural Design at the Architecture
Department of Sint-Lucas School of Architecture, Ghent

1978-1992 Professor Architectural Criticism at
KASK Ghent

AWARDS
& RECOGNITION

1979
Grand Prize of Rome

1980
Godecharle Award

1994
Premio Zerynthia Dialoghi tra Arte e
Architectura

1969
Publication 'Het lelijkste land
ter wereld' Renaat Braem

1973
Oprichting A+

1983
Competition Carrefour
de l'Europe, Brussels

1985
Start Architecture Program
deSingel, Antwerp

1988
Manifestation Architectuur
als buur, Ghent

1971
'Bouwen in België'
Geert Bekaert
with Francis Strauven

1983
Oprichting Stichting
Architektuurmuseum,
Ghent

1986
Art Manifestation
Chambres d'Amis
Initiatief '86, Ghent

1989
Competiton Sea Trade
Centre, Zeebrugge

1996-2012
Market Hall and
Central Squares,
Ghent
with Marie-José
Van Hee

1997-1999
Redesign Leopold De
Waelplaats and Museum-
square, Antwerp with
Marie-José Van Hee
architecten, Cristina Iglesias

2000-2004
Chamber Music Hall,
Gaasbeek

2003-2009
Whitechapel Art
Gallery,
London

2009-2012
Central Square and
Riverbanks, Deinze
with Marie-José Van Hee
architecten,
Benoît Van Innis

2010-2014
City Archives,
Bordeaux

1997-2003
Renovation Museum
Boijmans van Beuningen,
Rotterdam

1998-2002
Concert Hall,
Bruges

1999-2006
St-Felix Warehouse,
Antwerp

2009-...
Renovation University Library,
Ghent

2010-2012
Het Huis Middelheim,
Antwerp

2015-...
Flemish Radio
& Television Company,
Brussels
with Dierendonckblancke

1997
'Arquitectura de Flandes,
Col.legi d'Arquitectes de
Catalunya,
Barcelona

2009
'Pacing through
Architecture'
Bozar, Brussels
Exhibition and
publication

2012
13th Biennale di Venezia
on invitation from curator
David Chipperfield
with Marie-José Van Hee,
Cristina Iglesias and
Maarten Vanden Abeele

2014
SLOW (36h)
'Kunstenfestival van de
traagheid',
Concertgebouw, Brugge

2016
Hilde Daem:
Chairman of Herita

2000
2000-2007
Chairman of the Welstandscommissie, Antwerp

2016

1998
'Werk in architectuur:
Paul Robbrecht
en Hilde Daem'

2009
'Robbrecht en Daem:
Pacing through Architecture'

1997-1998 Professor in Architectural Design at AA School

1999-2009 Professor at Architectural Design and urban planning
at the University of Ghent

1997
Flemish Cultural Prize for
Architecture
with Marie-José Van Hee

1999, 2003
Nomination 6th Mies
van der Rohe Award for
European Architecture,
Barcelona

2008
Member of the Royal Academy for
Sciences and the Arts of Belgium

2009
Public Space Award
Market Hall -
Reconstruction Korenmarkt,
E. Braunplein and surroundings, Ghent

1990-1993
Competition Stad aan
de Stroom, Antwerp

1992
Coalition agreement Flemish government: first mention of architecture and
design policy as well as cultural subsidies
for architecture.

1995
Stéphane Beel 1992 (Fine Arts)
Luc Deleu 1995
Marie-José Van Hee en Robbrecht en Daem
1997

1997
Competition Beursschouwburg,
Brussels

2001
Foundation
Flemish
Architecture
Institute

2002
Policy document 'Urban Policy',
Flemish government. Subsidies
for urban renewal. Founding of
urban development corporations in Antwerp and Ghent.

1991
'Architetti della Fiandra'
Biënnale Venice

1994
First Flanders Architectural
Yearbook

1997
'Arquitectura de Flandes',
Barcelona

1999
Coalition agreement: b0b Van Reeth
appointed first Flemish Government
Architect.

Marie-José Van Hee
Timeline

SELECTED PROJECTS

1987-1989
Bank Branch and apartment
BACOB, Ukkel
with J. Van Dessel

1990-1993
House, office and
warehouse
Van Hee - Coppens,
Deinze

1991-1993
Pharmacist and residence
Van Backlé - De Feu,
Wemmel

1983-1986
House
Derks - Lowie,
Ghent

1988-1991
House, Showroom
and Warehouse Pay,
Laken
with J. Van Dessel

1990-1997
House Van Hee,
Ghent
with E. Claessens,
T. Vandenbussche

1997-1999
Redesign Leopold De
Waelplaats and
Museum Square,
Antwerp
with Robbrecht en Daem
architecten, C. Iglesias

EXHIBITIONS & PUBLICATIONS

1991
'Architetti della Fiandra'
5th International Architecture
Exhibition,
Venice

1993
'Marie-José Van Hee,
ontwerpen
1977-1993'
deSingel, Antwerp
Exhibition and
publication

1996
'Nouvelle architecture
en Flandre'
Arc en Rive Centre
d'Architecture,
Bordeaux

1997
'Arquitectura de Flandes',
Col.legi d'Arquitectes
de Catalunya, Barcelona

FREELANCE

1950
born

1968
1968 - 1974
Study at Sint-Lucas Ghent

1974
Degree in architecture
Sint-Lucas Ghent

1974-1986
Freelance
at 'Groep
Planning',
Brussels

1986-1990
Bureau VDVH &
ASSOC,
Brussels

1990
Start of her own
practice

1993
'Marie-José Van
Hee, ontwerpen
1977-1993'

BIOGRAPHY

TEACHING

1991

1991-2015 Professor in architectural design at the Architecture Department of Sint-Lucas School of Architecture, Ghent

AWARDS & RECOGNITION

1993
Provincial Prize Architecture 1993
for residence, office and warehouse
for Van Hee - Coppens in Deinze

1997
Flemish Cultural Prize
for Architecture with
Paul Robbrecht and
Hilde Daem

1969
Publication 'Het lelijkste land
ter wereld' Renaat Braem

1973
Oprichting A+

1983
Competition Carrefour
de l'Europe, Brussels

1985
Start Architecture Program
deSingel, Antwerp

1988
Manifestation Architectuur
als buur, Ghent

1971
'Bouwen in België'
Geert Bekaert
with Francis Strauven

1983
Oprichting Stichting
Architektuurmuseum,
Ghent

1986
Art Manifestation
Chambres d'Amis
Initiatief '86, Ghent

1989
Competiton Sea Trade
Centre, Zeebrugge

1999-2002
Renovation ModeNatie, ModeMuseum, ModeAcademie, Bookshop and Brasserie, Antwerp
with D. Verhaeghe, Bureau Bouwtechniek, L. Burm, D. Goyens, S. Hagiwara, F. Reumers.

2005-2011
House Van Aelten - Oosterlinck, Opwijk
with M. Deboutte, W. Voorspoels, D. Verhaeghe

2007-2013
House and apartment Ketelvest, Ghent
with S. De Vocht

2008-2013
Storm wall and flood adjustments Blankenberge
with MAAT ontwerpers, Witteveen en Bos

2009-2016
Apartments and house Van Gysel, Kallo
with M. Vanderghote

2013-...
Verapazbrug, Ghent
with MAAT ontwerpers, Witteveen en Bos

1999-2002
House Vanleemput - Oosterlinck with D. Verhaeghe, Wetteren

2003-2010
Offices and Apartment Bailleul with D. Verhaeghe, J. Baes, Ghent

2006-2011
House in Zuidzande, NL
with S. De Vocht

1996-2012
Market Hall and Central Squares, Ghent
with Robbrecht en Daem architecten

2008-2013
House and dental Practice Degryse-Gunst, Torhout

2009-2015
House Braeckman, Gavere
with I. Janda, J. Langerock, M. Deboutte

2009-2013
Central Square and Riverbanks, Deinze
with Robbrecht en Daem architecten, Benoît Van Innis

1999-2000
'Homeward, Contemporary architecture in Flandres'
Traveling exhibition Venice, Rome, Antwerp, Grenoble, ...

2002
'One-hundred houses for one-hundred European architects of the 20th century', Traveling exhibition Triennale di Milano, Milaan; deSingel, Antwerp

2012
13th Biennale di Venezia on invitation from curator David Chipperfield
with Marie-José Van Hee, Christina Iglesias and Maarten Vanden Abeele

2014
SLOW (36h) 'Kunstenfestival van de traagheid', Concertgebouw, Bruges

---

OWN PRACTICE

2002
'Marie-José Van Hee Architect'

2016

2016 Visiting Professor of Architectural Design, ETH Zürich, CH

2009
Award Publieke Ruimte 2009 for Public Space Award Market Hall-Reconstruction Korenmarkt, E. Braunplein and surroundings, Ghent

1999
Nomination 6th Mies van der Rohe Award for European Architecture, Barcelona

2008
Member of the Royal Academy for Sciences and the Arts of Belgium

---

1990-1993
Competition Stad aan de Stroom, Antwerp

1992
Coalition agreement Flemish government: first mention of architecture and design policy as well as cultural subsidies for architecture.

1995
Stéphane Beel 1992 (Fine Arts)
Luc Deleu 1995
Marie-José Van Hee en Robbrecht en Daem 1997

1997
Competition Beursschouwburg, Brussels

2001
Foundation Flemish Architecture Institute

2002
Policy document 'Urban Policy', Flemish government. Subsidies for urban renewal. Founding of urban development corporations in Antwerp and Ghent.

1991
'Architetti della Fiandra' Biënnale Venice

1994
First Flanders Architectural Yearbook

1997
'Arquitectura de Flandes', Barcelona

1999
Coalition agreement: b0b Van Reeth appointed first Flemish Government Architect.

Marc Dubois
Timeline

1978
'Gaston Eysselinck architect en meubeldesigner'

1984
'Vijf Europese Kathedralen'

1987
'Buismeubelen in België tijdens het Interbellum'

1991
'1980-1990 / Fragmenten van architectuur in België'

1996
'De rijwoning in Vlaanderen'

SELECTED PUBLICATIONS

1983
'Albert Van huffel 1877-1935'

1986
'De Fatale ontgoocheling / Architect Gaston Eysselinck / Zijn werk te Oostende 1945- 1953'

1988
'Een nieuw hart voor Gent / Internationale Ideeënwedstrijd voor de centrumpleinen'

1993
'Tendenze dell' architettura contemporanea / Belgio Architettura gli ultimi vant'anni'

1996
'De Tafel / The Table'

CURATOR EXHIBITIONS, a selection

1978
'Architect Gaston Eysselinck' Museum voor Sierkunst en Vormgeving, Ghent

1981-1985
Exhibitions on Albert Van huffel, Álvaro Siza Museum voor Sierkunst en Vormgeving, Ghent

1987
'Buismeubelen in België tijdens het Interbellum' Museum voor Sierkunst en Vormgeving, Ghent

---

1979
co-founder ARCHIPEL

1981
1981-1985
co-operator Wonen-TA BK

co-founder S/AM
Stichting Architektuur-museum

1985-1993
Chairman S/AM

1988
co-founder association Architectuurpromotie Ghent

1950
born

1968
1968 - 1974
Study at Sint-Lucas Ghent

1974
Degree in architecture Sint-Lucas Ghent

1975
1975-1977
Internship architect Marcel Molleman

1977
1977-1985
KCML member West-Vlaanderen

1978
1978-1980
self-employed architect

1980
co-founder Interbellum

1983
1983-...
Editorial member Vlaanderen

1985
1985-1995
KCML member Oost-Vlaanderen

1986
1986-1994
Editorial member Archis

BIOGRAPHY & OTHER PROFESSIONAL ENGAGEMENTS

TEACHING

1980-1983 teacher at Henry Van de Velde Institute, Antwerp

1984-1990 Secretary CAO
(Centrum voor Architectuuronderzoek Sint-Lucas, Ghent)
1984-1990 Editor in chief CAO Tijdingen

1978 Assistant at the Architecture Department of Sint-Lucas School of Architecture, Ghent

AWARDS & RECOGNITION

1969
Publication 'Het lelijkste land ter wereld' Renaat Braem

1973
Oprichting A+

1983
Competition Carrefour de l'Europe, Brussels

1985
Start Architecture Program deSingel, Antwerp

1988
Manifestation Architectuur als buur, Ghent

1971
'Bouwen in België' Geert Bekaert with Francis Strauven

1983
Oprichting Stichting Architektuurmuseum, Ghent

1986
Art Manifestation Chambres d'Amis Initiatief '86, Ghent

1989
Competiton Sea Trade Centre, Zeebrugge

1997
'Álvaro Siza'

1999
'Philippe Samyn /
Architecture And
Engineering
1990-2000'

2002
'Nieuwe Architectuur
in Brugge Contempo-
rary Architecture in
Bruges'

2003
'Woning/
House Gaston
Eysselinck
1930-1931'

2005
'Tussen binnenstad en
spoor Leuven 2003 /
Philippe Samyn and
Partners Architects
& Engineers'

2010
'Vincent Van Duysen -
Complete Works'

2010
'New Orleans
Álvaro Siza
Rotterdam'

2011
'Crematorium Heimolen
Claus en Kaan Architecten'

1998
'De compacte
woning op prijs
gesteld'

2001
'Álvaro Siza in Maastricht'

2003
'Lens°Ass
Architecten'

2003
'Stations & Steden /
Eurostation 10 jaar
onderweg'

2006
'Huis van de Stad / Lommel'

2008
'Kortrijk Stad
van Architec-
tuur en Design'

2010
'Kortrijk Stad
van Architectuur
en Design'

1991
'Architetti della Fiandra'
5th International Architecture
Exhibition, Venice

1996
'De Tafel'
Stichting Interieur,
Kortrijk

1997
'Arquitectura de
Flandes', Col.legi
d'Arquitectes de
Catalunya, Barcelona

1998
'Licht & Design'
Stichting Interieur,
Kortrijk

2003
'Gaston Eysselinck/
Fragiele Duurzaamheid
Designmuseum,
Ghent

2006
'Geo Henderick,
La Merveilleuse
Architecture'
Designmuseum,
Ghent

2006-2008
Exhibitions architects
Witte Zaal
Sint-Lucas, Ghent

2009-2010
Design X50,
Kortrijk

1993
1993-...
Member CICA
International Committee
of Architectural Critics

1996
1996, 1998
Director Biënnale
INTERIEUR Kortrijk

2006
2006-2008
Curator of various
exhibitions,
Witte Zaal, Sint Lucas,
Ghent

2009
2009-2013
Council for Culture
West-Vlaanderen

1989
1989-...
Architecture reviewer
Knack

1992
1992-2015
Advisor Mies van
der Rohe Pavilion
Award

1993
1993-1998
Editorial member
Architecture Review
Flanders

1996
co-founder
cAD (Centrum
Architectuur
en Design)

1996
1996-...
Correspondent
CASABELLA

1999
1999-2008
Member commision
Architecture and
design of the Flemish
Community

2005
2005-2013
Design consultant
Kortrijk

2007
2007-...
Council for Culture
West-Vlaanderen

1990-1994
Yearbook Sint Lucas with Jacques De Visscher.

1996-2008 Teacher at Piet Zwart Institute, Willem De Kooning Academie of the
university of Rotterdam, department MA Retail Design

1991-2015 Assistant, Docent and Professor Architectural History at the Architecture Department of Sint-Lucas School of Architecture, Ghent

1997
Recognition of professional prominence by
VLOR (Vlaamse Onderwijsraad)

2003
Architecture Award Nomination
of the Flemish community

2002
Policy document 'Urban Policy',
Flemish government. Subsidies
for urban renewal. Founding of
urban development corporations in Antwerp and Ghent.

2001
Foundation
Flemish
Architecture
Institute

1990-1993
Competition Stad aan
de Stroom, Antwerp

1992
Coalition agreement Flemish government: first mention of architecture and
design policy as well as cultural subsidies
for architecture.

1995
Stéphane Beel 1992 (Fine Arts)
Luc Deleu 1995
Marie-José Van Hee en Robbrecht en Daem
1997

1997
Competition Beursschouwburg,
Brussels

1991
'Architetti della Fiandra'
Biënnale Venice

1994
First Flanders Architectural
Yearbook

1997
'Arquitectura de Flandes',
Barcelona

1999
Coalition agreement: b0b Van Reeth
appointed first Flemish Government
Architect.

Bibliography

Breathing Life into Bricks: the Legacy of the 1970s
Lara Schrijver

- Braem, Renaat. *Het lelijkste land ter wereld*. Brussels: ASP and CVAa, 2010 [orig. Leuven: Davidsfonds, 1968].
- Caragonne, Alexander. *The Texas Rangers: Notes from an architectural underground*. Cambridge, MA: MIT Press, 1995.
- Carson, Rachel. *Silent Spring*. Boston, MA: Houghton Mifflin, 1962.
- De Caigny, Sofie and Katrien Vandermarliere. 'More than punctual interventions'.
- Drexler, Arthur. 'Preface'. In *Five Architects*, exhibition catalogue. 1. New York: Wittenborn & Company, 1972.
- Colquhoun, Alan. 'Form and Figure'. *Oppositions* 12, Spring (1978): 28 37.
- Glazer, Nathan. 'The Schools of the Minor Professions'. *Minerva* 12, no. 3 (1974): 346-364.
- Gutman, Robert. 'The Entrepreneurial Profession'. *Progressive Architecture* 5 (1977): 55-58.
- Hardin, Garrett. 'Tragedy of the Commons'. *Science* 168, no. 3859 (1968): 1243-1248.
- Kruft, Hanno Walter. *A History of Architectural Theory from Vitruvius to the Present*. New York: Princeton Architectural Press, 1994.
- Mann, William, Kristiaan Borret and André Loeckx. *Marie-José Van Hee, architect*. Ghent: Ludion, 2002.
- Mannheim, Karl. 'The Problem of Generations'. In *Essays on the Sociology of Knowledge* edited by Paul Kecsemeti, 276-322. London: Routledge, 1952. Originally published in 1928.
- Merrill, Michael. *Louis Kahn Drawing to Find Out: The Dominican Motherhouse and the Patient Search for Architecture*. Zurich: Lars Müller Publishers, 2010.
- Portoghesi, Paolo, ed. *The Presence of the Past*. First International Exhibition of Architecture, La Biennale di Venezia 1980, exhibition catalogue. Venezia: Edizione La Biennale di Venezia, 1980.
- Rittel, Horst and Melvin Webber. 'Dilemmas in a general theory of planning'. *Policy Sciences* 4, (1973): 153-169.
- Rowe, Colin. 'The Mathematics of the Ideal Villa'. *Architectural Review* (1947): 101-104.
- Scott Brown, Denise. 'On Architectural Formalism and Social Concern'. *Oppositions* 5, Summer (1976): 99-112.
- Simon, Herbert. *The Sciences of the Artificial*. Cambridge: MIT Press, 1969.
- Sterken, Sven. '*Ghostwriters of the Young Flemish Architecture*'.
- Ungers, Oswald Mathias. 'Architecture's Right to an Autonomous Language'. In *The Presence of the Past*, First International Exhibition of Architecture, La Biennale di Venezia 1980, exhibition catalogue, edited by Paolo Portoghesi, 319-324. Venezia: Edizione La Biennale di Venezia, 1980.
- Van Dijk, Hans. *Bouwmeesters. Portret van een generatie*. Rotterdam: 010 Publishers, 2009.
- Venturi, Robert. *Complexity and Contradiction in Architecture*. New York: Museum of Modern Art, 1966.
- Viollet-le-Duc, Discourses on Architecture book V. transl., Henry Van Brunt. Boston: James R. Osgood and Co., 1875. [orig. *Entretiens sur l'Architecture* 1863].
- Van Sande, Hera and Yves Schoonjans. 'A Constellation of Scattered Points: Crisis in Design Mentality at the Sint-Lucas Institute (1969-1974)'.

A Constellation of Scattered Points: Crisis in Design Mentality at the Sint-Lucas Institute (1969-1974)
Hera Van Sande and Yves Schoonjans

- Rugg, Harold. *Imagination*. New York: Harper and Row Publishers, 1963.
- Schaeverbeke, Robin. 'Zie tekening - Uitdagingen voor de Tekenpedagogie op Sint-Lucas.' In *Tekenen & betekenen: opstellen over het architectuurinstituut Sint-Lucas 1862-2012*, edited by Rajesh Heynickx, Yves Schoonjans, and Sven Sterken, 32-39. Leuven: Leuven University Press, 2012.
- Sennett, Richard. *The Craftsman*. New Haven: Yale University Press, 2008.
- Solovyova, Irina. *The role of the autobiographical experiences with emotional significance of an architect in design conjecturing*. PhD diss., Texas A&M University, 2008.
- Strauven, Francis. 'De Negatie van de Eigen Bouwcultuur.' *Archis* 9 (1987): 12-17.
- Vandist, Geertrui. 'Christian Kieckens en de Barok.' Interview 2008, University of Ghent. Online in: *TXT_INT_CK*, [http://www.christiankieckens.be/downloads/pdf/236.pdf, last consulted on 8 September 2015].
- Van de Perre, Dirk. *Op de grens van twee werelden. Beeld van het architectuuronderwijs aan het Sint-Lucasinstituut te Gent*

in de periode 1919-1965/1974. Ghent: Provincial Government of East Flanders, 2003.

- Van Gerrewey, Christophe. 'Saintluquismen - 150 jaar Kritiek op Sint-Lucas.' In *Tekenen & betekenen: opstellen over het architectuurinstituut Sint-Lucas 1862-2012*, edited by Rajesh Heynickx, Yves Schoonjans, and Sven Sterken, 92-101. Leuven: Leuven University Press, 2012.
- Van Reeth, bOb. Interview in B-nieuws, no.16, 2003.
- Wuytack, Karel. 'De beeldentuin - Een plek van educatie, reflectie en contestatie.' In *Tekenen & betekenen: opstellen over het architectuurinstituut Sint-Lucas 1862-2012*, edited by Rajesh Heynickx, Yves Schoonjans, and Sven Sterken, 70-79. Leuven: Leuven University Press, 2012.

More than Punctual Interventions: Cultural Events, Competitions and Public Debate as Impetus for Architectural Culture in Flanders, 1974-2000
Sofie De Caigny and Katrien Vandermarliere

- Bekaert, Geert. 'Wie over architectuur wil spreken, sta op en zwijg.' *Wonen TA/BK 11* (1983): 10-27.
- Bekaert, Geert. 'Belgische architectuur als gemeenplaats. De afwezigheid van een architectonische cultuur als uitdaging.' *Archis* 9, September (1987): 10-11.
- Bekaert, Geert. *Sea Trade Center Zeebrugge*. Antwerpen: De Standaard Uitgeverij, 1990.
- Bekaert, Geert. *Hedendaagse architectuur in België*. Tielt: Lannoo, 1995.
- Cassiman, Bart, Paul Robbrecht, and Hilde Daem, eds. 'De architectuur en het beeld'. deSingel, Antwerp, 2-28 May 1989. Catalogue, Antwerp: deSingel, 1989.
- Deleu, Luc. *Postfuturisme?* deSingel, Antwerp, 1 January – 1 March 1987. Catalogue, Antwerp: deSingel, 1987.
- Dubois, Marc. 'Prijsvraag WISH'84: een nieuwe impuls voor Vlaanderen', *Wonen TA/BK 4* (1984): 7.
- Dubois, Marc. 'Algemeen opzet van het jaarboek', *Jaarboek Architectuur Vlaanderen 1990-1993*. Ministry of the Flemish Community, 1994: 12-17.
- Dubois, Marc. 'Subsidies architectuur 1996 en 1997'. *Jaarboek Architectuur Vlaanderen 1996-97*. Ministry of the Flemish Community, 1998: 220-222.
- Grafe, Christoph et al. Normcore. Die Radikalität des Normalen in Flandern. *Arch+ Zeitschrift fûr Architektur und Städtebau* (2015).
- Grafe, Christoph. 'Die Erfindung einer Architekturkultur. Bemerkungen zu den Wurzeln der Architektur und ihrer Lehre in Flandern'. Normcore. Die Radikalität des Normalen in Flandern'. *Arch+. Zeitschrift fûr Architektur und Städtebau* 220 (2015): 4-9.
- Heynen, Hilde. 'Ter inleiding. De plaats van architectuur in Vlaanderen'. *Jaarboek Architectuur Vlaanderen 1994-95*. Ministry of the Flemish Community, 1996: 10-21.
- Loeckx, André. *Stadsvernieuwingsprojecten in Vlaanderen. Ontwerpend onderzoek en capacitybuilding*. Amsterdam: SUN Publishers, 2009.
- Lootsma, Bart. *Superdutch*. Rotterdam: NAi Publishers, 2000.
- Puttemans, Pierre. 'Geschiedenis van de Bouwkunst in België'. Moderne Bouwkunst in België. (Brussels: Vokaer, 1975).
- Strauven, Francis. '150 jaar architectuur en stedenbouw in België. Hoe België zijn huidige aanblik kreeg'. *Wonen TA/BK* 12 (1980): 7-22.
- Uyttenhove, Pieter. *Tussen kant en wal. De 19de-eeuwse gordel van Antwerpen: elementen voor een cultuur van de stad*. Turnhout: Brepols en Studio Open Stad, 1993.
- Vandermarliere, Katrien. 'Het experiment is een constante geworden'. *A+* 253 (2015): 36-40.
- Van Doorne, Geert, and Jo Lefebure, eds. 'Naar een architectuur-beleid voor Gent?'. In *Architectuur als Buur*. Turnhout: Brepols, 1988.
- Van Synghel, Koen. 'Schouwburg tussen grunge en gadgets', *De Standaard*, 7 February, 2004.

'Torn between Two Loves': Tentative Encounters between Art and Architecture by Christian Kieckens, Robbrecht en Daem architecten and Marie-José Van Hee
Birgit Cleppe

- Balau, Raymond. 'Displacement. Interview with Paul Robbrecht'. In *Werk in Architectuur. Paul Robbrecht and Hilde Daem*, by Steven Jacobs (Ghent: Ludion, 1998): 32. Originally published in A+ 119 (1992): 47-49.
- Balau, Raymond. 'Gebouw K'. In Balau, Raymond, Marc Dubois, Christian Kieckens, William Mann, Peter Swinnen,

Katrien Vandermarliere, and Koen Van Synghel, 99. *Christian Kieckens: zoeken, denken, bouwen*. Ghent: Ludion, 2001.

- Bekaert, Geert. 'S.M.A.K. Over de aangeboren angst voor architectuur'. In *Collected essays Part 7*, by Geert Bekaert, eds. Van Gerrewey, Christophe and Mil De Kooning, 473-482. Ghent: WZW, 2009. Originally published in *De Witte Raaf* 82 (November-December, 1999): 15-16.
- Bekaert, Geert. 'Als de dood voor architectuur'. In *Collected essays Part 5*, by Geert Bekaert, eds. Van Gerrewey, Christophe and Mil De Kooning, 127-128. Ghent: WZW, 2009. Originally published in *K&C 1* (September, 1986): 27.
- Borret, Kristiaan. 'De juiste afstand'. In *Marie-José Van Hee Architect*, by Loeckx, André, William Mann, and Kristiaan Borret, 96-107. Ghent: Ludion, 2002.
- Brams, Koen. 'Wat zegt u de tentoonstelling Dear ICC?' *De Witte Raaf* 114 (March-April, 2005).
- Cassiman, Bart. *Paul Robbrecht Hilde Daem: De architectuur en het beeld*. Antwerp: deSingel. 1989.
- Davidts, Wouter. *Museumarchitectuur van Centre Pompidou tot Tate Modern: verschuivingen in het artistieke begrip van openbaarheid en hun impact op het programma van het museum voor hedendaagse kunst*. Ph.D. diss., Ghent University, 2003).
- Delbeke, Maarten. 'Ephemeral principles'. In *Robbrecht en Daem: Pacing through Architecture*, by Stefan Devoldere, Maarten Delbeke, Iwan Strauven, and Kristien Daem, 181-193. (Cologne: Verlag Walther König, 2009).
- Devoldere, Stefan, Maarten Delbeke, Iwan Strauven, and Kristien Daem. *Robbrecht en Daem: Pacing through Architecture*. Cologne: Verlag Walther König, 2009.
- Dubois, Marc. 'Nieuw museum zonder verzameling voor Antwerpen'. *Wonen/TABK* 8 (1985): 3.
- Dubois, Marc. 'Een galerie-woning. Paul Robbrecht and Hilde Daem: verbouwing galerie Hufkens'. *Archis* 2 (1993): 56-57.
- Dubois, Marc. 'XS in meervoud' in: Balau, Raymond, Marc Dubois, Christian Kieckens, Peter Swinnen, Koen Van Synghel, Katrien Vandermarliere. *Christian Kieckens: Zoeken, Denken, Bouwen*, Ghent: Ludion, 2001, 66-81.
- Hoet, Jan et al., *Museum Zoekt Museum: Projecten Voor Een Autonoom Museum Van Hedendaagse Kunst in Confrontatie Met Opties En Realisaties In Binnen- En Buitenland*. Ghent: City Museum of Contemporary Art, 1983.
- Jacobs, Steven. 'Een schrijn in het dorp. Stéphane Beels ontwerp voor het Raveel-museum'. In *De Witte Raaf* 63 (September-October, 1996).
- Jacobs, Steven. *Werk in architectuur. Paul Robbrecht en Hilde Daem*. Ghent: Ludion, 1998.
- Kieckens, Christian. In conversation with Peter Swinnen. In Balau, Raymond et al., *Christian Kieckens: Zoeken, Denken, Bouwen*. Ghent: Ludion, 2001: 12.
- Liefooghe, Maarten and Stefaan Vervoort. 'Een revelerend gesprek: de figuren van Thomas Schütte in Het Huis van Robbrecht en Daem'. *De Witte Raaf* 158 (July-August, 2012).
- Monnier, Gérard. *L'art et ses institutions en France. De la Révolution à nos jours*. Paris: Editions Gallimard, 1995.
- Robbrecht, Paul. 'A conversation, November 1997. Farshid Moussavi and Paul Robbrecht'. In *Werk in Architectuur. Paul Robbrecht and Hilde Daem*, by Steven Jacobs, 145. Ghent: Ludion, 1998.
- Robbrecht, Paul. 'De gewijzigde betekenis van het Rationalisme in de hedendaagse Architectuur (The changed meaning of rationalism in contemporary architecture)', *Het Gewad*, 4, 1981, 7-8.
- Robbrecht, Paul. 'De plaats van de kunst. Raadgevingen en uitspraken, verwijten'. In *Werk in Architectuur. Paul Robbrecht and Hilde Daem*, by Steven Jacobs, 16. Originally published in Vlees & Beton, 8, s.d., 15-18.
- Schubert, Anna Luise. 'Wohnhaus and Praxis'. *Arch+ 220* (Summer 2015): 30-33.
- Exhibition in MVHK on 5 April – 4 May 1986, see Marc Dubois, 'Jan Hoet en de architectuur' (Jan Hoet and architecture), text published online, 2014, 3: http://www.marcdubois.be/cms/resources/jan-hoet-tekst-met-beelden-1.pdf last consulted 11/10/2015.

Ghostwriters of the Young Flemish Architecture: Marc Dubois, Christian Kieckens and the Architecture Museum Foundation, 1983-1992

Sven Sterken

- Bekaert, Geert. 'Wie over architectuur wil spreken, sta op en zwijge ...'. In *Verzamelde Opstellen, deel 4 – De Kromme Weg. 1981-1985*, by Geert Bekaert, eds. Van Gerrewey, Christophe and Mil de Kooning, 305-331. Gent: WZW Editions & Productions, 2008.
- Bekaert, Geert. *Hedendaagse architectuur in België*. Tielt: Lannoo, 1996.
- Bekaert, Geert. 'Architetti della Fiandra', *Ons Erfdeel* 35, no. 2 (1992): 286-288.
- Bucquoye, Monique. 'Een museum voor bouwmeesters'. *Knack* (Ghent edition), 10 August, 1983: 11-12.
- *Bulletin S/AM* 0 (1983).
- *Bulletin S/AM* 2 (1984).

- *Bulletin S/AM* 1 (1992).
- Cuyvers, Wim, Dirk De Meyer, Johan Decoker, and Xaveer De Geyter. *Jonge architecten (in Vlaanderen)*. Gent: Stichting Architektuur Museum, 1990.
- 'De Stichting Architektuur Museum: Utopie of noodzaak', *S/AM* 0 (1983): 1.
- Dubois, Marc, ed. De woning als architectuurtypologie. Gent: Stichting Architektuur Museum, 1985.
- Dubois, Marc. 'Van Diamant tot Kubus'. *S/AM* 1 (1990): 11-13.
- Dubois, Marc, and Christian Kieckens eds., *Architetti della Fiandra*. Gent: Stichting Architektuur Museum, 1991.
- Kieckens, Christian, ed. *Architektuurmusea*. Gent: Stichting Architektuur Museum, 1984.
- Kieckens, Christian, ed. *Jonge Architekten in België*. Gent: Stichting Architektuur Museum, 1986.
- Kieckens, Christian. 'Competition for branch of BAC Savings Bank in Mechelen'. *S/AM* 2 (1987): 12-20.
- Kieckens, Christian, ed., *Jonge Interieur Ontwerpers*. Gent: Stichting Architektuur Museum, 1988.
- Letter to the members of the Architecture Museum Foundation, 19 April, 1993, 2p., Archive *S/AM*, APA.
- Neutelings, Willem Jan. 'Maximalisme. Het einde van het Minimalisme en de goede smaak'. *A+* 204 (2007): 82-91.
- 'Open letter to ministers De Wael, D'Hondt, Geens, Olivier, and anyone else who becomes involved in building and renovation at one point or another', archive of S/AM, APA.
- Sterken, Sven and Els Vervloesem. 'Bij de wissel van de wacht. Een *status questionis* van de recente beleidsinitiatieven inzake architectuur'. In *Jaarboek Architectuur Vlaanderen 04-05*, 11-25. Antwerpen: Vlaams Architectuurinstituut, 2006.
- Strauven, Francis. 'De negatie van een eigen bouwcultuur'. *Archis* 9 (1987): 12-17.
- Vandermarliere, Katrien. *Mein Erstes Haus – Recent werk van jonge Vlamingen*. Antwerpen: deSingel, 1994.
- Vandereycken, K. 'Architectuurwedstrijd Gewestelijke Zetel BAC te Brugge 1987'. *S/AM* 1 (1988): 6-9.

The Architectural Practice as Breeding Ground for Interior and Furniture Design
Fredie Floré

- Balau, Raymond, Marc Dubois, Christian Kieckens, William Mann, Peter Swinnen, Katrien Vandermarliere, and Koen Van Synghel. *Christian Kieckens: zoeken, denken, bouwen*. Ghent: Ludion, 2001.
- Bekaert, Geert. 'De averechtse metropool'. In *Design Made in Belgium 1900-1994*, 5-15. Kortrijk: Stichting Interieur, 1994.
- Demeyer, Hervé, Marc Dubois, and Lieven Daenens. *Gaston Eysselinck, architekt en meubeldesigner (1907-1953)*. Ghent: Snoeck-Ducaju, 1978.
- De Vos, Els, Inge Somers, Bart Eeckhout. 'Three profiles of 'interior architects' in Postwar Flanders: the historic distinction between practitioners with a degree, domestic advisers, and interior decorators.' *Journal of Interior Design* 40, no. 2 (2015): 37-57.
- Dubois, Marc. *Albert Van huffel. 1877-1935*. Ghent: Snoeck-Ducaju, 1983.
- Dubois, Marc. *Architect Gaston Eysselinck: zijn werk te Oostende 1945-1953: de fatale ontgoocheling*. Bruges: Province of West Flanders, 1986.
- Dubois, Marc. *Buismeubelen in België. Tijdens het interbellum*. Ghent: Museum of Decorative Arts, 1987.
- Dubois, Marc and Christian Kieckens, eds. *Architetti [della Fiandra]*. Bruges: die Keure, 1991.
- Dubois, Marc, ed. *de TAFEL*. Kortrijk: Stichting Interieur vzw, 1996.
- Dubois, Marc, *Gaston Eysselinck 1930-1931: woning Gent*. Oostkamp: Stichting Kunstboek, 2003.
- Fallan, Kjetil. *Design History. Understanding Theory and Method*. Oxford: Berg Publishers, 2010.
- Floré, Fredie. 'Blinde vlek in de historiek van het Design museum Gent', *De Witte Raaf* 148 (2010): 13. DOI: http://www.dewitteraaf.be/artikel/detail/nl/3577.
- Gimeno-Martinez, Javier and Jasmijn Verlinden. 'From Museum of Decorative Arts to Design Museum: The Case of the Design museum Gent'. *Design and Culture* 2, no. 3 (2010): 259-284.
- Jacobs, Steven. 'Onvergetelijke plaatsen'. In *Werk in architectuur: Paul Robbrecht en Hilde Daem*, Jacobs, Steven, Paul Robbrecht, and Hilde Daem, 6-60. Ghent: Ludion, 1998.
- Kieckens, Christian, ed. *Jonge interieurontwerpers*. Ghent: Stichting Architektuurmuseum, 1988.
- Kieckens, Christian and Jos Vanderperren, eds. *Crescendo: Architectuur 1980 Werkgroep Deetaai*. Wezembeek-Oppem: DEETAAI, 1980.
- Lees-Maffei, Grace. 'Introduction: Professionalization as a Focus in Interior Design History'. *Journal of Design History* 21, no. 1 (2008): 1-18.
- Loeckx, André. 'Het derde huis'. In *Marie-José Van Hee. Architect*, André Loeckx, William Mann and Kristiaan Borret. Ghent: Ludion, 2002: 6-41.
- Loos, Adolf. 'Die Abschaffung der Möbel'. *Stichting Architektuurmuseum* 4, no. 4 (1987): 10-13. Originally published in 1924.

- Lueg, Gabriele. 'From Aalto to Zumthor – Furniture by Architects'. In *Furniture by Architects. From Aalto to Zumthor*, edited by Petra Hesse and Gabriele Lueg, 20-31. Cologne: Verlag Walther König, 2012.
- Page, Marian. *Furniture Designed by Architects*. London: The Architectural Press Ltd., 1983.
- Payne, Alina. *From Ornament to Object. Genealogies of Architectural Modernism*. New Haven/London: Yale University Press, 2012.
- Spitz, René. 'Dreams of life on dentists' chairs or The designer chair and the architect's image.' In *Furniture by Architects. From Aalto to Zumthor*, edited by Petra Hesse and Gabriele Lueg, 82-91. Cologne: Verlag Walther König, 2002.
- Strauven, Francis. 'Stichting Architektuurmuseum (S/AM) 1983-1992.' In *Repertorium van de architectuur in België van 1830 tot heden*, edited by Anne Van Loo, 519. Antwerp: Mercatorfonds, 2003.
- Vanfleteren, Erik, ed. *Denk-beelden. Meubelideeën na 1980*. Ghent: St.-Lucas Faculty of Architecture, 1987.

Architecture between Dwelling and Spatial Systematics: The Early Works of the Generation of '74
Caroline Voet

- Bruggemans, Jan. 'Flirt op het raakpunt van heden en verleden'. In *CRESCENDO 1. architectuur 1980*, the DEETAAI Study Group (Jos Vanderperren, Christian Kieckens), 6–7. Wezenbeek-Oppem: DEETAAI, 1980.
- Dubois, Marc. 'Het thematiseren als redding'. In *S/AM* 02/03 (April-September 1990): 4-7.
- Fujii, Hiromi and Fawcett, Chris. *Hiromi Fujii: architecture and projects in the '70 – '80*. Brussels: CIAUD-ICASD, 1981.
- Kahn, Louis. 'The Room, the Street, and Human Agreement'. In *Louis I. Kahn, Writings, Lectures, Interviews*, edited by Alessandra Latour. 263-269. New York: Rizzoli International, 1991. Originally published in *1/A Journal* 56 (1971).
- Kieckens, Christian, ed. *Architectuurmusea*. Ghent: Stichting Architektuurmuseum, 1985.
- Kieckens, Christian. 'Stoa'. In *S/AM* 02/03 (April-September 1990): 8-10.
- Kieckens, Christian. 'Interieur 80'. In *CRESCENDO 1. architectuur 1980*, the DEETAAI Study Group (Jos Vanderperren, Christian Kieckens), 60-62. Wezenbeek-Oppem: DEETAAI, 1980.
- Kieckens, Christian. Lecture 2014x1642, Joker week on 'The Corniche'. Ghent University. 2 April 2014.
- Loeckx, André. 'Het Derde Huis'. In *Marie-José Van Hee: Architect*. 6-41. Ghent: Ludion, 2002.
- Merrill, Michael. *Louis Kahn: Drawing to find out: The Dominican Motherhouse and the Patient Search for Architecture*. Zürich: Lars Muller Publishers, 2010.
- Norberg-Schulz, Christian. *Existence, Space and Architecture*. London: Praeger Publishers, 1971.
- Norberg-Schulz, Christian. 'Lo spazio nell'archittetura post-guariniana', in V. Viale (ed.). *Guarino Guarini e l'internazionalità del barocco*, 411-437. Torino: Accademia delle Scienze di Torino, 1970.
- Portoghesi, Paolo. *Borromini, architettura come linguaggio*. Milan: Electa, 1967.
- Robbrecht, Paul. Conversation with the author, 26 August 2015, Ghent.
- Robbrecht, Paul (Projects from 1984). In Dubois, Marc, ed. *De woning als architectuurtypologie*. Ghent: Stichting Architektuurmuseum, 1985.
- Robbrecht, Paul and Daem, Hilde. 'Klein Openluchtmuseum voor Architekturen' In Kieckens, Christian, ed. *Architectuurmusea*, 10-15. Ghent: Stichting Architektuurmuseum, 1984.
- Rowe, Colin. 'The Mathematics of the Ideal Villa: Palladio and Le Corbusier Compared', in *The Mathematics of the Ideal Villa and Other Essays* (Cambridge, MA: MIT Press, 1976): 1-28. Originally published in Architectural Review (1947).
- Ungers, Oswald Mathias. *Architecture comme thème*. Paris: Electa Monieur, 1983.
- Vanderperren, Jos. 'The house between the history and now'. In *CRESCENDO 1. architectuur 1980*, the DEETAAI Study Group (Jos Vanderperren, Christian Kieckens), 74-76. Wezenbeek-Oppem: DEETAAI, 1980.
- Vanderperren, Jos and Kennes, José. Dossier: Guarino Guarini. Part 1: 'The Systematic Spatial world of Guarino Guarini'. In A+31, September (1976): 67-97.
- Van Hee, Marie-José. 'Beschouwingen omtrent tuinen in de middeleeuwen tot in de tijd van Lodewijk XIX' [Reflections on gardens in the Middle Ages up to the period of Louis XIV]. Master's Thesis, Hoger Instituut Sint-Lucas Ghent, 1973-1974.
- Venturi, Robert. *Complexity and Contradiction in Architecture*. New York: Museum of Modern Art, 1966.
- Victoir, Jozef. 'Introduction'. In *CRESCENDO 1. architectuur 1980*, the DEETAAI Study Group (Jos Vanderperren, Christian Kieckens), 8-11. Wezenbeek-Oppem: DEETAAI, 1980.

Belgian Adventures in the Baroque
Maarten Delbeke

- *Architectuur te Gent: analyses. 24 maart – 7 mei 1978, Museum voor Sierkunst*, Gent. Ghent/Schaarbeek:

Museum of Decorative Art/Sint-Lukas, 1978.

- *[Form is one Function too]. Christian Kieckens architektuur 1990–1993.* Aalst: Christian Kieckens, 1993.
- Bruggemans, Jan. 'Flirt op het raakpunt van heden en verleden'. In *CRESCENDO 1. architectuur* 1980, the DEETAAI Study Group (Jos Vanderperren, Christian Kieckens), 6–7. Wezenbeek-Oppem: DEETAAI, 1980.
- Claes, Jacques. *De dingen en hun ruimte. Metabletische studie van de perspectivische en van de niet-perspectivische ruimte.* Antwerp: Nederlandse boekhandel, 1970.
- De Bruyne, Pieter. Epilogue to Vanderperren, Kennes, *De systematische ruimtelijke wereld van Guarino Guarini.*
- De Bruyne, Pieter, José Kennes, Frank Jennen, Bernard Lefever, Jos Vanderperren, *Analyse van het kunsthistorisch bouwwerk. 23 maart – 12 mei 1978, Museum voor Sierkunsten, Gent.* Schaarbeek: Higher Sint-Lucas Institute, 1978.
- De Meyer, Dirk. Acknowledgments in *Johann Santini Aichel. Architectuur en ambiguïteit*, Ph.D. diss., TU Eindhoven, 1997.
- Delbeke, Maarten. 'Mannerism and Meaning in Robert Venturi's 'Complexity and Contradiction in Architecture''. *Journal of Architecture* 15, 3 (2010): 267–82.
- Delbeke, Maarten. 'Architecten en kritiek. Bedenkingen bij 200 nummers van A+'. *A+* 200 (2006).
- Hill, Michael. 'Practical and symbolical geometry in Borromini's San Carlo alle Quattro Fontane'. *Journal of the Society of Architectural Historians* 72, 4 (2013): 555–83.
- Kieckens, Christian. 'Konstante en metamorfose'. In *[Form is one Function too]. Christian Kieckens architektuur 1990–1993.* Aalst: Christian Kieckens, 1993, 7.
- Kieckens, Christian. 'Learning from ...'. In *Pieter De Bruyne. Pionier van het postmoderne*, eds. Christian Kieckens, Eva Storgaard, [catalogue Design Museum Ghent 7 July – 21 October, 2012], 216–23. Brussels: ASP, 2012.
- Kieckens, Christian. *[IMG_BAROCK]* http://www.christiankieckens.be/downloads/pdf/232.pdf.
- Lauvland, Gro. 'The 'Recurrence' of the Baroque in Architecture: Giedion and Norberg-Schulz's approaches to constancy and change'. In *The baroque in architectural culture 1880-1980*, eds. Andrew Leach, John Macarthur, Maarten Delbeke, 223–30. Aldershot: Ashgate, 2015.
- Micheli, Sylvia. 'Between history and design. The baroque legacy in the work of Paolo Portoghesi'. In *The baroque in architectural culture 1880-1980*, eds. Andrew Leach, John Macarthur, Maarten Delbeke, 195–210. Aldershot: Ashgate, 2015.
- Norberg-Schulz, Christian. *Existence, Space & Architecture.* London: Studio Vista, 1971.
- Portoghesi, Paolo. *Borromini. Architettura come linguaggio.* Rome/Milaan: Ugo Bozzi/Electa, 1967.
- Storgaard, Eva. 'Pieter De Bruyne (1931–1987). Meubilair, interieurs en gebouwen'. In *Pieter De Bruyne. Pionier van het postmoderne*, eds. Christian Kieckens, Eva Storgaard, [catalogue Design Museum Ghent 7 July – 21 October, 2012], 20–151. Brussels: ASP, 2012.
- Storgaard, Eva. 'Vanuit de blauwe kamer. Scandinavische invloeden op Sint-Lucas (1950-1980)'. In *Tekenen & Betekenen. Opstellen over het architectuurinstituut Sint-Lucas 1862-2012*, eds. Heynninckx, Rajesh, Yves Schoonjans and Sven Sterken, 110–18. Leuven: Leuven University Press, 2012.
- Van de Perre, Dirk. *Op de grens van twee werelden. Beeld van het architectuuronderwijs van het Sint-Lucasinstituut te Gent in de periode 1919 – 1965/74.* Ghent: Provincial Government of East Flanders, 2003.
- Vanderperren, Jos en José Kennes. 'Dossier, deel 1. De systematische ruimtelijke wereld van Guarino Guarini'. *A+* 31 (September 1976): 67–97.
- Vanderperren, Jos, and José Kennes. *De systematische ruimtelijke wereld van Guarino Guarini.* Unpublished thesis, Sint-Lucas Schaarbeek, 1974.
- Vanderperren, Jos and José Kennes. 'Dossier, deel 2. Projekten'. *A+* 31 (September 1976).
- Vanderperren, Jos. '10 Brusselse woningen'. In *Dimensies van onze Stedelijke Omgeving, 17 november – 23 december 1979.* Antwerp: ICC, 1979.
- Venturi, Robert. *Complexity and Contradiction in Architecture.* New York: Museum of Modern Art, 1966.

Venturi's Discipline
Dirk Somers

- Venturi, Robert. *Complexity and Contradiction in Architecture.* New York: Museum of Modern Art, 1966.
- Venturi, Robert, Scott Brown, Denise, Izenour, Steven, *Learning from Las Vegas*, Cambridge, MA: MIT Press, 1972.

List of Authors

Birgit Cleppe (°1984) studied architecture at the University of Ghent and the Politecnico di Milano. She is currently completing a doctorate on European experimental art documentaries (1940-1960) at the Department of Art, Music and Theater Studies (UGent). She worked on the exhibition The Wonder Years. 30 years of Flemish architecture in models with the Flemish Architecture Institute and was project leader of the Architecture Book Flanders and the exhibition Wisselland. Previously, she was researcher at the Department of Architecture and Urban Planning (UGent) and was assistant curator of the exhibition bOb Van Reeth: Architect, in Bozar. She has published in e-tcetera, De Groene Amsterdammer, A+ and De Witte Raaf.

Sofie De Caigny (°1977) holds a PhD (2007, KU Leuven) in architectural history, published as Bouwen aan een nieuwe thuis. Wooncultuur in Vlaanderen (Leuven University Press, 2010), and a master's degree in cultural management (2001, Universitat de Barcelona). She is coordinator at the Centre for Flemish Architectural Archives (CVAa), the heritage department of the Flemish Architecture Institute (VAi). In this position, she manages projects on the conservation, digitization, dissemination and publication of digital architectural records. She has published on dwelling culture in the interwar period, architecture of the reconstruction after the First World War, the history of architectural education and on contemporary architecture in Flanders. Since 2014, she is Secretary General of ICAM, the International Confederation of Architectural Museums.

Fredie Floré (°1974) is associate professor of history and theory of interior architecture and design at KU Leuven, Faculty of Architecture. She holds a PhD on the history of home advice discourses in Belgium between 1945 and 1958 (Ghent University 2006; published as Lessen in goed wonen, Leuven University Press, 2010). Her current research focuses on the history of representations of living, architecture, interior and design in the second half of the 20th century. Floré is a board member of the International Conferences of Design History and Studies (ICDHS) and has published numerous articles and chapters in Belgian and foreign books and journals, including The Journal of Architecture, Architectural History, Interiors, Journal of Design History and De Witte Raaf. With Cammie McAtee, she is currently finalising the manuscript of The Politics of Furniture: Identity, Diplomacy and Persuasion in Post-War Interiors (Routledge 2017), an edited volume with contributions by an international selection of architectural and design historians.

William Mann (°1966) is an architect and is a director of Witherford Watson Mann Architects. He studied at Cambridge and Harvard Universities, and worked for Christian Kieckens 1993-1995 and Robbrecht en Daem architecten 1999-2002. Witherford Watson Mann's work focuses on the complex interdependencies of the city, through housing, public space and institutional buildings. They collaborated with Robbrecht en Daem on the adaptation of a disused library for the Whitechapel Gallery, London. They were awarded the 2013 RIBA Stirling Prize for their work at Astley Castle, binding its ruins into a strong new construction. William has written on cities, architecture and regeneration for Architecture + Urbanism, OASE, 2G and the Flanders Architecture Yearbook.

Dirk Somers (°1976) studied architecture in Antwerp and Milan and graduated in Urban and Environmental Planning at KU Leuven. In 1999 he received the title of Young Flemish Designer in the context of the first Meesterproef (Proof of Mastery) initiated by the Flemish government architect. In 2001 he founded Huiswerk Architecten together with Erik Wieërs. As a passionate designer, he built a repertoire with Huiswerk Architecten that received both national and international acclaim. In October 2011, Huiswerk Architecten ceased to exist and Dirk Somers has set up a new practice: Bovenbouw Architectuur. Bovenbouw Architectuur has recently had exhibitions at the Biënnale in Venice (2012), at the Architekturgalerie München (2013) and in 2014 in deSingel International Art Campus in Antwerp. Since 2003 Dirk Somers is teaching Architectural Design at Delft University of Technology. From September 2011 on he is also design professor at Ghent University. Besides that Dirk regularly holds lectures on topics such as tectonics, materialization and urban architecture and often takes part at workshops and juries at universities in Flanders and abroad.

Katrien Vandermarliere (°1962) is an art historian and was responsible for the public architecture program in the International Art Center deSingel Antwerp (1991-2002). She was curator for more than 70 exhibitions with international and Belgian contemporary architects, planners, and landscape designers. She was member of the editorial board of the Flemish Architecture yearbook (1992-2000) and Director of the Flemish Architecture institute (2002-2010). Nationally, she has had particular influence in the public communication of architecture to a non-professional public. Internationally, she was commissioner for the Belgian Pavilion for the International Architecture Biennale twice and received the Golden Lion award in 2004 for the best pavilion contribution.

From 2011 until 2014 she worked as curator for the Flemish Architecture Institute and deSingel International Art Campus. Since 2014 Katrien is head of communication for the engineering practice Ney & Partners alongside her freelance work as curator and editor. She has been a member of countless juries of architecture competitions, subsidy committees and think tanks to stimulate architecture culture in Flanders and abroad.

Eireen Schreurs (°1968) is an architect and researcher. Together with Like Bijlsma she runs the architecture firm SUBoffice. Their practice combines urban and architectural research with small-scale building projects, with a special focus on the collective domain and the house. Besides her work as an architect she holds a teaching and research position at the TU Delft, where she has set up a publication series on teaching positions called STUDIO and currently teaches graduation studios relating to issues of Craft in Architecture. As a researcher she is involved in a study on The New Craft School. She is a jury member of the Geert Bekaert Prize for design critic and has been a member of the editorial board of OASE.

Lara Schrijver (°1971) is professor in Architecture at the University of Antwerp, Faculty of Design Sciences, and was DAAD guest professor at the Dessau Institute of Architecture in 2013-2014. She holds degrees in architecture from Princeton University and Delft University of Technology, and received her Ph.D. from Eindhoven University of Technology. Before coming to Antwerp, she taught at Delft University of Technology and the Rotterdam Academy of Architecture. Her research focus is on 20th-century architecture and its theories. She is on the editorial board of Footprint journal, and was an editor for OASE for ten years, and served four years on the advisory committee of the Netherlands Fund for Architecture. Her work has been published in the Journal of Architecture, Architectural Theory Review, and Volume. Her book Radical Games (2009) was shortlisted for the 2011 CICA Bruno Zevi Book Award.

Sven Sterken (°1975) obtained a master's in architectural engineering from the universities of Paris, Pretoria and Ghent, and a PhD (2004) from the latter university with a doctoral thesis on the spatial and multimedia work of the composer Iannis Xenakis. At present, he is an associate professor at the Faculty of Architecture of Leuven University, where he teaches courses in architectural history and history of urbanism at both the bachelor and masters level. His current research focuses primarily on the architectural culture of the second half of the 20th century in Belgium, with a special interest in how architecture serves the territorial strategies of commercial, religious and political organizations. A former vice-president of the Belgian chapter of DOCOMOMO International (2012-2014), Sven Sterken is also actively involved in the debate about the conservation and future use of modern architecture.

Mechthild Stuhlmacher (°1963) studied music and architecture in Germany and the Netherlands and worked at various practices in the Netherlands and the UK. For many years she has been a member of the editorial team of the magazine OASE and of the editorial team of the architecture yearbook of Flanders and has since been involved in various other publication projects. She teaches architectural design at Delft University of Technology at the chair Interiors Buildings Cities and has regularly been invited for lectures and workshops internationally. Since 2001 she runs the architectural practice Korteknie

Stuhlmacher Architecten in Rotterdam, together with Rien Korteknie. The portfolio contains domestic and public buildings of different scales both in The Netherlands and in Belgium. With their work the architects feel in many ways related to the spatial, cultural and contextual concerns of their Flemish colleagues.

Caroline Voet (°1974) is doctoral assistant at the KU Leuven, Faculty of Architecture, Campus St-Lucas Ghent and Brussels, where she received her Ph.D. in 2013 on the work of the Dutch monk-architect Dom Hans van der Laan. She holds degrees in architecture from the Architectural Association in London and the Henry van de Velde Institute in Antwerp, where she both graduated with honours. Before teaching In Ghent, she taught at the AA and the VUB (Free University of Brussels). Her research focus is on spatial systematic and architectural methodology. Her work has been published in ARQ and Interiors. As a practicing architect she worked for Zaha Hadid in London and Christian Kieckens in Aalst/ Brussels. In 2005, she founded her own practice in Antwerp, working on reconversions, scenography and public interiors.

Maarten Delbeke (°1970) is professor of the History and Theory of Architecture at the Department of Architecture and Urban Planning at Ghent University. Previously he led the project The Quest for the Legitimacy of Architecture in Europe 1750-1850 at Leiden University, funded with a Vidi-grant from the Dutch Science Foundation. He publishes on the history and theory of art and architecture from the early modern period up to the present, and is an architectural critic. He is the author of The art of religion. Sforza Pallavicino and art theory in Bernini's Rome (Ashgate, 2012) and the co-editor of, amongst others, Bernini's Biographies. Critical Essays (Penn State, 2006), Foundation, Dedication and Consecration in Early Modern Europe (Brill, 2012) and The Baroque in Architectural Culture, 1880-1980 (Ashgate, 2015). He is the editor-in-chief of Architectural Histories, the online open access journal of the European Architectural History Network (EAHN).

Hera Van Sande (°1969) obtained her master in architectural engineering at the University of Ghent and at the Shibaura Kogyo University in Tokyo. She is professor Design Studio and Building Techniques at Vrije Universiteit Brussel and guest professor Design Studio at KU Leuven Faculty of Architecture. She holds a PhD (2008, Vrije Universiteit Brussel) in architectural engineering and history on the domain of identity search within Japanese modernist architecture. Her current research focuses on the spatial systematic of Japanese architecture and on the spatial qualities of minimal housing. She was editorial associate of Architecture + Urbanism from 2003 until 2009 and has collaborated with Toyo Ito on several projects since 2000. Currently she is also artistic director of the architectural association Archipel vzw and of the urban platform Oostende Werft vzw.

Yves Schoonjans (°1960) is professor in Architectural History and Theory at KU Leuven Faculty of Architecture and conducts research in the domain of recent architectural history and theory. His focus on informal architectural discourses runs along the parallel research lines of practices and discourses in a recent and contemporary context, and everyday local identity, appropriation and urban development. In 2009 he founded the Research group ARP (Architectural Culture of the Recent Past) with Sven Sterken & Rajesh Heynickx,

which tackles architecture as a wide cultural phenomenon and its relation to ideas, discourses and practices. In 2013 together with Kris Scheerlinck he initiated the 'Urban Projects, Collective Spaces and Local Identities' research group on collective spaces, architectural/urban culture, local identity and discourse. Recently he has fulfilled various management responsibilities, such as being head of the history and theory program from 2002 to 2008, director of the International Master of Architecture (2008-2010), director of master programs (2009-2013), vice-dean Internationalisation (2013-2015) and vice-chair of the Research Department (2013-).

Colophon

Editors	Sofie De Caigny, Lara Schrijver, Katrien Vandermarliere and Caroline Voet
Authors	Kristoffel Boghaert, Adam Caruso, Els Claessens, Birgit Cleppe, Sofie De Caigny, Maarten Delbeke, Pieter D'haeseleer, Jacques De Visscher, Fredie Floré, An Fonteyne, Tony Fretton, Hilde Heynen, Cristina Iglesias, William Mann, Yves Schoonjans, Eireen Schreurs, Lara Schrijver, Dirk Somers, Sven Sterken, Francis Strauven, Mechtild Stuhlmacher, Peter Swinnen, Patrick Van Caeckenbergh, Tania Vandenbussche, Katrien Vandermarliere, Hera van Sande, Koen Van Synghel, Paul Vermeulen and Caroline Voet.
Images and reproductions from	AWG Architecten (Antwerp), Architectuurarchief Provincie Antwerpen (Antwerp), Christian Kieckens Architects (Brussels), de Appel arts centre (Amsterdam), Design museum Ghent (Ghent), deSingel (Antwerp), Marc Dubois (Ghent), Marie-José Van Hee architecten (Ghent), Museum of London (London), Robbrecht en Daem architecten (Ghent), Städel Museum (Frankfurt am Main), Universiteitsbibliotheek Ghent (Ghent) and Vlaams Architectuurinstituut (Antwerp)
	Stills for the sketch series and initial research for timelines Fragile, Faculty of Architecture, KU Leuven, Campus Sint-Lucas, 2014-2015. Further design by Jins Callebaut, Ghan Oudhuis, Caroline Voet.
Translation	Data Translations International nv
Cover design and typesetting	Ann Van der Kinderen
Cover photo	© Bart Lenoir From left to right: Hilde Daem, Marc Dubois, Paul Robbrecht, Christian Kieckens, Marie-José Van Hee, deSingel, Antwerp 1997.

© 2016 KU Leuven, Faculty of Architecture - Centre for Flemish Architectural Archives, Architecture Institute Flanders
Leuven University Press / Universitaire Pers Leuven / Presses Universitaires de Louvain, Minderbroedersstraat 4, B-3000 Leuven (Belgium).

ISBN 978 94 6270 067 3
D / 2016 / 1869 / 17
NUR: 648